R.B. BENNETT
The Calgary Years

R.B. BENNETT
The Calgary Years

JAMES H. GRAY

UNIVERSITY OF TORONTO PRESS
Toronto Buffalo London

© University of Toronto Press 1991
Toronto Buffalo London
Printed in Canada

ISBN 0-8020-5975-9

Printed on acid-free paper

Canadian Cataloguing in Publication Data

Gray, James H., 1906–
    R.B. Bennett : the Calgary years
    Includes bibliographical references and index.
    ISBN 0-8020-5975-9
    1. Bennett, R.B. (Richard Bedford), 1870–1947.   2.
    Prime ministers – Canada – Biography.   3. Politicians
    – Alberta – Biography.   I. Title.
    FC576.B4G7 1991   971.062'3'092   C91-094625-6
    F1033.B4G7 1991

This book has been published with the help of the
Canada Council under its block grant program.

Contents

Preface

I first became interested in writing a biography of R.B. Bennett more than thirty years ago when I was very impressed by the profound changes two measures he had fathered in the 1930s made to western Canada: the Prairie Farm Rehabilitation Act and the Canadian Wheat Board. While I was getting around to the biography, I wrote and published a book about those changes, *Men against the Desert* (1967). A few years later, when I returned to the idea of the biography, I took a preliminary run at the finding aid for the Bennett Papers in the National Archives of Canada. It contained 627,000 separate microfilm entries. I fled in terror and the biography idea was filed and forgotten. Well, almost.

Bennett reappeared in two chapters in a book I was working on in the mid-1980s on Calgary lawyers, *Talk to My Lawyer!* (1987). The first event was his 1918 challenge to the government's order-in-council repealing the exemption of farmers and their sons from compulsory military service. The Alberta Court of Appeal voted four to one in his favour, but when the officers of the court tried to serve a writ of habeas corpus on the commandant of Fort Calgary and, later, to arrest him for contempt of court, they were turned back on both occasions by armed guards with weapons drawn. It was a confrontation that drove the war out of the newspaper headlines in Alberta for days on end. The second event occurred in 1922 and, in its own way, was almost as sensational. It was the break-up of the Lougheed and Bennett partnership. It occurred when Bennett went to England to feel out the possibility of moving to a legal practice in London but returned in a towering rage against Lougheed to re-establish his practice in Calgary and to stay in Canada.

Again I was fascinated with the idea of a Bennett biography, but was an approaching octogenarian the one to tackle so daunting a project? Certainly not! I talked to Professor Michael Bliss, biographer of Sir Joseph Flavelle, another Canadian millionaire, and co-editor of a moving book of letters to Bennett in the 1930s, *The Wretched of Canada* (1971), hoping he would take on the project. But he was not interested. He put me on to Professor Peter Waite, the biographer of Sir John Thompson, who he said was contemplating a biography of R.B. Bennett. Waite suggested we collaborate on a Bennett biography, with my doing the early years in New Brunswick and in Calgary – the years when Bennett, the successful lawyer and businessman, made his fortune – and he covering the later period when Bennett was prime minister and finally retired in England.

But there were problems. I was footloose and fancy free and could embark on the project at once. Waite was retiring from teaching in the Department of History at Dalhousie and had a number of commitments that would have to take precedence over the Bennett biography. As time passed these commitments became more time consuming and I was completing my segment before Waite could begin to write his, though he did manage an immense amount of research. It was for this reason that we decided on a two-volume biography.

I plunged into the Bennett Papers in the National Archives of Canada. I discovered that on his mother's death, Bennett had destroyed all the correspondence between them. Almost nothing survives of his correspondence with his brothers and sisters, and there is nothing extant of what must have been a voluminous correspondence between Bennett and Mrs Jennie Shirreff Eddy. It seems that Alice Millar, Bennett's trusted assistant for thirty years, destroyed a great deal of his correspondence when she was working on his papers at the University of New Brunswick after his death.

But there were research pluses as well as minuses. Through the good offices of a former student, Waite was able to obtain copies of Bennett's extensive correspondence, circa 1932–3, with his 'Dearest and Best Beloved' Hazel Colville. And I was able to gather in the details of his financial generosity not only to friends and acquaintances but to total strangers, and to piece together the details of his life with George, his drinking brother.

In writing this book I incurred many debts, and I want to acknowledge some of them here. I am particularly grateful to Dean Wilbur F. Bowker of the Institute of Law Research and Reform at the University of Alberta. Not only did he introduce me to the detailed pleadings of Lougheed versus Bennett, but he put me onto the long-forgotten effort by Bennett to upset the 1918 Conscription law. I am also indebted to the late J.J. Saucier, a former Bennett partner, who served as Bennett's personal secretary in Ottawa from 1932 to 1934 and handled most of his French-language correspondence. Prior to my tackling this book, Saucier and I had many conversations about his relations with Bennett during those years. Unfortunately, Saucier suffered a couple of strokes before I was able to get anything in writing or on tape from him. However, he did provide me with the monograph he wrote to mark the fiftieth anniversary of the law firm Bennett established after the break with Lougheed in 1922.

I profited immensely from Peter Waite's advice, encouragement, and research, and look forward to reading his views on Bennett. Among the archivists across Canada, Anthony Rees and Douglas Cass of the Glenbow Archives in Calgary deserve special mention for the extra miles they have gone in assisting this project. And Lynda Kabeary of the University of Calgary wrestled my imperfect typescripts into a readable format for the publisher. I thank them all. Finally, in researching the manuscript, I was assisted by a travelling grant from the Alberta Foundation for the Literary Arts.

Richard Bedford Bennett, MLA for Calgary, 1899

Bennett c. 1912

A sketch by C.H. Forrester from Bob Edwards's summer annual, 1920, depicting the 1898 departure of Bennett's boyhood friend Max Aitken for the east to seek his fortune.

The Duke and Duchess of Connaught (on the left) with Princess Patricia and Bennett at the 1912 Calgary Stampede

Bennett in a legal wig and gown

Bennett (centre) with Robert Borden, talking to a soldier of the Scottish regiment in London, England

Bennett in 1917

Bennett (fifth from left) with the Prince of Wales and a group at the EP
ranch, c. 1919

Bennett (centre) at the 1928 Calgary Stampede with William Parslow and
Pat Burns

Bennett talking with Mrs J.F. Macleod, 1930

Robert Borden with Bennett and Inspector Deane, RCMP

The Calgary Highlanders' farewell dinner for Bennett, 1939

R.B. BENNETT
The Calgary Years

CHAPTER ONE

Hopewell Cape, New Brunswick

The Jesuits have a maxim that goes something like this: 'Give me a child for the first seven years and you may do what you like with him afterwards.' With the communists, it took a little longer for the ideological casting to harden for, as Lenin said, in a speech to the commissars of education in Moscow in 1923: 'Give us the child for eight years and it will be a Bolshevist forever.' Either aphorist might have cited the life of Richard Bedford Bennett as living proof of the accuracy of his axiom. Richard was born to Henrietta Stiles and Henry Bennett on 3 July 1870. His mother 'had' him for the first sixteen years of his life and he was 'hers' forever. There is no better description of the actual situation than the one Bennett himself provides:

She was I suppose the main spring of my life. It was my ambition and joy to please her; to have her see that the care and effort she bestowed on me were not in vain. She had the finest mind I have known. She inspired within me such love of good literature as I have. I can hear her when I was but a child reciting Tennyson, Milton, Longfellow and Byron. She told me at her knee the stories of empires of old and my love of our great empire she taught me and the beauties of higher mathematics were unfolded to me by her master hand. Indeed all that I am or may be I owe, I will ever owe, to her. She was a teacher, guide, adviser, companion, counsellor, friend and above all an impartial and candid critic.[1]

There would be other children. Henry was born two years

after Richard but died at the age of four, Evelyn arrived in 1874, Ronald in 1876, then there was a five-year hiatus before George was born. Mildred did not arrive until 1889, when Richard was long gone from the nest. But there is no doubt that Richard was Henrietta's pride and joy and that he was his mother's son. From her he learned concentration on the matter at hand, the importance of hard work, and a reverence for the printed word, both sacred and profane. All this was accompanied by an abiding, unshakable faith in Methodist Christianity, which was reflected, among other things, in his lifelong abstention from alcohol and tobacco. 'I promised my mother I would never drink, and I never have,' he would boast in later life when he attended gatherings where alcohol was being served. For as long as she lived, Richard returned to her at Christmas, in complete disregard of his own convenience and concerns.

By birth and by training, Henrietta was a Wesleyan Methodist, and she brought the fundamentals of the Wesleyan faith to her marriage and to the management of the Bennett household.[2] Deeply dedicated to the work ethic, she considered sloth a sin while work was a virtue in its own right and not, as Genesis had it, a punishment for sin. Thrift, industry, honesty, sobriety, generosity, tolerance − all the virtues John Wesley had emphasized a hundred years before − were the basic virtues the Bennett children were taught at their mother's knee. Work as hard as you can, do the best you can, earn all you can, save all you can, and then give all you can. Time and again in his later life, Bennett's actions would only become explicable in recalling the lessons learned at his mother's knee.

Of Bennett's father, very little is known. Bennett seldom mentioned him and the few references to him elsewhere[3] are vague and unrevealing. A consensus might be that he was easy going and friendly but lacked aggressiveness, and that he had a difficult time providing for his growing family after his father closed their shipyard late in the 1870s. There were several hints that he may have had a liquor problem, which would explain his wife's overweening determination to commit her offspring to complete abstinence from alcoholic beverages. Lord Beaverbrook, who would have known, said the family lived on savings and the produce of their small farm. Certainly Richard learned very early in life that money was scarce. In the diaries he kept after he moved to Douglastown as a young teacher, he meticulously kept track of his every expenditure, down to and including the purchase of stamps and the pennies he dropped on collection plates.[4]

Until quite late in life, Bennett believed his forebears came to Nova Scotia as United Empire Loyalists. It was only during his term as prime minister, when he became something of a genealogy buff, that he discovered both sides of his family had settled in Nova Scotia well ahead of the American Revolution. A grandfather a couple of times removed, Captain Nathan Stiles, served with the British forces that took Louisburg in 1758 and Quebec in 1759. He was rewarded with 500 acres of land near Cornwallis in 1760. His other great-great grandfather, Zadok Bennett, was born in Lyme, Connecticut, and settled in Norton Township, Nova Scotia, in 1759 and received a grant of 500 acres in 1761. That was how it came to pass that Bennett's ancestors on both sides became identified with 'The King's Yankees' in the one British Atlantic coast colony that refused to join the thirteen in the revolt against King George III. When Nova Scotia was divided in two to make New Brunswick, both the Stiles and Bennetts found themselves in what became the new province's Albert County. Captain David Stiles had built himself a handsome house at Hopewell Hill, a hamlet ten miles down the road from Hopewell Cape, where Bennett's other grandfather, Nathan Bennett, had established Nathan Bennett and Son, Shipbuilders. His son, Henry J., married Henrietta Stiles in the Methodist church at Hopewell Hill on 22 September 1869.

For the young Bennetts the year 1870 was anything but an auspicious year in which to begin raising a family. The hiss of steam was signalling the death of shipyards everywhere in New Brunswick as the majestic clipper ships were falling prey to the Suez Canal and the steel-hulled, steam-powered new masters of the sea lanes. In the twenty-five years of its existence at Hopewell Cape, the Bennett shipyard had launched more than a dozen ocean-going cargo ships along with a number of smaller vessels for the river and coastal trades. The Bennett ships ranged from the *Albert*, launched in 1848, which was 56 feet long and 15 feet wide with two masts, to the *Sir John A. Macdonald*, which was completed in 1869 and was 175 feet long, 30 feet wide, and 30 feet deep, with three masts.[5] Nathan Bennett and Son were proud to name the best ship they ever built for the fountainhead of their Conservative party and Canada's first prime minister. Richard Bedford Bennett came by his Conservatism naturally.

Henrietta's baby, it so happened, was born in her parents' home at Hopewell Hill instead of in her own home at Hopewell Cape. She had taken the two-hour buggy ride to her mother's for a Sunday visit and the baby arrived unexpectedly. The mother and child remained at Hopewell Hill for a week before returning home to husband and father. The home they came back to was typical of those that lined the mile-long roadway that was Hopewell Cape's spine. Painted white, two storeys in height, it would in time prove adequate shelter for a family of five. Set well back from the road in the shelter of towering maple trees, it had a garden in front and a cowbarn in the rear. Beyond the barn were pasture lots and dyked fields of marsh hay stretching off towards the bank of the Petitcodiac River, which, below Hopewell Cape, became Shepody Bay and the northwest arm of the mighty Bay of Fundy. When the Fundy Tide was thrusting its tidal bore up the Petitcodiac River to Moncton, it was three miles wide below Hopewell Cape. When the tide was out it was a brownish mud flat for as far as the eye could see. From Hopewell's main dock, coastal ships carried lumber, gypsum rock, and plaster to Saint John and to the nearby American states.

Hopewell Cape,[6] at its peak the year Richard Bennett was born, had a population of 1800, a courthouse, Baptist church, town hall, school house, hotel, several general stores, and blacksmith shop. Five years later, when the Salisbury, Hillsborough, and Albert Railway reached Hopewell Cape from west of Moncton, the town became the county seat of Albert County. That did not save it from steady decline as the shipbuilding industry disappeared from the Petitcodiac River.

Henry Bennett was remembered mostly for the fact that he had a rough time making a living after his father closed their shipyard. They opened a general store in Hopewell Cape and, later on, Henry became involved in the development of some gypsum deposits. Scrounging a living left him little time for his eldest son. Henrietta, however, is well remembered as a friendly, cheerful, community conscious, neighbourly woman who was also quite clever.[7] She had taught school for six years before her marriage, in an era when girls regularly got no further education than the elementary grades. She was also remembered as a very religious person who saw to the spiritual upbringing of her brood. The village of Hopewell Cape had only a single church – Baptist – to serve its inhabitants. Though a dedicated Wesleyan Methodist herself, Henrietta regularly attended the Baptist service and enrolled son Richard in its Sunday school. The community was also visited by an itinerant Methodist minister who held services in the town hall. Henrietta never missed these meetings and took her children along. When she visited her parents' home at Hopewell Hill she took her family to the Methodist church. In addition to attendance at church and Sunday school, the Bennett children grew up in a home where Bible reading was regularly practised. Richard's pupils at Douglastown recalled seeing him carrying a Bible on his journeys back and forth to Chatham. He not only attended church twice every Sunday, but also taught Sunday school, at an age when most of his contemporaries had vastly different ideas about how best to spend a Sunday afternoon.[8]

Young Dick's secular education was even more intensive than his religious education. He spent the daylight hours being drilled in the three Rs at the school across the street, and the evening hours being re-drilled by his mother around the kitchen table at home. In both schools he was an enthusiastic student, eager to learn to the point of earning him such nicknames as 'smart aleck' and 'show-off' among his classmates. Alma Russell recalled an episode at normal school where pupils amused themselves by composing rhymed couplet's to describe each other.[9] Bennett's couplet was:

First there came Bennett, conceited and young,
Who never quite knew when to hold his quick tongue.

The intensity of Henrietta's commitment to her son's education is illustrated by her reaction to a contest in which he competed with a neighbour's daughter. William Jones, the school-
master, worked hard to involve the community in the school, and
on this occasion he persuaded a local merchant to offer a prize to
the student with the best record in punctuality, deportment, and
diligence. The contest would be settled by consulting the attendance register, the record of student grades, and the teacher's
notation of student behaviour in the classroom.[10] Carrie Reid
and Dick Bennett vigorously competed for the prize – a well-
read copy of a book of Longfellow's poems. When the prize was
awarded to Carrie, Mrs Bennett was resentful it had not gone to
her son. She recalled an occasion when the Reid girl had fainted
in class and had been brought home at recess. That, Mrs Bennett
insisted, in a protest to the school principal, certainly blotched
Carrie's attendance record. The prize, ergo, should go to her son,
whose record was perfect. The attendance record was rechecked
and it transpired that on the day in question Carrie had returned
to school after the noon hour. Mrs Bennett's protest was rejected
and Carrie kept the prize. Mrs Bennett's acceptance of the
decision was less than gracious.

The rift passed quickly, however, for the Reids were the next-
door neighbours of the Bennetts' and Hattie Reid was Henrietta
Bennett's best friend. All the Bennett children called Mrs Reid
'Auntie Hattie.' Mrs Reid's husband was a master mariner and,
when he was away at sea for prolonged periods, Henry Bennett
and Dick took care of the Reid family chores. When Richard was
about twelve he developed a crush on one of Carrie's friends,
Maud Pye. The trouble was Mrs Pye had no use for young Dick
and sent him away whenever he came around. Dick used to
discuss his infatuation with Carrie, and sought her advice and
assistance.

There are few records of Bennett's Hopewell years. He seems
to have been a loner who would rather sit on the school steps

reading a book than become involved in schoolyard games.[11] Max Aitken thought that Bennett's boyhood conformed pretty well with the norm for country boys. In a word, he did the chores – milked and pastured the cows, helped his mother with the garden, cut and split wood for the stove, carried out the ashes, cleaned the barn, and fixed the fences. Since the Bennetts lived across from the school, there was no opportunity for the leisurely long walks home from school when friendships grew, games were played, and devilment was planned.

Jones was a tireless organizer of extracurricular activities for his students. He delighted in staging tableaux of famous episodes in British history in which the pupils could recite poetry that celebrated the events. Young Dick never missed a chance to participate. One of the tableaux centred on the tragic life and death of Mary, Queen of Scots. Dick got the star part of the tableau in which he recited a poem while holding the headsman's axe aloft as Mary kneeled to place her neck upon the block.[12] Another Jones innovation was a mock parliament in which the students restaged debates of events in Canadian history. The mock parliaments proved such a success that they were restaged for the community in the church hall. As Carrie Reid recalled: 'For the mock parliament, we who participated chose our own parties. My people were Liberal and Dick's were Conservative, so we were on opposite sides . . . There were times that Dick and I almost hated each other. If I had been a boy we should probably have come to blows. He had a quick temper and when he got angry he always turned as white as a ghost.' The legendary Bennett temper of his Calgary years was already well developed in his school days.

Dick Bennett's childhood education was not limited to religion and the school curriculum. There was also the British Empire in all its glory. Students learned that the British Empire was the epitome of all that was good, true, and beautiful. 'Memory work' was still a part of every school's curriculum, and it was natural for teachers to turn to the glorifiers of empire for learning material, such as Tennyson's 'Charge of the Light Brigade' and the anthems 'God Save the Queen' and 'The Maple Leaf Forever':

Wolfe the dauntless hero came,
And planted firm Britannia's flag
On Canada's fair domain.

The motherland with which Canada and Canadians were
being bonded was best described by another anthem – 'Rule
Britannia':

> When Britain first at Heaven's command
> Arose from out the azure main,
> This was the charter of the land
> And guardian angels sung this strain:
> Rule Britannia, Britannia rule the waves!
> Britons never, never, never shall be slaves.

One additional ingredient in the process of imbuing children
with the glories of empire was the big map of the world that
hung in every schoolroom. It was the Mercator projection, with
all the British territories sharply emphasized in red. Seven or
eight years of anthem singing and poetry reciting was enough to
bind the young minds of the empire. The map, along with the
Union Jack that accompanied it, was the clincher.

Still another source of Britishana that was available to Richard
Bennett and his fellow students was the newspaper. Henry Ben-
nett subscribed to three newspapers in all, the *Saint John Daily
Sun* and two Albert County weeklies, the *Maple Leaf* and the
Observer. Ronald Bennett, recalling his childhood, said that all
three were well read by the entire family.[13]

Canadian newspapers generally paid as close attention to news
developments in London as their finances and distance would
permit, and few Canadian newspapers ever went to press without
a budget of cabled British news. A succession of items such as the
following might run on for half a column in any issue of the *Saint
John Sun*:

London: The Berlin correspondent of *The Times* reports that the
Emperor's health is much improved and he is up and about again.

London: It is reported from Cairo that Khartoum has fallen to the Mahta Muslims.

London: Two squadrons of the Navy are on orders to sail for Alexandria on Friday.

Much of this coverage was terse, but there were occasions when even the *Saint John Sun* let itself go. The story on the murders of Lord Frederick Cavendish and Thomas Burke by a group of Irish nationalists in a Dublin park was given columns of space. Events such as these were likely to set the ten-year-old Richard Bennett off on a string of questions about Gladstone and Parnell, and what home rule for the Irish was all about. They set off hours of discussion around the Bennett kitchen table.

In the main, though, the *Saint John Sun* served to fertilize the seeds of Richard's interest in Canadian politics that William Jones had planted with his mock parliaments in the Hopewell school. The *Sun*, in its support of Sir John A. Macdonald and the Liberal-Conservative party of Canada, took political partisanship to a new high. During election campaigns it found space for the complete texts of Conservative leaders' speeches, while limiting publicity for the Liberals to a third of that space. The *Sun*'s editor did not wait for conservative leaders to answer Liberal criticism – he did it for them in lengthy editorials. Then he took on the editors of all the Liberal newspapers in the Maritime provinces. From using the *Sun* as a mine from which to extract material for his mock parliament speeches, young Bennett naturally turned to it when he became involved in the real thing, the federal election campaign of February 1887.

By the time Bennett was fifteen he had learned all the Hopewell school had to teach him and was enrolled in the Department of Education teacher's course in Fredericton. He obtained his second-class certificate and taught in the elementary grades in the village school at Irishtown, a hamlet five miles north of Moncton. He soon became involved in the 1887 election. The campaign-room doors of all political parties were always open for volunteer workers, particularly in mid-winter campaigns when canvassers struggled as much against the weather as they did against political opponents. But while Bennett was prepared to lick stamps, deliver handbills, and knock on doors, what he most wanted to do was to make speeches. The Liberal-Conservative candidate in the Bennetts' Albert County federal constituency was R.C. Weldon, an authentic Maritime intellectual who had a doctorate in international law from Yale University, was the co-founder of the Dalhousie University Law School, had become its first dean, and was in the process of revolutionizing the way in which a legal education was acquired in Canada. Weldon was able to look beyond the callow, thin Dick Bennett and discover hidden qualities that justified his being turned loose on an unsuspecting rural electorate. As his brother Ronald would remember years later, Bennett proved a very able platform performer and he handled adult hecklers, who tried to disrupt his speeches, like a veteran.[14]

When Bennett got his first-class teaching certificate in 1888 he received an appointment as teacher-principal of the Douglastown school and supervisor of three other smaller schools in the general area. Whatever qualms the school trustees may have had over giving the position to an inexperienced eighteen-year-old were outweighed by the record he had achieved at the Fredericton Normal School. Douglastown was a village on the north shore of the Miramichi River midway between Newcastle and Chatham. The postman at Douglastown hired a teamster to drive into Newcastle three times a week to pick up the incoming mail and deliver the outgoing mail at the railway station. When Bennett first got off the train one late August afternoon at Newcastle, he hitched a ride with the teamster. Like all strangers in town, he was subjected to overt visual inspection from the natives, who stopped and stared as he sat rigidly erect outside the post-office general store, dressed in a white shirt and tie and a next-to-new suit, with a half-size-too-large bowler hat resting on his ears.[15] Alma Russell remembered him as a very young, very thin, very tall, very freckled schoolboy. He was waiting, presumably, the return of the teamster from the store to drive him and his heavy carton of books to Aunt Lizzie McLean's boarding house.

The Douglastown school contained four multi-grade classrooms with a total of 159 pupils. Bennett himself taught the three senior grades – six, seven, and eight. Several of his pupils were almost as old as he was, but he had it over them physically, at least as far as height was concerned. He was already nudging six feet, though he was rail-thin with a complexion that was embarrassingly feminine. Because he carried himself always stiffly erect, he had no trouble dominating the classrooms of his school. Even then Bennett was deeply concerned with the clothes he wore, a concern that stayed with him throughout his life. His salary at Douglastown was reputed to be $50 per term, about enough to keep him in food and clothing.

Dick Bennett is remembered fondly, by his female students at least, for the care he showed for his students. He was severely insistent that the lessons he taught be learned by his students; but for those having difficulties he had endless patience and gave generously of his time to pupils who demonstrated an eagerness to learn. Annie Morrison recalled in particular the extra attention he gave students whose efforts impressed him.[16] She and several other girls in her class were planning to enrol in normal school when they completed the eighth grade at Douglastown. When that come to Bennett's attention, he set up a special course of studies for them to ease their passage through normal school.

Although Bennett was a stern disciplinarian, he did not believe in corporal punishment and did not possess a strap. He maintained strict discipline in his classrooms by imposing other penalties for misbehaviour. They took the form of lines to be written at recess or after school, a hundred at a time; poetry to be memorized and recited before the class; and a report of the changing exterior scene, written while standing by the classroom window for an hour and writing on a slate.[16]

In an era long before educational frills were invented, the courses he taught were heavily weighted with fundamentals – reading, writing, arithmetic, and spelling, reinforced with geometry, algebra, British and Canadian history, physics, and biology. Some idea of the content of the courses can be obtained from the mere recital of the questions that turned up on the examinations Bennett set.[17] The spelling test for grades seven and eight contained one hundred multi-syllabic words to be spelled correctly, fifty of them also to be defined. Such words as convulsive, immeasurably, unparalleled, disembarkation, equanimity, haranguing, imperceptible, perturbed, manoeuvre, and so on. One question on the British history test read: 'Name the sovereigns of the Brunswick period of British history and their leading features. Name and briefly describe six important events of Queen Victoria's reign, giving dates where possible.' For the Canadian history test the pupils were asked to write all they knew of the United Empire Loyalists, Frontenac, Montcalm, William Johnson, Braddock, Wolfe, Murray, and Vaudreuil. In botany they had to identify the families to which wheat, strawberries, onions, gooseberries, and dandelions belonged, and know the difference between exogens and endogens.

The examining system in vogue was to list six or seven questions for each subject, of which the pupil could answer five so long as the answers filled the paper. The scope of the grade-school curriculum in New Brunswick in 1888 is impressive, and in Douglastown it was all coming from one young teacher, not from a half-dozen specialists. Bennett must have had to do a lot of boning up throughout the year to prepare the lessons that would enable the pupils to pass the exams. Fortunately, he developed a good memory. Once a fact went into his memory bank it was not only there forever but was subject to instant recall – a fact that would impress many fellow lawyers and politicians throughout his life. Moreover, Bennett genuinely loved teaching, a fact reflected in his devotion to speech making once he had mastered the art. In many of his most notable speeches a listener had only to close his eyes to imagine Bennett back in a classroom lecturing his eighth-grade pupils.

The classes taught at Douglastown normally ran to eight or ten pupils per grade, though they could expand to twelve during the good weather and shrink to five or six during the winter. Bennett abhored this casual attitude to school attendance. In his farewell to teaching in 1890, he summed up his experience, breathlessly, in one non-stop sentence: 'During a stay of nearly two years in this place I have come to the conclusion that the material is not lacking here to produce pupils of more than ordinary ability but while I feel that such is the case I cannot but remark that unless the parents are aroused and awakened from the apathy with which they now view all matters connected with school work the fine abilities of their children will never be shown.'[18] The letter, undated, was addressed to the Board of School Trustees, District 6, Newcastle. Bennett also had some critical words for them: 'I would remark that the school officers are sadly deficient in their duties. During my stay here I have not been favoured by a visit from one of the trustees.'

When Bennett discovered a Sons of Temperance lodge in Douglastown he joined at once and was soon elected secretary. At his suggestion, the lodge staged a number of public debates on subjects chosen to bring the local residents out to the Temperance Hall. He also joined the Conservative party in Chatham and spoke for it whenever an opportunity arose. Opportunities could not arise too often for Bennett. He loved making speeches and he worked at becoming a polished speaker. He studied the techniques of orators who crossed his orbit, picking up tricks of voice control and gesture that enhanced performance. It was no accident that when Bennett later took the platform to launch his campaign for the North-West Territories Assembly, he dazzled his audience. In Douglastown, between formal speech making, Bennett's most active community involvement was with the cracker-barrel forums that gathered almost nightly in Bill Millar's general store. He participated so enthusiastically in the discussions that others backed away, considering the young schoolteacher a show-off too big for his britches.[19]

At Douglastown Bennett developed quickly into a social animal. He made friends easily and the diary he began in 1888 is full of names of new acquaintances he made and notes about dinners and teas he was invited to.[20] It was also at Douglastown-Chatham that Dick Bennett discovered girls. Although the diaries are concerned mainly with reports of the weather, church services, and the quality of the sermons preached, they also contain many girls' names. He met Mary Russel on the ferry, went to church with Jeanie McLean, saw Bertie Russell. Most of all there was A——

and Alma, and for 5 August 1890 there was this entry: 'The best day of all. Excursion with A———. Had one of the finest times of my existence on St. George. . . . The day was passed in usual routine work. The evening will never be forgotten.'

What made this particular evening so exciting can never be known. Nothing seems to have developed from any of these diarized encounters. An exception of sorts might be made in the case of Alma Russell, undoubtedly the 'A———' of the diaries. She reappeared occasionally in what were obviously casual encounters, meeting on the Douglastown to Chatham ferry, for example. She moved to Vancouver to live with her brother in 1892 and never married. Bennett visited her whenever he was in Vancouver and kept up a correspondence with her for the rest of his life.

Bennett was at Douglastown for only a couple of years, but it was during that stretch that he made several of his most enduring friendships. The larger towns, Newcastle and Chatham, were located ten miles apart on opposite banks of the Miramichi River. Douglastown was a hamlet midway between and, during the summer, communication with all three was by the steam ferry *Miramichi*. It was while he was standing on the dock at Douglastown waiting for the ferry to take him to Newcastle that Bennett first met Max Aitken – or, rather, that Aitken first made Bennett's acquaintance. If Bennett had been aware at all of Aitken's presence on the dock it could only have been to wonder what this little boy – he was an undersized ten-year-old at the time but looked no more than eight – was doing wandering around on the dock all by himself. What Bennett was about to discover was that this little boy was Master Precocious himself, had been born brassy with an adult mind, thought nothing of engaging total strangers in conversation, and showed a near genius for arousing people's interest. He had already so captivated the captain and purser of the *Miramichi* that they welcomed him to ride with them up and down the river in the wheelhouse whenever the spirit moved him. It moved him frequently, because he had already developed a well-honed passion for making money and the ferry gave him three communities in which to operate.

Within the combined community there was a soapmaker with a new scam to attract purchasers to his products. To purchasers of his soap who saved the wrappers and returned a specified number to the company, he would award a new bicycle. Young Max borrowed enough money to buy a carton of soap, then went selling it door to door up and down the Miramichi at wholesale price, provided the purchaser would remove the wrapper and give it back to him. He collected enough soap wrappers to get the bicycle, and took it with him wherever he went on the ferry.[21]

Max Aitken, that day, was captivated by the well-dressed young stranger in the too-big bowler hat, walked up to him, introduced himself, and started to talk. By the time the ferry arrived to carry them to Newcastle, Bennett would have discovered that Aitken was the third son in a family of nine children, that his father was a minister at the Newcastle Presbyterian church, that his favourite authors were Scott, Stevenson, and Thackery, that he liked to read in the quiet of the cow barn, and that he hated school because he had to study Latin and French as well as English. By the time the ferry reached Newcastle Bennett had agreed to walk home with Max and stay for dinner. Thereafter, while Bennett lived in Douglastown, young Aitken looked him up whenever he was in the neighbourhood. Despite the nine-year difference in their age, when such a gap almost made an enduring friendship impossible, their relationship lasted a lifetime.

It was a friendship between two people who had almost nothing in common. Bennett had a temper to go with the bright auburn hair he had inherited from his mother. Aitken, in his whole life, was never angry with anybody; even if he was momentarily provoked, he did not let it show. Bennett would turn white, bluster, and sputter. Aitken would break into the broad grin for which he became famous and demonstrate his mastery of the soft answer that turned away wrath. Bennett was a deep believer in Wesleyan Protestantism but, like many another minister's son, Aiken took a cavalier, take-it-or-leave-it attitude towards his father's Presbyterianism. He loved teasing Bennett about religion, without Bennett's ever discovering he was 'putting him on.' As Aitken wrote: 'It was my habit during our early relationship, if

I wished to rouse him, to discuss doctrinal questions. In particular I dwelt upon the Presbyterian doctrine of predestination. A poem I had picked up would drive him to paroxysms of fury and monumental abuse. It went thus:

> I know that God is wroth with me For I was born in sin.
> My heart is exceedingly vile Damnation dwells therein.
> Awake I sin, asleep I sin, I sin with every breath.
> When Adam fell he went to hell, And damned us all to death.[22]

There is a certain mystery about Bennett's second Miramichi friendship. Did Bennett choose the law as his lifetime occupation because of his friendship with Lemuel J. Tweedie, Chatham's most prominent lawyer and Conservative provincial politician, or had he already decided on a legal career when he got his teaching position at Douglastown and selected Tweedie as the patron who would take him on as a part-time articled clerk? The evidence seems to be that he came to Tweedie by way of the law rather than the other way round. Dean Weldon was full of enthusiasm for Dalhousie Law School when Bennett helped out with his 1887 campaign for parliament. It is difficult to believe that Weldon would have overlooked a chance to recommend law as a career and his school to teach it. His enthusiasm would have struck home, but Bennett was in no position to yield to Weldon's blandishment. He could not afford Dalhousie. He had to take the teaching job to save some money before he could contemplate Dalhousie.

In the meantime, he would do what every other embryo lawyer in the Maritimes had been doing: he would sign up as a part-time articled student in a law office. That entailed taking the Friday afternoon ferry to Chatham, staying overnight with the Tweedie family, working all day Saturday in Tweedie's law office, staying again with the Tweedies on Saturday night, attending the Methodist church with them Sunday morning and evening, and returning to church to teach Sunday school in the afternoon.[23] During the summer break in 1889 he became a full-time student in Chatham.

It was while Bennett was commuting between the Douglas-town school and the Tweedie law office that he first met Joseph T. 'Harry' Shirreff and his sister Jennie. Harry worked as a teller in the Bank of Montreal, but it is not a matter of record how Bennett came to know the Shirreff family. The father was one of Chatham's most prominent citizens, who had been high sheriff of Northumberland County for twenty-five years. A casual friendship sprung up between the Shirreffs and Dick Bennett, though Harry was five years older than Bennett and his sister four years older. Jennie, some months after they met, left Chatham to enrol in a nurse's training course in Massachusetts, and Harry received a promotion in the bank and departed for Ontario. Three years later Jennie, having completed her course, got a job at the Halifax General Hospital. Harry joined her when he went to work for the E.B. Eddy Company as sales manager in the Halifax office, and the three-way friendship was renewed when Bennett was at Dalhousie Law School from the fall of 1890 until the spring of 1893. Bennett, however, was back in Chatham as Tweedie's junior partner when Jennie met and married Harry's boss in 1894 and moved to Hull. On E.B. Eddy's death in 1906 Jennie inherited control of the E.B. Eddy Company, the forest products giant that sprawled the banks of the Ottawa River opposite the Parliament Buildings.[24] Several years later, when she developed a need for some sound financial advice, Jennie took steps to renew their friendship, with spectacular financial consequences for Bennett.

Bennett seems to have realized that qualifying as a lawyer by the articling route, combined with teaching school, was going to take forever – or at least longer than he was willing to spend at it. There are hints of dissatisfaction in his diary. While Tweedie was away from the office during sessions of the legislature, work piled up and there was little for Bennett to do; then, when Tweedie returned, there would be a rush to catch up. Most of the time Bennett was engaged in routine office clerical procedures and in running messages, and he did not like the other lawyers with whom Tweedie was associated. In the spring of 1890 he submitted his resignation to the school board and told Tweedie he would be enrolling at Dalhousie in the fall. Tweedie provided him with a summer job, with bed and board thrown in, while he waited for the opening of the law school in the fall.

A couple of months after Bennett enrolled at Dalhousie, there was an opening for an assistant in the university library. Bennett applied to fill it on a part-time basis and, when Dr Weldon endorsed his application, he got the job, which substantially eased his financial pressures during his years at the university. The law studies Bennett had been able to do in Tweedie's office paid rich dividends at Dalhousie. In his freshman year he finished first in his class in crimes, first in contracts, and second in constitutional history, standings that were about par for the rest of his attendance at Dalhousie. In his second year he obtained first- or second-class honours in four of his five courses, and did the same in his graduating year. Indeed, during his three years at Dalhousie, where he took a total of fourteen courses of study, his marks fell below 65 per cent in only two courses in which he had passing grades.[25]

It was probably towards the close of his freshman year at Dalhousie, as he was nearing his twenty-first birthday, that Bennett became seriously entangled in one of the commonest of all male rites of passage – the selection of the signature that would identify him to all comers, forevermore, his 'sign,' his 'shingle,' his 'moniker.' Should the name he would inscribe on all the legal documents he would soon be signing, on his bank-book, his cheques, and on notes he would endorse, be R.B. Bennett, Richard B. Bennett, Richard Bedford Bennett, or R. Bedford Bennett? He tried them all and ended by selecting none. Instead he chose 'Rich. B. Bennett.' Not a simple 'Rich. B. Bennett' along a dotted line, however. Instead, it was a complicated piece of penmanship that would take endless hours, stretching into days, even weeks, of practice to get right.[26] He stopped abruptly at the end of the first four letters of his Christian name, but did not use a simple dot to signify the abbreviation; rather, he made an upward stroke from the bottom of the 'h' to the top of the capital 'B,' where he inscribed a small circle and made a down stroke and an up stroke to begin the capital 'B.' Then the script was tilted upward at a forty-five-degree angle so that the bottom of the final 't' in Bennett was much higher than the top of the first 'R' in Rich.

It took the passage of thirteen years to bring the signature down to a level plane, and another dozen years for him to reduce it to a simple R.B. Bennett.

Tweedie, of course, fully endorsed Bennett's decision to enrol at Dalhousie and created a summer job for him from May to September each year. When Bennett graduated, Tweedie brought him into his office to practise and soon afterward formed the partnership of Tweedie and Bennett.

It was about this time that Max Aitken resurfaced.[27] He had absorbed all the education the province of New Brunswick could provide by the time he was fifteen and was living by his wits in Newcastle as a 'stringer' for the *Montreal Star* – a part-time correspondent who was paid by the column-inch for the news reports he provided – and as a life-insurance agent. Then, at sixteen, with his friend Richard Bennett as a role model, he decided to study law and persuaded Bennett to sponsor him as an articled student. Tweedie and Bennett provided Aitken with a small back room in which to work at a typewriter with a temperamental ribbon and an ink-well with an imperfect set of pens.

Aitken did not really mind, though he occasionally railed against them in notes to Bennett. He was, in fact, rather infrequently to be found in his office. He simply transferred his insurance selling and *Star* reporting to Chatham. As Tweedie would remark later, 'there were times when I wondered whether Max was working for me or I was working for him.'[28]

The town of Chatham was incorporated by the New Brunswick legislature in 1896, which meant it would now function with an elected council. It was no problem for Aitken to persuade Bennett to become a candidate for the first Chatham town council. He then stage-managed his election. First Aitken drew up an election platform of promises calculated by the editor of the local newspaper to appeal to Chatham electors. Then he persuaded the newspaper to print up bundles of election pamphlets, which Aitken delivered up and down the streets of Chatham, stopping whenever the opportunity arose to add reinforcement to the pamphlet's message. Aitken's work paid off, and Bennett was elected to council by the margin of a single vote.

On election night, Bennett was fulsome in his praise of Aitken for winning the election for him. Sometime later in the evening he came across and read for the first time a copy of Aitken's election platform. The next morning he stormed into the Tweedie and Bennett office in a towering rage at Aitken for committing him to a number of promises that would be impossible to keep or to which he was resolutely opposed.

The storm abated. What neither Aitken nor the electors of Chatham knew was that Bennett was already well along in his negotiations with Sir James Lougheed to move to Calgary in a partnership. That move was made within months of the Chatham election and was a shock to Aitken. In a long letter to Bennett, in April 1897, filled with office gossip, he urged Bennett to return to Chatham and open an office. 'You are very popular in Chatham,' he wrote, 'and they think things would be different if you were on council. I have been told that I am beginning to resemble Bennett. I am trying to with all my might, – No smoking and no drinking now.'[29]

Despite the fact that Bennett seldom replied to any of Aitken's letters, he kept writing. 'Notwithstanding that you don't answer half my letters, I write on,' he penned in July. 'I do wish you would come back and open an office . . . Tweedie's business would all fall to you.' He closed with a notation that his father was well again and pressing him to go to Dalhousie, or article with a lawyer in Saint John. He did neither, but wrote to Bennett that fall that he would soon be on his way to Calgary, singing: 'For society I don't give a curse, Let friends and relatives be damned!'

As Aitken knew so well from past experience, that was the sort of thing that would not only get Bennett's attention but was sure to trigger one of his temper tantrums. For Aitken, they were a joy to behold.

CHAPTER TWO

Calgary, North-West Territories

As 1896 dawned, Richard Bedford Bennett had every reason to believe he had the world by the tail. At twenty-five he had settled nicely into a law partnership with Lemuel Tweedie, QC, who would go on to become premier and later lieutenant-governor of New Brunswick. Bennett had lately been elected an alderman of the newly incorporated city of Chatham, New Brunswick, a sure springboard into provincial politics in the province where his family had lived for over a century. A year later he was preparing, after a mind-numbing four-day train ride, to alight at the Calgary station to an environment light-years removed from anything he had previously experienced. The catalyst for this transition had been Calgary's richest man, loudest booster, and most successful lawyer, Senator James Lougheed.

James Alexander Lougheed was a late bloomer.[1] Born in Brampton, Ontario, in 1854, he followed the carpenter's trade for several years after completing high school. Then he decided to switch from carpentry to the law and, after graduating from Osgoode Hall and articling with a Toronto firm, he headed west to Medicine Hat, North-West Territories, in 1882. The construction headquarters for the Canadian Pacific Railway was located at Medicine Hat as its mainline was pushed westward towards Calgary and the Rockies. At Medicine Hat, Lougheed met William Van Horne and persuaded the railway builder to appoint him the CPR's solicitor in Calgary. Then he set off to get to Calgary and his new home before the railway got there.

The Calgary that welcomed Lougheed in 1883 had a Mounted Police post, two trading posts, a half-dozen log cabins, a collection of Indian tipis, a clapboard and tar-paper hotel, and two score tents, all concentrated within 250 yards of the confluence of the Elbow and the Bow rivers.[2] All were there, basically in anticipation that the CPR would build a station at or near Fort Calgary. It was also rumoured that the company had chosen Calgary as the base for its assault on the Rocky Mountain passes. If that were true, there would be all kinds of jobs building the town, and a lot of money would be made by squatters who laid claim to land near the railway station. Lougheed managed to buy one of the cabins, and settled down with the rest to await the arrival of the track layers.

Trying to guess the location of the CPR station was by no means confined to the Calgarians. Indeed, the CPR had been waging a guerrilla war with squatters and land speculators ever since its main line crossed the western boundary of Manitoba. In Saskatchewan, a group of speculators headed by Edgar Dewdney, the lieutenant-governor, bought up the land for a couple of miles around a spot on Wascana Creek they believed would be the location of Regina, the new capital of the Territories.[3] The railway builders, however, ten miles east of the creek site, veered their construction sharply to the north so that the station would be located in the centre of a mile-square tract of land owned by the company. The CPR station always became the centre of new towns like Brandon, Broadview, Moose Jaw, Swift Current, and Medicine Hat. Where it located its station was always in the centre of a square mile of land owned by the railway and from which it alone would profit from subdivision into and sale of building lots.

Three months after Lougheed reached Calgary, the CPR revealed the location of its station and announced it was going to hold an auction sale of the lots. The station was, naturally, to be built a half mile west of the Mounted Police fort in the centre of a square mile of land owned by the company and devoid of a single squatter. The town plan was a sixteen-by-sixteen block grid of streets divided into north side and south side by the CPR mainline running through the centre. The streets ran north and south and the avenues east and west. The avenues were all named, mostly for prominent CPR directors and officials, and the streets were numbered. Centre Street, which ran due north from the front door of the station, divided east side and west side. Atlantic Avenue, running east and west in front of the station, and Stephen Avenue, the next removed to the north, were designated as the main business streets.

When the lot sale ended, Lougheed emerged with thirty parcels strategically dotted along the main business streets.[4] For the next ten years he juggled his time between developing his downtown real estate and expanding his law practice, which soon boasted both the Hudson's Bay Company and the Bank of Montreal as clients as well as the CPR. Within five years he had three two- and three-storey sandstone business buildings on adjacent lots on Stephen Avenue. All contained retail stores at ground level and business offices on the second floor. In one of these, the Clarence Block, the firm of Lougheed and McCarter occupied the front suite of offices on the second floor.

In his first year in Calgary, Lougheed found time to woo and wed Isabella Hardisty, a niece of Richard Hardisty, the Territories' first senator, and the CPR's Lord Strathcona as well. The Hardistys had been in the service of the Hudson's Bay Company in the northwest for three generations, and Richard Hardisty was head of its western operation when he was appointed senator for the North-West Territories in 1888. When Hardisty was killed in an accident in 1889, Lougheed was named to the Senate to replace him by Sir John A. Macdonald.

The boom on which everyone in southern Alberta counted with the arrival of the railway failed to materialize, although Calgary fared better than any other community. Its population grew from 500 in 1884 to almost 4000 in 1891, and then stopped dead in its tracks. There followed, however, a period of almost prosperous stagnation. The construction of the Calgary and Edmonton Railway, a quasi-subsidiary of the CPR, and its extension to Fort Macleod made Calgary the distribution point for the north, south, and west. A large wholesale district gradually developed on the railway sidings south and north of the main line. The railway yards east of the station echoed to the sound of freight trains being broken up and reassembled, box cars being unloaded and reloaded. Underpinned by the CPR payroll, the city developed as the main financial centre of the foothills, a retail trade centre, and a steadily improving livestock packing industry.

The weekly *Alberta Tribune* carried the business cards of these law firms: Bernard and Bernard; J.B. Smith; W.R. Winter and J.R. Costigan. None of the leading lights of the legal profession in the Territories was involved in any precedent-setting litigation that merited the attention of any law journals. Conveyancing was the bread and butter of most practices, and the first order of business of the Calgary Bar Association, when it was organized in the spring of 1890, was to set up a minimum fee standard.[5] The highest minimum on the list was $10 for drawing ordinary mortgages, articles of partnership in duplicate, and building contracts, and for registering chattel mortgages. Swearing affidavits, making searches, and the like were $1. Bill collecting was of secondary importance in producing revenue for all lawyers. Since most households ran monthly accounts with their grocers, butchers, and bakers, delinquencies were common. The lawyers also placed insurance, supplied mortgage money, and acted as agents for rental properties.

Early in his career Lougheed discovered he had neither the talent nor the taste for the nuts and bolts of law practice. From his appointment to the Senate onward, his interest in politics jostled for his primary attention with his interest in finance. Though Calgary was entangled in a no-growth situation, he continued to develop his real estate holdings and, by 1895, had a half-dozen properties built and occupied. He also had his hand in a number of local commercial and industrial developments.

The solution for Lougheed's time problem was, of course, a partnership in which one partner looked after the store while the other was on the road. Lougheed, at forty-two, had run through several joint operations with local lawyers without much success and, in 1896, when his latest partner left, he decided to canvass farther afield. He consulted the dean of Dalhousie Law School for recommendations of likely candidates with certain particular skills. The partner would have to be adventurous enough to settle permanently on the western frontier, be prepared to take over and run the practice without direction from Lougheed, be a hard worker who could quickly adapt to all phases of the law, have a personality that would enable him to achieve an empathetic relationship with Lougheed's corporate clients, be capable of holding his own in the often cut-throat competition within the profession, have a reputation for probity and sobriety, and, above all else, be a political Conservative.

Dean Weldon remembered Bennett most favourably from even before his student days and was aware of the excellent start he was making on a career in Chatham. He recommended him to Lougheed with such feeling that the senator journeyed from Ottawa to Chatham to meet him and, later, to offer him the partnership.[6] It was done with Lougheed's usual jumping-up-and-down enthusiasm for his adopted constituency. He extolled not only the friendly reception Bennett would get in Calgary but the boundless opportunities he would find there. The richness and abundance of the natural resources of the country were everywhere apparent. And Lougheed's partner, because of the corporate connections he had already made, would be most favourably placed to exploit the opportunities. If Bennett were also interested in pursuing a political career, Lougheed could promise him assistance on that count too.

The idea of pursuing a legal career in the far west was one that had never occurred to Bennett. The offer took him completely by surprise but, despite Lougheed's blandishments, he withheld making a decision. Lougheed returned to Calgary to formalize his offer in writing. Eventually in the fall of 1896 a deal was struck. Bennett would join the Lougheed firm and, in the first year, would receive 20 per cent of the net earnings of the partnership up to $3750, and 30 per cent of the earnings above that figure. The following year each percentage figure was to increase by 5 per cent. Then the arrangement would be renegotiated.[7]

The Calgary that welcomed Richard Bedford Bennett on a late January morning in 1897 was a world Bennett never could have imagined. Having spent his entire twenty-six years in the verdant splendour of the 'forest primeval' that was New Brunswick, nothing could have prepared him for the desolation that met his eyes as he emerged from the CPR station on to Atlantic Avenue. The park along the station front was now covered with a skiff of dust-blackened snow. Off to one corner, the beginning of a shrubbery was abandoned to the winds of winter. Ahead of him Centre Street stretched unbroken to the Bow River a half mile to the north. To the right, to the left, and straight ahead were mud streets bordered with plank sidewalks.

The CPR station, freight sheds, and executive office building stretched for two blocks along the south side of Atlantic Avenue. Across the way, between Centre Street and First Street West, were the Palace, Windsor, and Dominion hotels, interspersed by vacant lots and large livery stables. To the right, from Centre Street to First Street East, were the Yale, Empire, and Grand Central hotels, likewise separated by livery stables and empty lots.

The livery stables and empty lots were very much a part of the Calgary scene. The stables, with their attached benches for leisure taking, were convenient town and country meeting places. Business people on excursions to bank or railway station paused at each stable to see who was in town. The empty lots were convenient parking places for farm wagons and for cowboys' horses while their owners were in the neighbourhood. Cow ponies were seldom if ever stabled. Most of all, the vacant lots were piling grounds for manure from the livery stables; by midsummer, when the wind came just behind the rain, they pungently attested to the fact that Calgary was very much a horse town. Beyond the interstices provided by the stable yards were the backsides of Stephen Avenue – an unbroken stretch of two- and three-storey dull-gray and red-brick commercial buildings that extended from First Street West to First Street East, the business centre of pioneer Calgary.

After downtown Calgary was destroyed by fire in 1886, the city turned almost exclusively to brick and locally quarried sandstone as a building material. Its lustreless gray surface seemed to soak up sunlight, to absorb it instead of reflecting it. On the brightest of days downtown Calgary turned a sombre face to the world, and on overcast days it was downright depressing. From horizon to horizon there was not a tree to be seen, and the clouds of dust being blown around by a swirling wind accentuated the unalloyed dullness of the landscape, particularly in the early morning gloom. It was enough to persuade a young Maritimer to turn on his heel and take the next eastbound train out of town.

But not the young, cerebral Mr Bennett who was not given to reacting to external stimuli. He had not come to Calgary for the scenery but to embark on a two-pronged career that would take him to the top of the legal profession and to the office of prime minister of Canada. He had absorbed enough of Lougheed's enthusiasm for the future of the country to believe that Calgary might launch him on successful flights of both fancies, even if the capital of Canada did not eventually transfer to Alberta, as Lougheed foresaw. He could hardly wait to get started and, when he spotted the flag-pole atop the Bank of Montreal on Stephen Avenue, where Lougheed said it would be, he pulled his overcoat up over his ears and strode off purposefully for the Alberta Hotel, across the street from the bank, where a room was reserved for him. The trunks full of law books he had brought with him could be delivered to the Lougheed and Bennett office later.

The three-storey, fifty-room Alberta Hotel was the best in Calgary and was obliquely across the street from the Clarence Block, where Bennett's shingle would hang for the next twenty-five years of his professional life. It also had the largest dining room and the longest bar in the west. It was thus the favourite meeting place and watering hole for the city's business and professional community, as well as the neighbouring ranchers and farmers.

The fact that Senator Lougheed had a new partner coming in from the east had been noised about town for several weeks. Then, on the day of his arrival, the weekly *Tribune* carried two items, though neither one could have been called headline news:

The last N.W.T. Gazette announces the appointments of L.C. Fulmer of

Banff, James Walker of Calgary and George Hamilton of Calgary as licensed commissioners and Richard B. Bennett as an Advocate.

Richard B. Bennett, barrister, Chatham, N.B. has moved to Calgary to join one of our legal firms.

There could have been no doubt in anyone's mind that R.B. Bennett was that partner when he moved up to the desk in the Alberta Hotel that morning to register. His black bowler hat, white scarf, stylishly cut overcoat, sharply pressed pants, and polished shoes identified him from 100 feet as a stranger in a town where short 'reefer' coats and never-pressed frontier pants were the accepted norm in men's clothing. As Bennett was finishing registering, a couple of local citizens approached to introduce themselves and welcome him to Calgary. One invited Bennett to accompany him into the bar for a drink. 'Thank you very much,' said Bennett, 'but I don't drink.'

The other stranger, after introducing himself, reached into his vest pocket for his cigar case, drew out a smoke, and offered it to Bennett. 'Thank you very much,' said Bennett, 'but I don't smoke.'

A third Calgarian who had been listening to the exchange turned to the desk clerk. 'Boy oh boy,' he said, 'there's a guy who's got no future in this man's town!'

This apocryphal anecdote, which surfaces occasionally in journalistic probings of Calgary's 'colourful' roots, accentuates the 'wildwestness' of its pioneer era in a way it hardly deserves.

Because it was both a jumping-off place for the hinterland and a layover place between trains, Calgary was served by more than a normal quota of hotels and, hence, hotel bar rooms where liquor was sold. While the CPR provided daily service each way on its transcontinental line, it offered only twice-weekly service north to Edmonton and south to Fort Macleod, a six-hour journey either way. Missed train connections were the order of the day, particularly in winter, so the hotels were frequently filled with wayfarers with time on their hands. They rubbed elbows in the bars with the settlers who came into the city for supplies and waited overnight to get an early start on their long journeys home. A greater than normal floating population undoubtedly increased the amount of boozing that went on in Calgary and the bar-room brawling that erupted and occasionally spilled out onto the streets. Nor was it uncommon for liquored-up cowboys to stage impromptu horse races down Stephen Avenue and, in the process, frighten tethered farm teams into tearing loose from their hitching posts to join the race.

But Calgary was also home to several thousand sober, pious, and hard-working people whose regular nine-hour days, six days a week, left little time or inclination for carousing. For most of them, what was mainly on their minds was saving enough out of their summer's wages to carry them through the winter, when the economy slowed to a halt. That was a milieu in which young Mr Bennett would come to feel very much at home. As for the non-drinking recreational facilities, Calgary was indeed a wasteland. It had a handsome Opera House, but it was dark most of the time. There were no theatres or dance halls, though there was dancing at the hotel dining rooms occasionally. That suited Bennett, too, because his hardshell Methodist faith had no accommodation for contrived amusements, dancing, and card playing. In his native New Brunswick he had developed no interest in games, sports, or athletics, which was just as well because the only sporting events in Calgary were occasional cricket matches between pick-up teams of 'The English' and 'The Rest.' Some young Americans tried to work up an interest in baseball with only moderate success.

Once Richard Bennett was comfortably settled into his new home town he discovered that Calgary was populated by his kind of people – overwhelmingly, even awesomely so. When the Canadian government completed its census for 1901 it reported that the Anglo-Saxon Protestants outnumbered all the 'lesser breeds' by something like ten to one. The nose counting by racial origins identified 1982 English, 1117 Scots, 1004 Irish, 400 Scandinavian, along with 197 German, 125 French, and 64 Chinese. Of the Protestants, 1293 were Presbyterians, 1253 Anglicans, 950 Methodists, 345 Baptists, and 221 Lutherans. The

Roman Catholics numbered only 537. Uncounted in the government census was the intensity of the Protestant work ethic in Calgary. The long hours of sunshine made it possible for the building trades to extend their normal fifty-four hours a week well into the seventy-two-hour range, increasing their pay packets from around $2.50 to well over $3.00 a day.

Calgary was not exactly a city of churches, but there were enough to satisfy the needs of the citizenry. In addition to the Catholic, Anglican, Presbyterian, Methodist, and Baptist churches, there was a Salvation Army Citadel and a German Lutheran congregation that met in the homes of its adherents. At the time of Bennett's arrival, the nation was in the throes of the early run-up to the national prohibition plebiscite of 1898. It was in the prohibition campaign, in which the Methodist church was most active, that Bennett made his political debut in Alberta, when he carried the 'Dry' message to the communities in the Calgary area.

The CPR westbound train, in 1897, arrived in Calgary at around 3 pm, when it was on time. In the winter it was so infrequently on time that few Calgarians bothered to meet it. Senator Lougheed was among those Calgarians. He waited until after breakfast to saunter down to the hotel, where he was in time to help his young partner unpack his clothes and assist him in stretching out the wrinkles that had accumulated over the journey westward. Later that day Lougheed took him around to the court house and to their offices. That evening Bennett accompanied the Lougheed family to an operatic concert at Hull's Opera House by Madam Albani, the Italian diva. As it happened, the weather had turned bitterly cold in Calgary that week and it was a moot point who shivered most, the touring players on the stage or the huddling audience in their seats. Forty-two years later, on his farewell visit to Calgary, Bennett would most vividly recall his experience, that first week, of almost losing his way in a blizzard as he walked the eight blocks from the Alberta Hotel to Lougheed's home to keep a dinner engagement.[8]

The Lougheed and Bennett law office took up the front half of the second floor of the Clarence Block, which was across the street and fifty yards east of the Alberta Hotel. The senator had the more westerly of the two private offices, and Bennett was assigned the other. Between the two was the general office for the secretaries and a couple of students and clerks. The other half of the second floor was occupied by the offices of two other lawyers and an insurance and real estate agency.

Bennett settled comfortably into his new office and his new city. He became a permanent guest of the Albert Hotel, occupying a third-floor room and taking his meals in the hotel dining room. For the next two years Bennett's time was equally divided between the Alberta Hotel and his office. Lougheed had equipped his offices with acetyne gas lights, which provided much better illumination for reading than the coal oil lamps of the Alberta Hotel. After finishing supper, RB usually repaired to the Lougheed and Bennett office for three or four hours of recreational reading. His hotel-room reading was usually confined to a single chapter from the Bible, his bedtime reading ritual all his life.

Bennett fitted into the social life of the city as easily as he did into his new professional career, though it was more a peripheral involvement than an active participation. The senator had him to dinner and introduced him into his circle of friends. They in turn had Bennett to dinner, particularly when they needed an unattached male to even up the seating arrangements. He had followed his father into the Masonic Order in Hopewell, and he renewed the fellowship when he arrived in Calgary, along with membership in the First Methodist Church.[9] Lougheed, a fellow Methodist, took Bennett to church on his first Sunday in Calgary. It was the beginning of a long commitment that would culminate with Bennett's purchase of a handsome set of chimes for the church's bell tower in 1927. The church, when Bennett joined, was beset with problems rooted in its long and steady decline in membership. The church members were inclined to attribute the decline to the deficiencies of their current minister, and their disenchantment with the Rev. V.R. Vrooman, a recent appointee, was reaching a point where an active movement to replace him was developing. Bennett was caught up in the movement and was entrusted by the board of management with drafting a resolution to ease his departure. A couple of years later, when the board decided to build a larger edifice, Bennett was given the responsibility of purchasing the site at First Street West and Seventh Avenue.

Aside from these episodes, Bennett seems to have played little part in the active management of the church's affairs. He attended the evening service and taught in the Sunday school, but that seems to have been it. The Calgary newspapers (there were four at the time) gave extensive news coverage to the activities of all religious organizations and fraternal societies, particularly the Masonic Order. Bennett's name never turned up in any of these news reports. Aside from church attendance, he tended to keep to himself. Despite the best efforts of the community to fit him into its social life, he led a lonely life during his first year in Calgary.

It may well have been that it was a need for companionship that impelled Bennett to arrange to have his brother George join him. In any event, when Bennett was home for Christmas in 1897, it was agreed that when George completed high school in 1898, he would enrol at the Mount Allison Academy and Commercial College in Sackville, New Brunswick, to prepare himself for a career in business. The *Calgary Herald*, on 19 January 1899, noted that when Bennett returned from his annual Christmas holiday in New Brunswick, he was accompanied by his brother George, who was taking up residence in Calgary. The residence he took up was the joint occupancy with his brother of a large front room in Mrs Moore's rooming house at 222 Reinach Avenue, later Fourth Avenue West. It was a room they would share for the next five years. In fact, they only slept there and went their separate ways.

Unquestionably through Bennett's influence, George got a job as a ledger keeper at the Bank of Montreal. Unlike his brother, the outgoing George made friends easily and was soon moving in his own circle. While RB continued to take his meals at the Alberta Hotel, George's ledger keeper's salary dictated that he 'board' at Mrs Moore's. When Mrs Moore moved to Sixth Avenue the house was taken over by two widowed sisters, Sarah and

Emma Smith. They would remain R.B. Bennett's landladies for the next twenty years. Even after he had acquired a Mount Royal mansion and upwards of $1 million in assets, home remained a furnished front room on Fourth Avenue.[10]

For those twenty years, Bennett's Calgary would be bounded by his lodgings on Fourth Avenue West, the Alberta Hotel where he took his meals, the Clarence Block, the law courts on Seventh Avenue, and the First Methodist Church on Second Street West. His taking of meals at the Alberta Hotel has become deeply etched in Calgary folklore. A creature of habit, Bennett tended to gravitate to the same table at the back of the hotel dining room. As time passed it became known as 'the Bennett table,' at which his friends frequently joined him at noon for the exchange of badinage and gossip and for business discussions. Though Bennett never told a joke, he enjoyed the persiflage that lightened the lunch hour. Nor was the hour always devoid of serious conversation. It was a place for Bennett's friends to raise problems and ventilate grievances, some of which were grist for Bennett's mill. Thus, a discussion of freight rates or stock saddles might find its way into a Bennett Territorial Assembly animadversion on Alberta's freight-rate disabilities. In the beginning, however, Bennett ate at the Alberta Hotel because it was handy, the food was good, and the price – twenty-five cents – reasonable, even by the low Calgary standard. Lunch-time companionship developed later.[11]

Bennett's entry into the profession in Calgary was formally announced on 13 February 1897, when the Lougheed and Bennett business card made its appearance in the columns of the *Alberta Tribune* and the *Calgary Herald*. It listed the firm's most important clients – the Bank of Montreal, Great West Life, Ontario Loan and Debenture Company, and Berbeck Investment Company. By then Bennett had already made his first appearance in court, as reported in the *Tribune* on 6 February 1897: 'On Thursday before Mr. Justice Rouleau in chambers, the application of John Donahue for a writ of certiorari to quash a conviction under a by-law of the City of Calgary, under which he was fined for operating a billiard table without a license, was argued.

R.B. Bennett appeared for the appellant and A.L. Sifton for the city.'

There was something almost prophetic in the legal collision, for Arthur Sifton became the target for the almost virulent personal animus that Bennett sometimes developed for political opponents. Yet the two men had many things in common: both were deeply committed Methodists, both were teetotallers. In 1895 Sifton had helped launch the 'provincial status for Alberta' campaign, which Bennett joined and used to precipitate his own entry into Alberta politics in 1898. But Sifton was a Liberal, and that in itself was a mortal sin. He was, moreover, the brother of Sir Clifford Sifton, Laurier's super-powered minister of the interior, which was worse.

Bennett lost no time in joining the Methodist church on his arrival in Calgary. It was the church, in a way, that opened the door into politics for him. The pastors of most Protestant churches were active in the Prohibition drive of 1897, and Bennett enlisted immediately as a volunteer speaker for the cause. He appeared at meetings in the winter of 1897-8 as far north as Red Deer. Later on, when he decided to run for the North-West Territories Assembly, his 'Dry' stand was used in a slanderous campaign against him.[12]

The other major political handicap Bennett had to overcome was the fact that his firm represented the CPR in Calgary. Although it was the lifeline of Alberta and the rest of the Prairies, the CPR was well on its way to becoming, at the turn of the century, the favourite whipping boy of the Prairie West. That attitude was summed up in an apocryphal story that circulated the country for fifty years. It concerned the farmer who came home to discover that his only daughter had lost her virginity to the hired man and was now palpably pregnant. The father threw his hat on the floor, jumped on it, and cried: 'Goddam the C.P.R.!'

Behind this attitude were many causes. Merchants complained about freight and express rates, about delays in receiving shipments, about damage to goods in transit. Farmers complained of freight rates, losses of livestock in transit, damage to grain in transit, and delays in movement of livestock and in obtaining box cars for grain shipments. In the cities and towns there were complaints of unsafe and inadequate crossings of the railway tracks. In the country there were endless complaints of livestock being killed by the trains. Underlying everything was disenchantment with the slowness of the settlement of the west and the lack of construction of branch railway lines to open up the country. It took the CPR an unconscionable time to learn how to run a railway, even to bringing its original trackage up to a standard that would enable it to maintain schedules in face of the vagaries of western weather.

Moreover, the CPR had, over a period of ten years, developed a singularly effective means of dealing with complaints. It ignored them! To the farmer pounding the table and demanding compensation for his train-slaughtered cows there was a simple question: What were the cows doing trespassing on the property of the CPR? To the citizenry held up at road crossings, what was a few minutes delay for a handful compared with the need of hundreds to get their merchandise? Associating with the CPR won no popularity contests.

Bennett's first order of business as James Lougheed's partner was to familiarize himself with the legal and political realities of the North-West Territories. Civil law did not present much of a problem, since it only meant substituting the special aspects of a grain and livestock economy for those of a lumbering and fishing economy. The double-barrelled criminal law branch, however, took a little getting used to. The North-West Mounted Police was a law unto itself when it came to the criminal code. It could arrest a thief, try him in the Mounted Police Barracks before the area superintendent who was acting as a magistrate, and become his jailer, if the superintendent-magistrate deemed a jail sentence necessary. The city magistrate functioned when offences took place within Calgary, though he was mainly concerned with cases involving city by-laws. In major criminal cases the trial was by the Queen's Bench judge for the 'Provisional District of Alberta,' as the future Province of Alberta was officially designated.

If there was anything this young lawyer needed throughout 1897 it was clients for his legal services. Southern Alberta, and

Calgary with it, had not yet achieved the status of 'next year country.' At best it was very much the 'year after the year after next year country.' In the year before Bennett's arrival, the Department of the Interior had managed to fill only 1857 applications for homesteads for all of western Canada.[13] Even this paltry number had to be discounted to 1400 by the cancellation of 457 homesteads taken up in previous years. Clifford Sifton was only beginning to reorganize the interior department and his intensive drive to lure American, British, and European farmers to the Prairies was not even being prepared for launching yet. Calgarians were not given to suing each other, and the legal work that was generated seldom justified large fees. Nor was the volume of work available to the Lougheed and Bennett partnership great enough to keep both lawyers busy, even though the senator was absent from the city much of the time. As Bennett would recall forty years later in an interview with Frederick Griffin of the *Toronto Star*, if conditions had been any better anywhere else he'd have gone there. During his first year in Calgary, his earnings had not exceeded $1000.[14]

Too much should not be made of the $1000 figure. Bennett could have lived very well indeed on it. Several years later, when Calgary was in the throes of the big boom, an insight can be gained into his cost of living from a letter he wrote to a friend in Hopewell Hill concerning a vacant high school principalship. Board and lodging for a single man cost at least $26 a month. Bennett paid $33. A man and wife with two children could expect to pay at least $75 a month. Houses were scarce and expensive – $15 to $30 a month. But on the where-there's-smoke-there's-fire principle, it might be assumed that Bennett did start looking around for an alternative turf within a couple of months of his arrival in Calgary. On 17 March 1897 the *Calgary Herald* carried the following short paragraph: 'The Herald is authorized to contradict the report in the Revelstoke Herald that Mr. R.B. Bennett was about to locate in Revelstoke.' Yet if Bennett had not contemplated moving to Revelstoke, why not?

In contrast with stagnating Calgary, the interior of British Columbia was spectacularly alive. In the winter of 1896–7 its mountains were acrawl with prospectors searching for even more fabulous deposits of gold, silver, copper, lead, and zinc than had already been discovered. Enough coal had been staked out in the East Kootenays alone to fire all the furnaces in Canada. In the wake of the gold, silver, and base metal discoveries, American capital was flowing in to build the mines, mills, smelters, and refineries needed to bring the prospects into production. The benefits from such activity would accrue to the United States over a branch line of the Northern Pacific Railway that had recently been completed between Spokane and Grand Forks, British Columbia.

Out of all this arose a steadily mounting agitation for the construction of a railway from Lethbridge to Nelson through the Crowsnest Pass. Such a government-built railway would break the CPR monopoly. It would preserve for Canada and Canadians the benefits from processing British Columbia's ore in Canada. The pleas for a Crow's Nest Pass railway that had gone forward to the Conservative administration had gone unanswered. Then, hard upon the election of the Laurier Liberals in 1896, the minister of railways and canals, A.G. Blair, came west with promises that seemed to commit the new government to the project. Not only would it immediately embark on the construction of the railway, but it would be a government-owned project that would break the hated CPR transportation monopoly. Calgarians sat back happily and waited for construction to begin. The euphoria evaporated with the publication in the Toronto *Globe* in February 1897 of the report that the railway would be built by the CPR.

Calgary had long regarded the eastern interior of British Columbia as a potentially rich commercial colony of the city, and a Crow's Nest Pass railway as its way of penetrating that market. When the *Globe* story broke it sent the town into a panic, for it indicated that the CPR's monopoly on the setting of freight rates would continue. The public protest meeting the mayor called on 2 March 1897 introduced the newly arrived R.B. Bennett to the longest standing, longest running, most vexatious of all Prairie grievances: freight rates! It was this meeting that aroused in Bennett his life-long interest in Canadian transportation policy.

As a newcomer in town, Bennett was prepared to sit and listen to the business and professional leaders of southern Alberta making common cause against the CPR. Liberal leaders like A.L. Sifton joined Conservatives like Senator Lougheed in oratorical assaults on the freight, express, and passenger rate-making policies of the CPR.

The resolution before the meeting was simple and to the point: 'Be it resolved that the Dominion Government build the road.' There was scarcely an extant Albertan who did not have a favourite horror story based on the CPR. A.L. McCarthy, the meeting chairman, cited two. For the people of Rat Portage, Ontario, 135 miles *east* of Winnipeg, who wanted to go to Toronto, it was cheaper to buy a ticket to Winnipeg and go from there, passing through Rat Portage en route, than to board an eastbound train at Rat Portage. And it was cheaper to travel from Nelson, British Columbia, to Toronto through Calgary than it was from Calgary to Toronto. Business people cited other examples – the low cost per ton-mile of moving goods in Ontario and Quebec compared with the high costs on the prairies. Government ownership was regarded as the only way of escape from CPR rate making.

The unanimously passed resolution of 2 March fared no better in Liberal Ottawa than the previous importuning had in Conservative Ottawa. It foundered on the rock of Clifford Sifton's intransigent opposition to government ownership. Still, Sifton drove a hard bargain with the CPR.[15] Instead of the demanded subsidy of $20,000 a mile, he got the company to accept $11,000. And to dampen the public outrage over freight rates, the rate on all grain shipped from western Canada was reduced by three cents per 100 pounds. Westbound rates on a large number of commodities were also substantially reduced, from 10 per cent to 33⅓ per cent. Perhaps most important of all, the CPR was to first get government approval of the freight rates it would charge on the Crow's Nest Pass Railway, along with the rates it would establish for moving goods from the Canadian Northern Railway over the CPR.

By the time the bill to formalize the deal with the CPR was working its way through parliament in the summer of 1897, the firm of Lougheed and Bennett had been bitten by the gold bug. Word of the fabulous discoveries in the Klondike exploded across the world when steamers docking at Seattle and San Francisco began discharging prospectors from the Yukon with pockets full of the gold dust they had taken from their claims the previous winter. The world-wide gold rush for the Klondike was on. Soon the trains reaching Edmonton were disgorging coveys of tenderfeet eager to begin the long overland trek to the Yukon. In Calgary the Board of Trade organized a mass meeting in mid-August 1897, to lay the foundation for turning Calgary into the main jumping-off point for the Klondike.[16]

This meeting marked the emergence of Bennett as a Calgary civic booster of unbounded enthusiasm. Even the *Montreal Star*, he said, had recognized in its columns that Calgary was an ideal outfitting point for Yukon-bound gold seekers. Inquiries were being received from all over the world. He urged the city to get busy and prepare a booklet of helpful hints for gold seekers, advertising Calgary's advantage as an outfitting centre. The booklet could be widely circulated, even sent to the office of the Canadian high commissioner in London. Bennett was named by the meeting to a committee to discuss with Sir Thomas Shaughnessy, vice-president at the CPR, the possibility of building a railway extension to the Yukon.

In the meantime, Senator Lougheed had organized several prospecting parties to search for gold along the Elbow River west of Calgary and into the mountains beyond. In November 1897 the firm of Lougheed and Bennett announced that at the next session of the Territorial Assembly it would apply for incorporation of the Klondike-Alberta Transportation Company to move goods and people from the Saskatchewan River to the Liard and Peace rivers en route to the Yukon.

The extent of Bennett's financial involvement in Lougheed's gold-mining sorties can only be guessed at, for his limited financial resources left little margin for investment in prospecting syndicates or in gold and base-metal mining companies. But regardless of the depth of the gold-bug's bite, it left Bennett permanently infected.[17] For the rest of his life, resource development was something he could not resist. He was into mining promotions with John I. McFarland, into prospecting syndicates with C.C. Cross and W.R. Hull. When he was cataloguing his shareholding in 1939, his list contained the names of a dozen mining companies in which he had long held shares, then of little or no value, as well as another dozen of substantial value, including 500 shares of Kerr Addison, 1000 Wright Hargrave, 50 Hudson's Bay, 15,000 Lebel Oro, and unstated numbers in Imperial Oil and International Petroleum.

Bennett's public appearances in Calgary in civic and temperance crusades did not compensate, however, for the absence of something else he had enjoyed immensely in New Brunswick: partisan party political confrontations. Participation in the political process had been the spice of Bennett's life in New Brunswick where:

> Every little Canadian born alive
> is either a little Liberal or Conservative.

Lougheed, Paddy Nolan, Dr R.G. Brett, and James Riley were all Conservatives, but where was the Conservative party? Where was the political party activity he could become involved in to round out his life? There was none, and for a very simple reason. The North-West Territories was in the process of evolving from Crown Colony status into self-governing status and had not yet reached a point of responsible government by political parties.

The North-West Territories, formerly Rupert's Land, became the *property* of the Dominion of Canada in 1870 by right of purchase from the Hudson's Bay Company. As befitted an imperial power, Ottawa forthwith dispatched a lieutenant-governor to take possession of and govern its colony.[18] The North-West Territories Act, Statutes of Canada, 1875, chapter 49, provided a temporary form of government pending the arrival of an expected flow of immigrants who would permanently settle it. This first government consisted of a lieutenant-governor, appointed by the Governor General in Council, who would 'administer the government under instruction from time to time given him by Order in Council or by the Secretary of State of Canada.'

The lieutenant-governor, 'with the advice of the Queen's Privy Council for Canada,' was empowered to appoint up to five persons, including the stipendiary magistrates, to a council to aid in the administration of the Territories. There was provision in the act to expand the membership of the council to twenty-one as the settlements grew. A general rewriting of the act took place in 1885 when the advisory council became the Legislative Assembly, and the limit to the elected membership was raised to twenty-two plus a maximum of three legal experts appointed by Ottawa. These appointees would participate in all the proceedings of the assembly, but would not vote.

The business of the assembly was limited to whatever was presented to it in the Speech from the Throne. In composing the speech, the lieutenant-governor had an advisory committee of four, which he selected from the membership of the assembly. The assembly was empowered to pass ordinances for local and municipal taxation, property and civil rights, public health, roads, licensing of inns, injury to public morals, police, nuisances, and generally all matters of merely local or private nature.

The legislation limited the spending of the assembly to whatever money Ottawa supplied. It did *not* provide for the adoption of the British system of responsible government by political parties. The administration for the Territories was completely subservient to the political party in power in Ottawa. It was, however, a form of administration that made very good sense – there was nobody there to govern except Indians when it was first appointed. In 1882 there were scarcely 5000 white settlers between Manitoba and the Rockies. Mostly they were settled in what would become eastern Saskatchewan, in the vicinity of Mounted Police posts at Regina, Fort Macleod, and Calgary and around the old trading post at Edmonton. Nevertheless, settlers were filtering in and, by 1883, five additional members were elected to the advisory council and the Territories capital was firmly established in Regina.

By the time the North-West Rebellion had run its course in 1885, the full quota of twenty-two members was reached, but it was still strictly an advisory body without power to originate fiscal legislation. It was still devoid of political parties and it stayed that way for twenty years, largely through the dominant influence of F.W.G. Haultain, a brilliant young lawyer who had settled at Fort Macleod in 1884 and was elected to the assembly in 1887. He was chosen to the lieutenant-governor's advisory council, and his skill as a spokesman for the administration soon elevated him to the role of de facto 'premier' of the Territories. Although Haultain was a dedicated Conservative, he became the accepted spokesman for the assembly in negotiations with Liberal Ottawa. Moreover, he was the intransigent champion of the non-partisan form of Legislative Assembly that prevailed. This was the situation that existed when Bennett eventually lifted his attention from his law books to contemplate the political opportunities available to him in his new environment. There was none, unless he could ignite a responsible-government provincial-status crusade to re-place the present system. His participation in the Prohibition campaign was Bennett's spring training camp for the political big leagues.

The unexpected arrival of Max Aitken in Calgary in the spring of 1898 was unquestionably a factor in Bennett's decision to run for the Territorial Assembly in the November 1898 election. Aitken had master-minded and work-horsed Bennett's successful run for a seat on the Chatham town council in 1895. After Bennett left for the west, Aitken no longer found the atmosphere in Tweedie's law office tolerable and he left to take a job in a bank. Then he enrolled briefly in the Saint John Law School, before heading west to seek his fame and fortune. Bennett was delighted to see him, and there was much getting together for old-times' sake — until, that is, Aitken's first business venture. He and a new business partner succeeded in persuading the Union Bank to lend them $250 with which to buy a bowling alley across the street from Bennett's office.[19]

Bennett was outraged that a friend of his could be so uncouth as to associate with the low-life Calgarian habitués of bars, pool rooms, and bowling halls. Their relationship ruptured temporarily, with Bennett ordering Aitken out of his office and off the premises. Relations were restored weeks later when the assembly election was called and Aitken volunteered to run Bennett's campaign in Calgary.

Another dividend Bennett collected on the trail for Prohibition was the friendship of George Cloakey, an effervescent land agent from Olds.[20] Cloakey was not a Prohibitionist but he was fascinated by Bennett's platform mastery. He cultivated his friendship and became his first campaign manager and long-serving political counsellor. Whether it was Max Aitken, George Cloakey, or Sir James Lougheed who persuaded Bennett to run for the Calgary West seat is lost to history, but the fact he decided to run early in the race is indicated by a brief notice that appeared on 25 June 1898 in the *Alberta Tribune* to the effect that R.B. Bennett was likely to give C.O. Critchley, the sitting member, a vigorous challenge in the upcoming election.

One of the advantages of the system in place was that anybody could run without bothering to get a nomination from any political party. All that was required was a deposit of $100 to pay for ballots and a notice of intention in a newspaper. Bennett inserted his formal notice in the *Herald* for the 4 November election on 30 August and hit the campaign trail.

The people of Alberta in the summer of 1898 were far too busy trying to become established, whether on farms, ranches, or in business, or practising a trade, to be overly attentive to what governments were up to, in Regina or in Ottawa. But a consensus was growing among people who had time to think about it that everything was likely to improve if the Territories were granted provincial status and the right to run their own affairs, as in Manitoba, British Columbia, and Ontario. In 1896 the Laurier administration had amended the North-West Territories Act to provide an increased measure of autonomy, but since Ottawa still controlled the purse strings and the patronage, self-government was more apparent than real. It was perhaps inevitable, when the election was called, that provincial status would become the major issue of the campaign.

Provincial status had been the subject of desultory discussion for many months, but nothing had come of it because, it was claimed, the population was not large enough to make provincial status feasible. The waters were also muddied by the how-big-a-province argument. One school of thought headed by Haultain maintained that the whole area between Manitoba and British Columbia should be one province. Others argued for two provinces roughly the size of present-day Alberta and Saskatchewan. Though he was by no means alone, it was Bennett who seized the issue of immediate provincial status for Alberta, with Calgary as the capital.

Ordinarily, anyone as young as Bennett and so new to the country would have had two strikes against him when the election took place. Such sentiment was substantially diluted, however, by the general disenchantment that existed with the performance of the members of the assembly. Non-partisanship turned out to be, on examination, synonymous with rubber-stamping of administration policy. Since the entire executive except for Haultain was straight-grain Liberal, the pioneer settlers of Conservative persuasion tended to see any newcomer as an improvement on the sitting members.

As the election approached, there was no burning issue of 'throw the rascals out' because there was no apparent rascality in the assembly. Nobody accused any of the members of anything except being bumbling incompetents. A lot of people seemed to agree with the general attitude expressed in Bob Edwards's *Wetaskiwin Free Lance*: get rid of all the sitting members and elect a new bunch. The sitting members for Calgary West and Calgary East both sampled the political currents and decided not to run for re-election. There was, in short, a considerable ground swell in favour of new blood in the assembly, and Bennett was about as new as anyone could get. In a young man's country, as southern Alberta certainly was, being a twenty-eight-year-old lawyer was not in itself totally offensive to the electors.

The Calgary West constituency extended from Fish Creek in

the south to the village of Olds in the north, a distance of seventy miles, and from Centre Street in Calgary to Jumping Pound in the ranching country west of Calgary. Within this area, George Cloakey knew just about everybody and set up a number of ranch-house and town-hall meetings for Bennett.[21] Sometimes Bennett hired a horse and buggy and made his own way to the meeting. When he did, he was often late because of his unfamiliarity with the local landmarks on the trails. When he went with Cloakey he got there on time. In Calgary, Max Aitken took over preparation and distribution of printed material.

The gregarious Aitken was a tireless canvasser. It was well that he was because Calgary homesites were so scattered that he frequently had to walk a half-dozen blocks to deliver a half-dozen handbills. Then he discovered the 'Mission' district south of the railway tracks along the Elbow River, where the older houses were more closely placed. He focused his attention there and turned it into a Bennett stronghold.

Coming as the campaign did in the midst of harvest, it was well nigh impossible to get the farmers and their families together for a meeting. Bennett came to regard a few listeners as all that could be expected. However, George Cloakey arranged for a good meeting in Olds on 9 September. By this time there were two other candidates in the race for Calgary West, and a third would be in the field before election day. James Muir, QC, was a veteran Calgary lawyer and W.W. Stuart a prominent rancher. The last man in the field was James Riley, a Calgary pioneer and one of the largest land owners on the north side of the Bow River. Bennett, Muir, and Riley were Conservatives and Stuart was the only Liberal on the ballot. Bennett and Muir collided head on at the campaign meeting in Olds.[22]

In arranging the meeting in Olds, Cloakey did not invite the other candidates to share the platform, a courtesy usually extended in pioneer election meetings. Bennett's theme that evening was the need for vigorous new ideas from vigorous new representatives in the assembly. Midway through his speech, when hecklers began to question his knowledge of farm and ranch problems and to chide him on his too recent arrival in the country, Bennett lost his temper and launched an attack on the aged and decrepit candidates who were opposing him. Did they, he demanded, want one of his opponents to represent them? Played-out old men between sixty and seventy? Disappointed office seekers with worn-out ideas? Or did they want a young man, an energetic man with elastic ideas who would not hesitate to represent them with vigour and imagination?

When he concluded his emotional appeal, who should be waiting in front of the hall but the 'ancient and worn out' James Muir, who challenged him on all counts. He shouted denunciation at Bennett, who shouted back. Eventually the confrontation became so menacing that a Mounted Police constable who was in the audience came forward, separated the two men, and tried to escort Bennett out of the building. Whereupon Bennett rounded on the constable with such vehemence that the policeman backed off.

In a small town like Olds, with a population of a couple of hundred, the uproar at the election meeting was naturally on everybody's tongue the next day. Bennett was no longer an anonymous character who had blown in from Calgary. He was somebody to reckon with, and George Cloakey went back again and again in the weeks that followed to build on the public awareness base that developed out of the meeting.

As far as Calgary itself was concerned, Bennett kicked off his campaign on 27 September with one of the biggest political meetings ever seen in the town.[23] He hired the Hull Opera House for the meeting and invited all his opponents to share his platform. He made a special effort to persuade the electors to bring their wives along to see the political process at work. As the *Herald* would report, the ladies comfortably filled the dress circle of the Opera House and took a lively interest in proceedings, even though it would be another eighteen years before they would be permitted to mark a ballot. Bennett, while he avoided the suffragette issue, welcomed the women to the meeting and urged them to become more involved in the issues that were facing the people of Alberta and Canada.[24]

Bennett met his relationship with the CPR head on in his

speech. If the interests of the railway company ever came into conflict with the interests of the people of Calgary it would be the people who would command his support, he promised. To emphasize that point, he said one of his main concerns was to get the government to finance the construction of a railway from Fort Macleod, the terminus of the Calgary and Edmonton Railway, to Jim Hill's Northern Pacific Railway in Montana. Immigrants from the United States could then gain direct access to the Calgary area. He pointed out that the Canadian Railway Act required all railway companies to give other railways access to their trackage in order to serve the public need. To the cheers of the crowd Bennett said he was a profound believer in the merits of competition, for the CPR as well as for other enterprises.

What set Bennett's major political speech off from the general run of local political oratory was the depth of the information he provided and the sureness of his grasp of his subject. His citation of chapter and verse of the Railway Act, along with a clear explanation of how it worked, was a case in point. Most important of all, Bennett spoke out strongly in favour of immediate provincial status for the Alberta area, with Calgary as the capital. In the meantime, he advocated government by political parties within the Territories. James Muir did not attend Bennett's meeting, but he sent a proxy speaker to ridicule Bennett's candidacy. How could the people of Calgary West take his candidacy seriously, he demanded, when 95 per cent of them had never heard of R.B. Bennett? Bennett, who was lacking both age and experience and knew nothing of the problems of the farmers or ranchers? Anyway, he said, all the issues raised by Bennett were old stuff to Calgary West, some of them going back ten years. Bennett admitted he was a recent arrival in Calgary, but with some emotion he declared he was permanently committed to the city and to serving its interest in every possible way. In dress and bearing he might not have come from the Calgary mould, but there was no doubt in the minds of his listeners at the Opera House that night where Bennett's heart resided. He had become a Calgarian.

As the campaign proceeded, Bennett was to discover that politicians who embark on campaigns of personal abuse, as he had done when he attacked the age and decrepitude of his opponents, will themselves become the target for personal abuse. The brickbats flew around Bennett's head from all directions. A whispering campaign impugned his temperance convictions by spreading a story that witnesses had seen him reel down Stephen Avenue roaring drunk. There were rumours that his campaign workers were busy dispensing free whiskey out the back door of meetings while he was being totally straight-laced in his campaign oratory, even quoting scriptures.

There was some truth in the whiskey charge, because whiskey was a favourite lubricant of all western elections. The probabilities were, however, that the character assassination that featured the campaign might well have done Bennett as much good as it did harm. In any event, he was a comparatively easy winner over his three opponents: Bennett 291, Stuart 205, Muir 169, and Riley 47. Though Bennett did very well in Calgary, his real triumph was in Olds, where he polled ninety-three votes, double the total of his three opponents combined. Calgary took the election results very much in its stride, but Olds staged a monster victory bonfire that lasted well into the night.

For Bennett the election had been a wrenching experience, not alone for the personal abuse he had suffered. He had expected that the *Calgary Herald*, which was owned by a fellow Conservative, would at least give him a fair break in its columns. After all there was little, if anything, in his platform with which the editor of the *Herald* disagreed. The newspaper was also in favour of provincial status for Alberta, for competition in railway lines, for responsible government for Alberta, for the vesting of the title to its natural resources in Alberta. Instead of supporting him, however, the *Herald* peppered Bennett with critical comments during the campaign, gave only brief coverage of his meetings, and opened its columns to a series of lengthy expository articles from the pen of W.W. Stuart, Bennett's main opponent.

Once the election was over, the *Herald* made an effort to get back on side in what it undoubtedly regarded as a laudatory comment, but one that fell well short of that level. If Bennett would only 'guard against being carried away by the exuberance of his own verbosity,' the *Herald* wrote, the young member for Calgary West had it within his power to carve out a brilliant and successful career. The *Albertan*, which had supported him throughout the campaign and defended him against the abuse directed towards him, predicted that Bennett would make the voters proud for having elected him.

Ordinarily, after the excitement of an election campaign, the first appearance of a newly elected member of a public body is anti-climactic. Not so Richard Bennett. His first speech to the North-West Territories Legislative Assembly on 5 April 1899 was little short of sensational. It made the front pages of the newspapers in Regina and Calgary. The correspondent for the *Herald* wrote on 6 April: 'After Mr. Haultain had concluded his speech, Mr. Bennett replied in what is conceded to have been one of the most eloquent speeches ever heard in this house.'

Not only did the content of Bennett's speech have everybody sitting up and taking notice, he, on his first day in the assembly, out-manoeuvred the veteran F.W.G. Haultain. It had become Haultain's practice, as quantum premier of the Territories, to allow all the other members to make their presentations before he spoke. Mostly these speeches were concerned with such mundane matters as roads, bridges, and schools, the lack thereof, and the need of improvements thereto. Haultain could then provide general answers to each member and that would be the end of the 'Speech from the Throne.'

When the members returned to the hall after the supper adjournment, Haultain looked around for the next speaker and nobody rose. Specifically, he looked for Bennett, confident from Bennett's campaign oratory that he would have a lot to say. Bennett was not in his place and was nowhere to be seen. With no one else prepared to speak, Haultain rose to make his closing presentation. Before he was half-way through, Bennett took his seat to await the conclusion of Haultain's speech so he could start his own. He had neatly deprived Haultain of the opportunity of immediately answering Bennett's criticisms and diminishing the impact of his speech. Instead the night was Bennett's exclusively, along with the newspaper headlines.

The Bennett tour-de-force was in essence an attack on Haultain's administration and all his works. As the youngest member making his first appearance in assembly, Bennett said he had expected to hear the great problems facing the country touched upon in the Speech from the Throne. But there was nothing of importance before them. Instead, it would be safe to conclude that the attorney-general (Haultain's official position) – the author of the Speech from the Throne – must have spent the previous six months studying up on dullness. Bennett said he had come to the House with a mandate from his constituency to deal with the problems of the country, among them the railways, the railway monopoly, the grain-elevator monopoly, and freight-rates discrimination. In place of the policy of drift, on which he said the government was embarked, he urged that the system of responsible government merited discussion. Haultain, in his belief that the people were not ready for responsible government, was confusing the people of eastern Assiniboia, Haultain's area of strongest support, with those of Alberta.

There was the most compelling of reasons why the demand for provincial status should be vigorously pursued, Bennett said. With provincial status, Alberta could use the credit of the province to sponsor the construction of railways essential to ending the railway monopoly and the discriminatory freight-rate structure that now existed. He cited the case of a Calgary saddlery company, which was charged $7000 more to move its supplies from Ontario to Calgary than it would have paid to move the supplies to Vancouver. It was sheer folly for Mr Haultain to plead that the railways and freight rates were a federal responsibility. Let Alberta obtain provincial status and it could make discriminatory freight rates very much its business.

And all this from the solicitor for the CPR!

During the election campaign the *Alberta Tribune* had suggested that Bennett was showing such qualities of mind and spirit that he might become a leader dissidents in the assembly could rally round to create an opposition party capable of defeating some of the less popular administrative measures. It was not to be. Bennett was to evince little talent for working with a group, or even interest in doing so. He continued to make speeches from time to time, particularly advocating the launching of a vigorous drive for provincial status, but he exerted surprisingly little real influence on the assembly.

The wide coverage Bennett's speeches received in the pioneer press of the Territory certainly widened awareness of his name, along with the recognition that here was a politician to be reckoned with. The Harris-Gouin attempted murder trial elevated him to the front rank of Territorial lawyers, at least in the eyes of his fellow Calgarians.

Whether defending Edward Harris in the Harris-Gouin shooting came to the Lougheed and Bennett firm by reason of Bennett's New Brunswick connection or from Lougheed's prominence in the national Conservative party is unknown. Harris, aged twenty-five, was the son of C.P. Harris, a prominent Moncton 'capitalist.' The young Mrs Harris, the femme fatal of the case, described by the local papers as pretty, petite, and nineteen but never by her given name, was the daughter of F.S. Archibald, who had been the chief engineer, under the Conservative government, of the Intercolonial Railway at Moncton. When the attempted murder charge was laid against young Harris, his father left immediately for Calgary to support his defence.[25]

The Harrises had been married less than a year when they arrived in Calgary in the spring of 1898 to check into the business opportunities available. Eventually their path crossed that of George Gouin, a man in his middle thirties and an established auctioneer and commission agent. Gouin took his meals at the Alberta Hotel and lived in a two-room bachelor suite in the Thomson Block, down the street from the hotel. Eventually Harris went into partnership with Gouin and the couple moved into rooms across the hall from Gouin.[26]

The firm's main stock in trade was agricultural products and implements. Buying and selling hay, coarse grains, cattle, and the like frequently took one of the partners as far afield as Edmonton. In addition to the business relationship, the Harrises and Gouin became very good friends, frequently attending church and taking their meals together at the Alberta Hotel.[27]

What developed, specifically, between Mrs Harris and Gouin was never spelled out at the ultimate trial. But by the early summer of 1899, Gouin and Mrs Harris were exchanging letters when he was away from Calgary, and by autumn Harris was becoming suspicious of the relationship of his wife and his partner. Unbeknownst to Harris, Gouin by this time had given Mrs Harris a key to his room. They exchanged notes by leaving them in Gouin's room.

On Saturday, 4 November 1899, Harris told his wife he proposed to spend the afternoon pigeon-shooting at the Calgary Gun Club. She said she would spend the afternoon visiting friends, mentioning a couple by name. At around 2 o'clock Harris hired a horse and buggy and headed for the club, a half-hour away on the western outskirts of the city. By four o'clock he was back in town and called at the homes of his wife's friends to pick her up. Neither had seen her, so Harris headed back to his room. As he approached the Thomson Block he noticed that the blinds were down in Gouin's bedroom window. He parked the horse and buggy in front of the building and went to his room. There he sat for some time, with his door open, listening for sounds from Gouin's room across the hall. At last he took a revolver from a bureau drawer, loaded it, and moved quietly into the hall. With great suddenness, he crashed into the door of Gouin's apartment, breaking it open and propelling himself headlong across the sitting room into the bedroom where his wife was standing by the window. Gouin, who earlier had heard Harris coming upstairs, was bent over behind his own door, watching Harris's door through the keyhole, apparently waiting for Harris to return to the horse and buggy and thus permit Mrs Harris to escape unseen from his room.

The force of Harris's charge sent Gouin sprawling on his back, partly stunned. Clambering to his feet, he rushed into the bedroom after Harris, grabbed him from behind, and spun him around to push him away from Mrs Harris. Then the men, in mutual bear-hugs, wrestled to the floor and, as they were rolling around, Harris shot Gouin in the abdomen. Mrs Harris screamed and ran from the room and down the hall to the office of Dr G.A.

Ings. Ings, who had heard the shot, hurried to Gouin's room, where the two men were still struggling on the floor. He pulled them apart, picked up the gun, examined Gouin's wound, and took him to the Holy Cross Hospital, a half a mile away. Gouin ultimately recovered.

Harris, after calling Ings's attention to the fact that the bed in the room had not been made up, accompanied the group to the street, got in his buggy, and drove off, in a flight from the scene of the crime. After driving to the hamlet of Midnapore, ten miles south, he changed his mind. He abandoned the horse and buggy, caught the train that had happened along, and returned to Calgary, where he surrendered to the police and was charged with attempted murder. Harris retained Bennett to defend him, and A.L. Sifton acted for the prosecution.

For Sifton, this was indeed the simplest of cases – a classic example of the eternal triangle. The family friend coveted the affection of another man's wife. The jealous husband armed himself with a loaded revolver, broke into the 'other man's' home, and shot the man he suspected of alienating his wife's affection. It was such an open-and-shut case that Sifton only called two witnesses, Gouin and Dr Ings, and did not even bother to call his eye-witness, Mrs Harris. It took him barely ten minutes to complete his address to the jury.[28]

But for ordinary Calgarians, it was by no means so simple. Calgary, despite some outward signs to the contrary, was a straight-laced community. There were the brothels 'across the river,' whose noisome excesses were frequently heard as far south as downtown. There were periodic outbursts of brawling around the downtown hotel bars. Excesses were to be expected, for this was a young man's town, in which there were 700 more single males than there were single females. But this was essentially a God-fearing, church-going, law-abiding community. In publishing its first report of the shooting in November, the *Calgary Herald* was almost apologetic for having to inflict the details of the sordid affair on its readers. It rationalized its action by noting that newspapers as far away as Winnipeg were pestering it for details of the shooting.

There was, moreover, more to the Harris-Gouin affair than simple violation of the criminal code. Canon law had also been violated. It had not been definitely established that adultery had been committed, that seduction had taken place, but there was no doubt that Gouin was guilty of coveting his neighbour's wife. Thinking himself on his deathbed at Holy Cross Hospital, Gouin had sent some jewellery to Mrs Harris via Dr Ings with the expression of his deepest love. She in turn had sent a ring to him. Under neither British common law, nor the codes of the various American states where adultery was forbidden by law, was it necessary to prove the commission of the act of adultery. The suspicion on the part of the husband that his wife was unfaithful was sufficient, under American law, to mitigate a charge of murder to one of manslaughter.[29] Under British common law, 'criminal conversation,' as it was called, was actionable for damages by a husband lacking proof that adultery had occurred. From the very beginning of the Harris-Gouin affair, Calgarians were on the side of the accused, a fact that would be demonstrated several times during the trial in January 1900.

Between the shooting in early November and the trial at the end of January, Bennett gathered material to enable him to stand the case on its head, as it were – to reverse the roles of accuser and accused. Calgary was no longer a small town in which everybody knew everybody else's business and suspected what could not be known. But George Gouin's reputation as a roué who played the field and left a number of distressed young ladies in the lurch was easily uncovered. In his almost vicious cross-examination of Gouin, Bennett questioned him about the names and dates and places of his other affairs in Calgary. Gouin confessed readily to having been on most affectionate terms with them all, but vigorously denied ever having had 'immoral' relations with them – and that also went for all the women who regularly visited him in his rooms.

Eventually, Mr Justice Rouleau, who was presiding, called a halt to Bennett's repetitious probing of Gouin's love life. Bennett's attack on Gouin and his way of life was transforming the courtroom jammed with spectators into a theatre in which the audience laughed and applauded Bennett's sallies as they would an actor's. His characterizations of Gouin as a 'cur,' 'homewrecker,' 'sensualist,' 'coward,' and 'despoiler of innocent women' evoked such a boisterous reaction that Rouleau brought his gavel into play. One more such outbreak, he warned, and he would clear the court. That happened when Bennett was barely ten minutes into his address of the jury, following a thunderclap of applause that shook the room. The sheriff then cleared the spectators from the building. They missed the best part of the show as Bennett put the finishing touches to the process of transforming the wounded victim of the gunshot into the villain of the piece. It took the jury just ten minutes to find Edward Harris not guilty of attempted murder.[30]

The Harris case made Richard Bedford Bennett in Calgary. He had taken a longshot case and had given it everything he had. Another barrister, perhaps most other barristers, might have concentrated on ameliorating the sentence that Harris's action deserved, even demanded. Bennett, in the jargon of the gaming tables, 'went for broke,' went all out to win an outright acquittal.

Curiously enough, the Harris–Gouin case was the only quasi-capital case Bennett ever took. Indeed, very few serious criminal cases ever found their way into the Lougheed and Bennett office. Bennett, of course, made regular visits to the police courts where bylaw infractions involved regular clients of the firm. Such cases became something of a nuisance after the Lord's Day Act became a pet enforcement project of the city police department. Nevertheless, without criminal law, Bennett's law practice expanded rapidly after 1900. By the spring of 1902 the Calgary *Albertan* could note, in listing the Supreme Court cases to be heard at the spring session, that of the seventeen mostly civil cases on the list, the Lougheed and Bennett firm was acting for five plaintiffs and five defendants.

With the Harris–Gouin case behind him, Bennett was off to Regina for the 1900 session of the Territorial Assembly and another debate over provincial status for Alberta. In the past year the last of the clouds of the ten-year world depression had lifted from the North-West Territories, along with the drought. The rains had come and the immigrants were arriving in steadily increasing numbers. Concern over the impact on the taxpayers of provincial status was diminishing. There were still plenty of issues undecided, however. Should a single province take in the entire territory between Manitoba and British Columbia, as Haultain wanted, or should two new provinces be created, as Bennett wanted?

At the 1900 session, Haultain, who had been strongly urging caution and delay, conceded that the time to demand provincial status had arrived. On 2 May the assembly approved sending a memorial to Ottawa demanding a full inquiry into the position of the Territories, and the terms and conditions for granting provincial status to the North-West Territories.

The 1900 session was scarcely out of the way when rumours began to spread that there was a federal election in the offing. The rumours turned out to be true and the election was called for 7 November 1900. Acting on that speculation during the summer, Conservatives like Senator Lougheed and J.P. Nolan began casting around for suitable candidates to oppose Frank Oliver, the Liberal member who had won the Alberta constituency with considerable ease in 1896. Oliver was the publisher of the *Edmonton Bulletin* and had been a member of the Territorial Assembly for the previous decade.

The election call found the Conservatives on the western frontier in a parlous state. There existed, on paper, a 'Liberal-Conservative Association.' It was made up mainly of a scattering of lawyers, doctors, and merchants in Edmonton-Strathcona, Calgary, and Fort Macleod. The election gave the Conservative-minded individuals an opportunity to coalesce into an active organization, and they did so with the expected birth pains. Invitations were sent out for a nominating convention to be held in Calgary. A total of fifty delegates turned up on 20 July, but when it was discovered that large areas of the south country were unrepresented, the convention was adjourned to round up more delegates.

There was another problem. Nobody could be certain whether F.W.G. Haultain would accept the nomination. If he would run he would be the unanimous choice of the Alberta Conservatives, but he had given no indication he was prepared to exchange a back bench in the House of Commons for his dominating position in the Territorial Assembly. In the end he refused to run. The convention was reconvened and, after four other nominees backed out, Bennett was the unanimous choice of the Conservatives to challenge Frank Oliver. Then everything flew apart.[31]

The Fort Macleod Tories, feigning outrage at the high-handed tactics of the 'Northerners,' called a convention of their own to draft Haultain as the nominee. But Haultain held firm in refusing to run, and ultimately the split was healed — sort of. Bennett was endorsed by the 'southerners' and he resigned from the assembly to run for the Alberta seat. Haultain, however, had been cut so deeply by Bennett's assembly attacks that he refused to endorse him or have any part in his campaign, thus destroying whatever small chance Bennett had of winning.

The superstar of the campaign was not R.B. Bennett but Frank Oliver, MP. The rake-thin, mustachioed Oliver had worked on newspapers in Toronto and Winnipeg and made his way to Edmonton by wagon train in 1876. To his editorship of the *Bulletin* he brought an inflamed hatred of Sir John A. Macdonald and all his works, particularly his handling of the Indian and half-breed problems. He was one of the original members of the Territorial Assembly, but lost his seat in 1885 over his outspoken criticism of the dominion government. After the rebellion of 1885, however, he concentrated his criticism on the CPR, the Hudson's Bay Company, and the land speculators, and was again elected to the assembly in 1888. When Alberta was allotted a seat in parliament, Oliver was urged to run as a Liberal, but refused. He refused again in 1891, but won the seat as an independent Liberal in the Laurier triumph of 1896.

Quickly co-opted into the Liberal party, Oliver had efficiently massaged the patronage interest of his constituency and became as familiar to the inhabitants of the hinterlands as he was to the settled areas. He was supported generously by the well-financed Liberal party that had an enthusiastic and efficient organization. Yet if doubt existed about the chances Bennett had of unseating Oliver, it remained deeply hidden as the Conservative campaign opened in Calgary on 17 September 1990.[32] Once again Bennett hired the Opera House for his campaign launching, and a sizeable crowd gathered in front even before the doors were open. Crispin Smith, the lawyer-musician, took his Fire Department Band on parade through downtown Calgary to advertise the meeting and to entertain the electors before the speech-making began. Once again the Opera House was comfortably filled, as it had been for Bennett's campaign for the Territorial Assembly two years before. He spoke for almost two hours, quoting chapter and verse from the Liberals' 1896 campaign platform to demonstrate how they had reneged 'on every promise they ever made.'

The impact the speech had on the crowd, and its worth as a political document, depended on which newspaper Calgarians read. It was an age in which politicians owned newspapers and newspapers slavishly followed the owner's party line. In the September–October campaign of 1900 the Calgary media switched sides. The *Alberta Tribune*, which had supported Bennett so enthusiastically in 1898, had been absorbed by the *Albertan*, a staunch supporter of Frank Oliver. The *Herald*, which had fought Bennett in 1898, became his supporter in 1900. It devoted three columns of space to his 'reopening gun' meeting and strongly supported him editorially. The *Albertan* boycotted Bennett's meeting and explained why it did not report a word of his speech: 'We give no report of the speech of Mr Bennett, first because it contains only misrepresentations which we do not care to publish and secondly because no opportunity was given to any Liberal to reply.' As for the speech itself, the *Albertan* said 'the electors were treated to a bitter and detailed attack on the acts of the present administration, a display of cheap and coarse wit, and a splendid imitation of Tupperian bluster, declamation and emptiness. The electors were entitled to hear something more self-restrained, moderate and earnest than they were treated to last Thursday. The light hearted flippancy of a boy, the wit and humor of the street and barroom, even though relieved occasionally by fictitious indignation and patriotic kite flying, will not attract or deceive the voters.'[33]

Over the next six weeks, Bennett worked full-time at getting elected. All-weather roads were still unknown in Alberta, so movement was by railway and horse and buggy. For Bennett, a speech in Edmonton was at least a two-day and perhaps a three-day affair. With frequent whistle stops, it took the train a minimum of five hours and sometimes up to eight hours to make the 175-mile run to the north. There was a small dividend to the whistle stopping: it enabled Bennett to spend time greeting the station platform crowds. Occasionally, depending on the amount of express, freight, and mail to be loaded and unloaded, he even had time for small set speeches.

Long before the federal election, Max Aitken had decided Calgary was not for him and had returned to New Brunswick via Edmonton. Once again Bennett enlisted the support of George Cloakey. In 1900 he was Bennett's guide to the outback, driving him by buggy and farm wagon into scores of farmyards in the constituency.

One of Cloakey's primary objectives in life was to revamp Bennett's platform style. As he kept telling him, he spoke so fast that most of his best stuff went over people's heads. Like most politicians of the era, Cloakey's idea of campaign oratory was to take a handful of simple ideas and reinforce them by endless repetition. But Bennett's oratorical style, even during his apprenticeship years, was never amenable to modification because it was an amalgam of an insatiable appetite for the printed word, a prodigious memory for facts, figures, and faces, an unmatched vocabulary, and a convert's dedication to the cause he was pleading. And this was true whether he was pleading a case in court, addressing a public meeting, or conversing with a friend across a dinner table. Nevertheless, Bennett did listen to Cloakey and conceded that a slower pace made sense. Occasionally, when he caught sight of Cloakey in the audience, he would apply the brakes. 'Oops,' he'd interject, 'here I go, speaking too fast again. If I don't go a little slower George Cloakey will be getting after me.' For a minute or two he would slow his pace, but when he was aroused by what he was saying he would be off again in a full flood of oratory.[34]

Bennett had other assets as a politician that more than made up for his machine-gun delivery. During those early campaigns in Alberta Bennett was tireless in his pursuit of the electors. He would go anywhere and everywhere Cloakey wanted him to go. He had a memory for names and faces that challenged belief. Cloakey recalled one example where Bennett had interrupted a farm wife in the midst of her bread making. She was covered with flour from head to toe, so they talked for only a moment and took their departure. A year later, when Bennett and Cloakey happened upon the woman again at a bazaar in Okotoks, Bennett remembered her by name and recalled their previous encounter.[35]

Oliver would have been more than a handful for Bennett even if he had a united, well-financed, and well-organized machine behind him, but he had none of these supports. Not only did Haultain refuse to endorse Bennett or speak on his behalf, but Lougheed himself took little part in the campaign. Indeed, the only prominent Conservative who took to the hustlings for Bennett was Dr R.G. Brett of Banff, whose name appeared in the newspapers several times as having spoken in support of Bennett.

It was, of course, a very dirty campaign. Bennett's pious Christian posture seemed a magnet for brickbats. Once again the stories about his being a secret boozer surfaced. As Bennett's mentor and tour conductor, Cloakey was a master of the *realpolitik* of the pioneer west. If a bottle of whiskey would nail down the votes of a group of cowboys, he made sure Bennett was engaged elsewhere when delivery was made. That also applied to the drinks on the house at Calgary hotel bars. It was a time when every politician's definition of an honest elector was 'one who stays bought.' From past experience, Cloakey had a pretty good idea which electors were worth buying with booze and which were not.

Despite the vigour of the Cloakey-Bennett assault on the electorate, Frank Oliver's great support in the north and the deep south was too much for them. Bennett was beaten 5203 votes to 4209.

Bennett had resigned from the Territorial Assembly to run for parliament. At the first opportunity, however, in a by-election in 1901, he reclaimed that seat and held it for the next four years.

That would not have happened if Haultain had had his way. Bennett, from his first speech onward in 1898, had seldom resisted the temptation to mix deep-cutting personal jibes with the issues he was discussing. Since Haultain dominated the administration of the Territories, Bennett kept him squarely in his sights for thrusts that could be driven in and broken off. One such related to a passage in the Throne Speech regarding the establishment of an irrigation experimental farm in the Calgary area. The speech announced that a site for this farm had been acquired by the government. In fact, while the deal had been done, title to the property would not pass until the assembly voted the money to pay for it. This technicality was the basis for Bennett's charging that Haultain had put falsehoods in the Throne Speech for the lieutenant-governor to read.

After a single session of fault finding and abuse, Haultain had had more than enough of R.B. Bennett.[36] Three days after the national election on 7 November 1900 he wrote to A.E. Cross, the member for Calgary East, to explore possible ways of keeping Bennett out of the assembly. It was not, he said, that he was keen to keep him out of the House: 'Without him the opposition will degenerate into a perfect farce, which will reflect on the whole institution.' But how, he wondered, could he remain aloof if Bennett, in the upcoming by-election, appealed to the constituency with the same arguments he used in the assembly? One possibility, Haultain suggested, might be to locate an outstanding Conservative who could be persuaded to run against Bennett as a government supporter. Did Cross know such a person, and what was his reaction to the idea? However Cross reacted, it was a stillborn notion, for no serious challenge was ever mounted to Bennett's grip on the Calgary West riding.

There were times over the ensuing months when Bennett would wonder whether being a member of the Territorial Assembly was more trouble than it was worth. At long last, the flood tide of American immigration was flowing strongly across southern Alberta. The villages along the Calgary and Edmonton Railway were doubling in population every six months, and the spaces between the towns were gradually being occupied by new-coming farmers. All this was creating a steady flow of profit from Bennett's real estate speculations. He had a network of agents scattered throughout the west disposing of his holdings to incoming settlers. Blocks of 2000–3000 acres of farm land could be acquired from the railway for $3 or $4 an acre with a 10 per cent down payment and the balance payable in equal instalments over a ten-year term. This land would be retailed in 160- and 320-acre farm-sized parcels on the same terms at perhaps a dollar per acre advance in price.[37] From 1901 onward that was the unbroken economic trend in western Canada – the price of farm land increased, from $3 an acre to $5 then $8 an acre; from $10 to $15 and ultimately to $20 an acre. All Bennett and the other land speculators had to do to earn a substantial profit was to take down a block or two of railway land, for the original down payment, subdivide it into farm-sized parcels, and sit back and wait for the incoming farmers. They were incoming in such numbers that the operation might be repeated several times during a year.

For Bennett the down side was that as new settlers became established on their farms they wanted services – mainly bridges, roads, and schools. The way they got them was by putting pressure on the nearest convenient members of the Territorial Assembly. The large letterbook Bennett kept from 1900 to 1904 is replete with correspondence with constituents about services, along with ensuing correspondence with the authorities in Regina with explanations why a road could not be built, culverts could not be supplied, bridges could not be immediately repaired.[38]

Bennett made every effort to take care of the needs of his constituents, but there is a great deal of internal evidence that he could not keep up with the demands. Many of his letters began with apologies for his tardiness in acknowledging receipt of the request or in getting to the problem. He was absent from the city, he was attending court in Fort Macleod, Lethbridge, or Red Deer. He was absent in eastern Canada or in the United States. Nor did the demands on his time by his constituents end there. There were merchants and agents in the small towns who felt the need to be appointed justices of the peace or commissioners of oaths. They wrote to Bennett to obtain the appointments and he had to write to Regina with a recommendation, which might lead to an exchange of several letters.

Along with the rising tide of land settlers who were making their impact on Calgary and Alberta were growing numbers of trained artisans attracted by the dawn-to-dark construction boom that was becoming a Calgary hallmark. At first, trades unionism in Calgary was confined largely to the railway running trades, shop crews, and coal miners. Then, in the spring of 1902, the brick-layers and stonemasons unions managed to sign with the contractors for a wage of $2.75 per day for a nine-hour day. Thus encouraged, the members of the carpenters union tried to get a similar agreement. They encountered a notable lack of interest from the fragmented housebuilders and general contractors, either for recognizing a union or for a minimum wage. After several attempts to get the employers to a meeting, and being rebuffed, the union went to Bennett for advice. He suggested they offer to arbitrate and agreed to represent them if the employers agreed. They refused, so the union called the carpenters out on strike on 7 July 1902.[39] After a week on the picket line the carpenters decided a public mass meeting was needed to put the pressure of public opinion on the contractors. Would Mr Bennett attend such a rally and make a speech in support of the carpenters? To the astonishment of the clientele of Lougheed and Bennett, and to most of Bennett's Calgary acquaintanceship as well, he would indeed.

After the union leaders spoke of their failed efforts to get the contractors to a meeting to discuss their proposals, Bennett was called to the platform. The speech that followed was a far cry from anything that might have been expected from a lawyer speaking for a fee. It was the sort of speech that would have done Keir Hardie or John L. Lewis proud, for he went far beyond the issue at hand. Of that issue, he said this was not a case of workers trying to grip capitalists by the throat. This was a case of reasonable men trying to get a dispute referred to arbitration. On the question of union recognition, it was the right of all Canadian citizens to belong to an organization to serve their interests. The lawyers had their organization protecting their interests, setting the fees they would receive for their work. Everyone should have this right and freedom. More, he urged all those who were not in unions to get out and get organized. As for wage rates, he contended it was in the interest of Calgary that the highest possible wages be paid in their pioneer economy so the workers could build decent homes for their families and afford a good education for their children. 'So long as I live,' Bennett concluded, 'I will give my best efforts to any labor organization which endeavors to uphold right causes, make better the homes of the people and helps to build a strong and reliant race.'[40]

This surely was a speech that no client of Lougheed and Bennett, no Calgary businessman, no regular diner at Bennett's Alberta Hotel table, and no building contractor would have expected to hear from R.B. Bennett. And whether or not it was Bennett who persuaded them, the contractors eventually came to terms with the carpenters union for $2.50 per nine-hour day.

At Lougheed and Bennett, meanwhile, the developing land boom had generated a great deal of law-office paper pushing as agreements for sale were drafted, liens registered, mortgages negotiated, and land titles transferred. It was all mainly routine, and, as the workload became heavier, additional bodies were hired. When it came to the barrister side of the profession − the court work − the situation was more complicated.

From the beginning of Lougheed's practice in Calgary, the firm had been identified with the CPR. When Bennett assumed charge of the office he became 'the CPR lawyer' as far as Calgary was concerned. The CPR chief counsel for Manitoba, the North-West Territories, and British Columbia was J.A.M. Aitkins of the Winnipeg firm of Aitkins, Loftus and Co. When disputes between the railway and the citizenry reached the 'lawyering' stage, company officials were required in the first instance to submit the statements of claim to the Aitkins office. If Aitkins decided that the claim should be settled, he would notify a local lawyer to negotiate a settlement at the best possible figure below a suggested maximum. The Lougheed and Bennett firm was Aitkins's agent in southern Alberta. When Aitkins said settle, Bennett settled. When Aitkins said go to trial, Bennett went to trial.

Once the decision was made to go to trial, the matter was entirely in Bennett's hands, except that Aitkins was kept aware of the progress of proceedings by regular reports. When the case was decided, the Bennett firm billed the Aitkins firm for its fees and disbursements. The system seemed to work satisfactorily until late in 1902, when Aitkins took strong objection to some of the bills being rendered and complained to Lougheed personally. Lougheed turned the letter over to Bennett when he returned from his Christmas visit home.[41] On 27 February 1903 Bennett fired off a trenchant reply to Aitkins in which he defended the settlement he had negotiated and the amount of his time the trial had consumed, and emphasized that in all cases the CPR was being asked to pay less than the Bennett office would have charged local clients for comparative work.

Though Bennett became increasingly busy with his law practice and his real estate operation after he won re-election to the Territorial Assembly, he could still find time to maintain his interest in federal politics, particularly after Robert Borden replaced Sir Charles Tupper as leader of the Liberal-Conservative party in February 1901. One of the new leader's primary concerns was the organizational disarray of the party. As soon as it could be managed, Borden took off on a grand tour of western Canada in early September 1902. The tour took him into every convenient nook and cranny in the west. He adopted the practice of picking up prominent local Tories and having them accompany the tour through their extended neighbourhoods. In Regina he met F.W.G. Haultain, and was delighted to discover that while he was an appointee of the Liberal Territorial establishment, he was a committed Conservative. Bennett met Borden for the first time when he joined the tour in Edmonton and spent three days en route to Calgary. As Borden would later recall, 'From Bennett in particular I received valuable and useful suggestions of policies which would appeal to the people of that province. He was than a young man of 32 overflowing with energy and enthusiasm. I felt confident that his future course in public life...would be conspicuous.'[42]

Among those 'valuable and useful' policies was unquestionably provincial status for Alberta and Saskatchewan. With it would come the demand for vesting crown land and minerals in the provinces, along with compensation for those natural resources already alienated. As for railway policy, Bennett's views were undergoing mild modification, but modification that would position him a couple of degrees off centre from Borden's own emerging convictions. In the beginning, Bennett had argued in the assembly that a provincial government could use its credit to build a railway from Fort Macleod to Jim Hill's Northern Pacific at Shelby, Montana. His speech could have been interpreted as a plea for government ownership. But could Alberta have a government-owned railway without its efficiency being vitiated by political patronage? On 3 June 1903 Bennett wrote Borden a long letter on a transportation policy for the west.[43]

Bennett was now against government subsidies to railways, whether in the form of cash, bond guarantees, or land grants. Western settlers required adequate transportation facilities, but the country, with the population it would have for the foreseeable future, simply could not afford three national transcontinental railways. Perhaps if the Canadian Northern and the Grand Trunk were put together and slimmed down, they could be made viable. Certainly the government must rigidly control the freight rates at a level the people of western Canada could afford to pay. But with such a patronage-ridden, inefficient example as the Intercolonial Railway before it, could government ownership be the answer? Bennett thought not.

Bennett did not allow disagreement with Borden on railway policy to retard his organizational activities. Within five months a call came out from Borden's office to the Conservatives in the North-West Territories to hold a regional organization convention on a polling-district basis. Then, when the next election was called, it would have a nucleus in place ready to be moulded into an organization. Bennett threw himself enthusiastically into rounding up delegates for the convention.[44] He wrote lengthy letters to everybody he knew in the hinterlands to press them to come to Moose Jaw. When he negotiated a cut-rate railway fare to get the delegates to the convention, it became the subject of another letter. When he got a package of printed material from Ottawa, it was distributed in advance of the convention.

In his correspondence with Borden he made no effort to hide his animosity towards Haultain. On 10 March he had written Borden: 'It is idle for us to attempt to understand Mr. Haultain's ways. He is a good Conservative but he appoints Grits... the assurance of fealty to a leader and loyalty to a party count in my judgement for very little when the physical evidence of the fealty and loyalty advances the interest of the opposing party.' Borden refused to take sides and wrote to Bennett that the convention should restrain itself in criticizing Haultain's administration and, in federal politics, invite his cooperation and assistance 'as long as he is disposed to remain with us.'

Held on 25 March 1903 at Moose Jaw, the convention was a great success on all counts. It attracted 140 delegates, at least one and frequently several delegates from most of the Territorial constituencies. It voted overwhelmingly, without Bennett taking any part in the debate, to place Conservative party candidates in every constituency at the next Territorial election. As Bennett wrote to Borden in his summary of the convention: 'I did not speak either in the committee or in the convention on the resolution... When you have your opponents beaten it is bad policy to create feelings over a sure result.' The convention went on to pass resolution after resolution that might have come directly from Bennett's 1899 assembly speeches. It called for immediate provincial status for Alberta, including the transfer of crown lands and minerals to the new provinces. Bennett even seconded a motion moved by Haultain criticizing the federal government for neglecting the interest of the Territories by its niggardly appropriations for vital services. After the resolution passed, Bennett informed Borden, he had a long talk with Haultain and 'from now on we will unite our best efforts to advance the interests of the party.'

By the time of the Conservative convention, Calgary was

bursting at every seam. The CPR had long since outgrown its east Calgary assembly yards and freight sheds. It was busy constructing the largest locomotive repair shop between Winnipeg and Vancouver in the Ogden area and constructing additional storage trackage. But the CPR, like other expanding Calgary enterprises, was held back by the lack of housing in Calgary for its expanding staff. Over the previous two years 150 houses had been built and there were still long waiting lists of people wanting accommodation. The demand for commercial space was equally pressing. For the Calgary legal profession, the sudden real estate boom brought a sharp increase in demand for the drawing of mortgages, registering titles, and vetting bills of sale. Each mortgage drawn had to have an insurance policy to protect the lending institution, and all law offices were also sales agents for fire and casualty insurance. The law office of Lougheed and Bennett was becoming swamped with work. The joint effort of the Canadian government and the Canadian Pacific Railway was taking hold. Over the next generation more than one million immigrants would find their way to western Canada from the United States alone.[45] The advance guard for that movement, the land agents seeking spreads of land to take home to sell to the disenchanted farmers of the U.S. middle west, was becoming so numerous that Bennett was forced to take up office space in the CPR land department to deal with them.

When Bennett made his first investment in real estate is not recorded, but it had to be early in his Calgary residence. Certainly no one could have been associated with James Lougheed for very long without becoming infected with his incurable addiction to Calgary real estate. It did not, in fact, take all that much money to 'get into real estate.' Nor was it even necessary for a real estate speculator to put substantial sums at risk.

Bennett by 1903 was wheeling and dealing on farm properties with potential buyers all across the country. In February of that year he was in touch with correspondents in Petrolia and Fairbank, Ontario, and in Bowden, Alberta, about the sale of farm lands.[46] That he was into real estate extensively may be inferred from an offer to a local agent: 'If you sell the land for $6.10 (an acre) I will make your commission $175 and we will prepare the papers etc. This is a larger commission than we usually pay. In fact we are selling our Assiniboia lands on a straight commission of 25 cents an acre.' Involvement of lawyers in real estate in Calgary was by no means confined to Lougheed and Bennett. As Bennett wrote to C.H. Barker of Nanaimo, British Columbia, who had inquired about establishing a practice in the North-West Territories: 'For pure law, there is not the very best chance in the Territories,' Bennett wrote, 'but for law mixed with speculation in real estate there are most excellent openings . . . Every member on the main line east of here is making money, most of them buy and sell real estate.'

There can be little doubt that Bennett was in a position, as solicitor for the CPR, to take advantage of 'inside information' in connection with its land sales. But inside information about CPR intentions had a very short 'confidential' life span. The railway was so keen to expand its land sales that a great deal of 'confidential inside information' moved into circulation from behind the public counter in the land department in the form of guesses about the immediate track-laying plans of the CPR. Bennett himself was quite free with information about its plans.[47] On 1 December 1903 he wrote to H.C. McLeod, general manager of the Bank of Nova Scotia in Toronto: 'The Canadian Pacific will spend several hundred thousand dollars here next year and building operation will be carried on very vigorously. I think you made no mistake in going to Wetaskiwin as my present advices are that the Canadian Pacific will reach that point with its Kirkella extension at a not distant date.'

The following year, Bennett intervened when he learned the Bank of Nova Scotia had bought a lot on Eighth Avenue and was contemplating erecting a building on it costing $10,000 to $12,000. It was none of his business, he wrote McLeod, but the bank was out of touch with Calgary building costs. For a building in keeping with the Bank of Nova Scotia's position in the community, it should figure on spending at least $15,000. The Merchants Bank, he had heard, would be spending at least that much plus an additional $10,000 for a building lot. As an extra piece of persuasive information, he noted that the CPR was contemplating spending $50,000 on a new station a block away from where the bank would be building. That, plus the $1 million the company was to spend on its great irrigation project, could be taken as evidence, he said, that Calgary's future was assured.

Bennett's correspondence contains a number of other letters boosting the town of Wetaskiwin as a terminus for a CPR branch line. The substance and form of Bennett's real estate operations also are indicated by this correspondence. He and his partners were wholesalers. They bought spreads of land from the CPR for the down payments demanded by the railway and, as prices rose over the years, then sold it in farm-sized packages to incoming settlers. The outstanding feature of land prices during the first decade of the century in western Canada was that they rose steadily as millions of acres of new land were put under the plough.

While Bennett was becoming ever more deeply involved in real estate and the innumerable opportunities for investment in Alberta enterprises, his main concern was still with his law practice. The aggressive, even belligerent, persona he had been developing in the Territories Assembly was coming to imbue his legal persona as well. He seemed to become more personally involved in his client's cases than many other lawyers, as exemplified by his handling of the Harris-Gouin attempted murder trial and the carpenters' strike.

There was also, floating near the surface of the Bennett psyche, a trait that turned the prosaic into the sensational when he became involved. A case in point was that of the fireguard ploughmen, as prosaic a dispute as the justice system of Calgary ever had before it.[48]

In the pioneer era, prairie fires started by sparks from railway engines became an ever-present hazard of the lives of settlers. In 1903 the Territorial Assembly passed a law requiring the CPR, in certain areas, to plough the grass on strips of land paralleling its right-of-way to prevent fires from spreading. As a crew of ploughmen was fulfilling the company's legal obligations, it came eventually onto the property of Mrs Jane Hastings, who took umbrage. A shouting match between the head ploughman, George Lloyd, and Mrs Hastings developed, culminating either or both in Mrs Hastings charging at Lloyd with a knife and/or Lloyd laying hands on and otherwise assaulting Mrs Hastings. In the end, Lloyd held Mrs Hastings away from the gate so his two helpers and their eight horses could get onto the Hastings place and proceed with their fireguard ploughing. Mrs Hastings went to the North-West Mounted Police and laid assault charges against Lloyd, who was arrested and remanded to appear before Colonel G.E. Sanders of the Mounted Police Court in Calgary.

The bemonocled Sanders was a native of British Columbia who had risen through the ranks of the NWMP to superintendent of the Calgary division in 1896. His service in the South African War had earned him his rank of colonel, and he emerged from that war with the broadest cultivated English accent west of Kingston, Ontario. He presided in magistrate court in the Calgary Mounted Police barracks, and later in the Calgary police court, as the personification of a martinet run amok. Among his *obiter dicta*: Calgary streets were overrun by saucy niggers! The testimony of Jews under oath could not be accepted! His idea of a lenient sentence for stealing a purse was twelve months in jail and twenty lashes.[49]

As counsel for the CPR, Bennett appeared with Lloyd before Sanders to answer the charges on 10 September 1904. After the examination of the complainant, one of Lloyd's witnesses was being examined when a dispute developed between Bennett and James Short, the prosecutor, over the law covering fireguard plowing. Bennett contended that under the Territories Fire Ordinance of 1903 the ploughmen were required to enter the property to plough the fireguard. Sanders interrupted the discussion to say that, for the purposes of this trial, he was not going to recognize the ordinance and was proceeding under the Criminal Code. Bennett objected strenuously, whereupon the magistrate called Sergeant Wilson of the NWMP to remove Bennett from the courtroom. With Bennett gesticulating and threatening to sue the magistrate and the policeman, Wilson took him firmly by the arm and escorted him from the room.

Lloyd, when peace was restored, protested that he could not proceed without a lawyer, so Sanders adjourned the case to enable him to retain a replacement for Bennett. Outside the barracks, Lloyd met Bennett, they talked, and returned to the courtroom together. Sanders refused to listen to Bennett, and once again ordered Sergeant Wilson to eject him. He then adjourned court until the afternoon. Again Bennett appeared and again he was ejected. In the end he settled for a seat among the spectators and watched as Sanders convicted Lloyd of assault and fined him $1.00 and costs. Bennett took an appeal to the Territories court and won reversal of the verdict.[50]

The imbroglio at the Mounted Police barracks naturally set Calgary on its ear and attracted attention as far away as Regina. Over the next twenty years, Bennett would reappear periodically in Sanders's courtroom, usually in hearings that included references by Bennett to Sanders's unfortunate deficiency in legal background and Sanders's rejoinders on the superior virtue of common sense over formal legal training. Bennett seldom, if ever, won a case before Sanders, but he usually appealed and won on appeal.

Another example of Bennett's becoming involved in a headline-making case almost by inadvertence was the celebrated city hall land-sale scandal. Public bodies, in the early west, tended to 'fly by the seat of their pants,' without undo attention to legal niceties, particularly in that grey area that separated private profit from public interest. As villages evolved into towns with councillors, elected official tended to 'look after' things on a casual, ad hoc basis. A councillor would investigate a citizen's complaint and recommend remedial measures to a town official. Town officials, needing supplies of gravel, lumber, or paper clips, would patronize a local merchantizer of such wares, who frequently happened to be a town councillor. As towns grew larger, new-coming merchants looked askance at entrenched interests that kept them from getting a share of the business. Ultimately, systems of public tendering for supplies were put in place, usually after considerable public outcrying. In Calgary it was not unusual for Bennett to be involved in the outcrying.

During the long depression of the 1890s a great deal of vacant land within the Calgary city limits had been taken over by the city for taxes. As the depression lifted, local housebuyers would occasionally buy lots from the city at prices set by the city council. The Calgary city council decided, in early spring, 1904, to compile an inventory of city lands and hold a land sale. The finance committee was instructed to catalogue the lands, price the lots, and inaugurate the sale. The job was done in a thirty-minute meeting of the aldermen in the city clerk's office. Then several aldermen got out pencil and paper and made up lists of the lots they wanted to buy for themselves. The city clerk immediately assigned these lots to them while they went off to the banks to negotiate loans.

Prior to the sale decision, a number of Calgarians, including Senator Lougheed, had put in bids for individual lots. None of these sales was approved. Nor did the city get around to advertising its land sale. But when prospective buyers heard by word of mouth of the sale and went to the city hall, they discovered all the best lots were already sold to the aldermen.

The grousing of the frozen-out bargain hunters quickly reached the Bennett table in the Alberta Hotel.[51] At the next meeting of the city council, Bennett appeared to speak for 'Calgary ratepayers' and to demand that the council rescind the land sales and have a special inquiry launched to investigate the actions of the aldermen on the finance committee. Out of the uproar that ensued, a judicial inquiry by Mr Justice Sifton was established. Bennett was cross-examiner at the hearing and saw his intervention vindicated when Sifton's report forced the resignation of two aldermen for corrupt practice in connection with the sale of lots.

The growing pains that were creating such spasms in the Calgary civic administration had been having an impact on the Lougheed and Bennett partnership as well. It had certainly accumulated a glittering assortment of corporation clients. In addition to the Bank of Montreal and Canadian Pacific Railway it had become a legal adviser to the Royal Bank, Bank of Nova Scotia, Bank of Commerce, Merchants Bank, Crown Trust, Union

Trust, Crown Life, Great West Life, Massey Harris, and R.G. Dun.

As the clientele increased, so did the Lougheed and Bennett staff. H.A. Allison joined the staff in 1903 and W.T. Taylor was hired a couple of years later. W.H. McLaws, who had articled with the firm, stayed on as a practising lawyer. Curiously enough, as the partnership grew and prospered, Lougheed's interest in it diminished. The sittings of the Canadian Senate were increasing in length and he was spending more time in Ottawa, Toronto, and Montreal. When he was at home his multiplicity of real estate interest had greater call on his time than his law practice. Eventually a completely new arrangement was made by the partners. Lougheed's share of the annual net income of the practice was reduced to $3000. His son was to be hired and his salary was to be charged against Lougheed's $3000. Bennett was to be entitled to 40 per cent of the annual net profits, and 60 per cent was to be divided among Allison, Taylor, and McLaws. Though he seldom used it, Lougheed retained his private office.[52]

Bennett then became the counsel for the CPR in Calgary at a retainer of $7500 a year and, when the Canadian Pacific Irrigation Colonization Company was formed, he moved into the CPR offices on an almost full-time basis. His CPR office was connected to his law office, a block and a half away, by a private telephone line. Thus Lougheed and Bennett evolved into a partnership without in-house partners. This was a great boon to the employees, one they could not have enjoyed when Bennett was there – they could smoke.

Though Bennett never touched liquor, he came in later life to be tolerant of those who did, but he never learned to tolerate smoking in any form. Not only was smoking forbidden to the employees of Lougheed and Bennett, but his clients could not smoke either, as Bennett himself frequently made plain.[53] The one exception was George Robinson, Bennett's oldest Calgary friend who, in the early days, rented an office in the Clarence Building. Robinson was an insurance and real estate agent who later doubled as Bennett's election campaign manager. To the horror of newly hired clerks, Robinson would saunter into Bennett's office with a cigar ablaze and continue smoking it until he chose to dispose of the butt.

Robinson was one of the few Calgarians who could tease Bennett with impunity and who never had his sallies squelched with a withering gaze. He could even kid Bennett about his monkish lifestyle. During election campaigns, country hotel keepers frequently nudged their room rates upwards when Bennett and party checked in. Once in Medicine Hat when that happened, Robinson expostulated, to the raucous amusement of the rest of their party: "Wow! for that rate I presume the women are included." RB laughed with the rest, but with a chuckle and not a guffaw.

It was Robinson, according to Calgary legend, who persuaded Bennett to become a pioneer Calgary motorist, but who had the good sense not to accompany him on his maiden drive through Calgary streets. That drive began on Stephen Avenue west of the Hudson's Bay store. Bennett was zooming merrily along when, as he approached Centre Street, he decided to turn north. As he made the turn, a boy suddenly loomed ahead of him on a bicycle. Bennett reached for the brake, turned the wheel, and collided sharply with the side of the Imperial bank. The bank wall withstood the collision better than the car. The accident gave birth to the legend that it ended Bennett's motor-owning career. The legend is without foundation. He immediately wrote to the Oldsmobile Motor Company in Detroit for some new brass headlights, mud guards, a steering column, and a new axle because, as he wrote the company, it was a very fine car and he was anxious to get it once more in operation. It turned out to be a forlorn hope. The Oldsmobile Company eventually replied that it did not have any spare parts in stock for Bennett's model. There then followed an exchange of additional letters and telegrams over the next several months, but no satisfaction seems to have been obtained by Bennett from the company. He never replaced the car while he lived in Calgary.

CHAPTER THREE

Frontier Politics

Propelled along by the population implosion from the United States and by the booming demand that was developing for both rural and urban real estate, the legal career of R.B. Bennett eventually sprouted, blossomed, and bore succulent fruit. The same, unhappily, could not be said for his life in politics. On the stump he was the closest thing to the consummate orator the foothills of Alberta had ever seen, but there is more to being a successful politician than silver-tongued oratory. There is an inner quality that comes into play after the last hurrahs have died down, a quality that enables speakers to etch their name deeply on the permanent records of the assembly to which they belong. However that quality is defined, Bennett did not have it. For all the influence he was able to exert on the course of events at the Territorial Assembly in Regina, he might just as well have stayed in Calgary.

The sheer power of his oratory on the hustings led many of his supporters to expect great things from him in the assembly. Perhaps he would emerge quickly as leader of the opposition and persuade the assembly to reverse some of F.W.G. Haultain's policies, or even replace Haultain himself as de facto premier. It never happened, possibly because the personal animus he exhibited towards Haultain or his ingrained penchant for resorting to personal abuse of his opponents alienated too many members of the assembly. His below-the-belt attack on A.L. Sifton in the budget debate of 1901 was a case in point. After two judicial recounts,

Sifton had lost the Banff riding in the election of 1898. The Laurier government promptly appointed him to the Executive Council of the Territories and Haultain put him in charge of preparing the 1901 budget. Bennett paid his disrespect to Sifton and his budget by chiding him about his election loss, charging that he never in his life had accomplished anything on his own and owed everything to the positions obtained for him by his brother, Sir Clifford Sifton, the minister of the interior.[1]

The real reason for Bennett's failure to leave a lasting impression on the history of the Legislative Assembly, however, may have lain elsewhere – in the fact that while 'Territorial Legislative Assembly' might have had a grandiose ring to the politicians who belonged to it, the model it most closely resembled was that of a backwoods county council. At the turn of the century it budgeted for less than $400,000, of which Ottawa supplied $350,000.[2] Part of the difference was made up by items such as liquor licence fees and marriage licences. The assembly's main concerns were with roads and bridges, schools and public health, and the occasional enactment of ordinances to regulate steer branding, coal mining, business, and industry. It is hardly surprising, over the five years Bennett represented Calgary West in the assembly, that he failed to leave enduring evidence of his influence on such 'affairs to state' as these. Neither, really, did anyone else.

As the assembly string was being run out, it must have occurred to Bennett that it was time and the population influx rather than anything he could do that would achieve his main political goals – autonomy for Alberta and increased railway construction. Time would take care of two of the subsidiary causes he had espoused in the assembly – the need for a law to compel employers to maintain safe working conditions for employees and be liable for accidents to workers, and the passage of a law to regulate bankruptcies. Time, too, changed the administration's stance of opposition to autonomy. Haultain by 1903 had swung in a complete circle and trenchantly supported it. When the Laurier administration ignored the pro-autonomy resolutions of the assembly, Haultain went to Ottawa, in 1904, to press Sir Wilfrid Laurier for action.[3] On the eve of the dominion election of 1904, Laurier promised that if his party were re-elected it would open autonomy negotiations.

If time was taking care of the issues that primarily concerned him, Bennett's own need for being politically involved diminished. Indeed, membership in the Territorial Assembly was becoming a bit of a nuisance. Until his mother died in 1914, Bennett always journeyed to New Brunswick to spend Christmas with her. That meant an absence from his growing law practice in Calgary from mid-December until mid-January. Then he was barely back in the office when he had to be off to Regina for a couple of weeks. The CPR was centralizing its western operations in Calgary and its demands on Bennett's time became increasingly pressing. All these demands had to be fitted in with those of his growing number of professional clients. As he would write to Max Aitken in July 1904: 'The court is in session here. I am very busy. Out of the 24 largest cases on the docket we had one side or the other in 20 and I lost only one and that will be appealed.'[4]

The CPR connection was time consuming in two main areas. The first was the rapid growth taking place in CPR litigation that accompanied the settler influx, in particular the defence of actions for damages. From the day of its first arrival in the west, the CPR's watchward seemed to be: 'We've got a railway to run: You get the hell out of our way and stay the hell out of our way!'

The railway trackage and the freight and passenger trains that ran over it belonged to the Canadian Pacific Railway Company Limited. Anyone or anything that ventured onto that property had to assume whatever risk was entailed in the action taken. That applied whether the venturer was a herd of horses stampeding across the open range at midnight or a wayfaring stranger slipping on an icy station platform and sliding under the wheels of a passing train. It also applied to company employees fatally injured on running-crew assignments. When people thought otherwise, they would have R.B. Bennett to contend with in court if they tried to collect damages. Given the antagonism felt towards the CPR in the turn-of-the-century west, the odds against the CPR winning a damage suit were overwhelming. Bennett was forced to dig deeper and deeper into English common law to find precedents for the case he was arguing, and he lost many more cases than he won. In the process he frequently drew rebukes from the bench for the course he was trying to pursue. That seemingly did not concern the railway. It remained more willing to be sued than to settle, more willing to appeal than to accept the judgments of trial courts.

The second area where CPR work was demanding of Bennett's time was in extraterritorial activities, particularly in British Columbia after 1904 where the railway was negotiating for branch lines and hotel sites. As a result, Bennett was frequently absent from the city.[5] When he was at home, he had an increasing volume of agricultural real estate business to do as a retailer-wholesaler of CPR land.

Equally time-consuming were the chores Bennett had to perform for his Territorial Assembly constituents. As the farm land began to fill up, the demand for passable roads and bridges mounted steadily. The pressure was exerted first on Bennett, who wrote almost daily to the civil servants in Regina, though he know full well that nothing could be done because of lack of money.[6] All of this made it easy for him to turn his back on his Conservative friends when they began organizing for the November 1904 federal election campaign. The nomination went elsewhere, and Bennett confined his activities to occasional speech-making. Whether Bennett's Methodist conscience would have allowed him to opt out of the race if he had known in July what he would know in December is indeed doubtful. The 'Manitoba Schools Question' was being fought all over again in the nether reaches of the Liberal party, and it was that struggle, more than any of the usual reasons given, that was delaying the granting of provincial status to the Territories.

Six years before, Sir Wilfrid Laurier had outraged the Catholic hierarchy, up to and including the Vatican itself, by signing the Laurier-Greenway compromise that confirmed the abolition of strictly denominational schools in Manitoba.[7] At the time of Confederation existing schools in Rupert's Land were operated by the Roman Catholic church and the Church of England. In

1890 the government of Manitoba abolished the denominational schools in favour of a system of non-sectarian 'national' schools. The action was anathema to the Roman Catholic community and kept eastern Canada in a turmoil for almost a decade. In the end a deal was done – the Laurier-Greenway compromise. The Manitoba Schools Act was amended to permit members of Catholic orders to be employed as teachers; Roman Catholic schools could be tax-supported in districts where the Catholics were in the majority; children could be given religious instruction during the last half hour of each day. But the Catholic schools were subject to inspection by the provincial Department of Education and were required to follow the same course of studies and to use the same textbooks as the public schools. The amendment was a far cry from the days when the Roman Catholic hierarchy had set the curriculum, dictated textbooks, and insisted that religious instruction be incorporated in all subjects. The campaign against the compromise was continued on all fronts by the church.

On 4 May 1904 the Toronto *News* ran the following story: 'The principal reason for the slowness in giving Autonomy to the West is that the Ottawa Government dare not give it. The hierarchy of the Roman Catholic Church has served notice that when a Bill to make a new province or provinces is drafted, it must contain a provision establishing Separate (Catholic) Schools. Should that be done Separate Schools would become a permanent portion of the western system.' The 'scoop' seemed to go largely unread, for no other Canadian paper picked it up or commented on it. But Laurier read it and went to his friend John Willison, the editor of the *News*, to persuade him to drop the issue until after the election.[8] The last thing Laurier needed was a refighting of the Manitoba Schools Question during the approaching federal election. Laurier's view was shared by the Catholic lay leaders. Senator R.W. Scott, who handled many of Laurier's relations with the Catholic church, told Msgr Sbarretti, the papal legate, 'Our only chance of success is by keeping the subject out of politics by avoiding all reference to it.'

The issue never did emerge during the campaign, but somewhere along the way Bennett became privy to what was going on. During his annual Christmas visit to his mother he was interviewed by the Saint John *Star* and on 24 December 1904 he was quoted as saying:

The opinion prevails that the neglect of the Federal Government to deal with the repeated demands of the Legislature for autonomy has been owing to the difficulty which surrounds the educational problem. Whether Separate Schools shall exist by law or whether they should be prohibited, is the first question calling for decision, and shall the new Province or Provinces be given full power to deal with the matter without any limitations whatever?

When, two months later, the first draft of the Autonomy Bill was introduced into the House of Commons, it quickly became apparent how accurate Bennett's information had been. The way section 16 dealing with education was drafted, it could have been interpreted to mean that the status quo ante to 1875 was being restored. When Sir Clifford Sifton discovered it, he rushed back to Ottawa from a health resort in Indiana and resigned from the cabinet. W.S. Fielding, the finance minister, threatened to resign. Laurier vigorously denied any such interpretation had been intended. He invited Sifton to redraft the clause to his and Fielding's satisfaction.

It was during the internecine controversy of the Liberal party over the Autonomy Bill that Bennett received word, on 10 March 1905, of the sudden death of his father at Hopewell Cape, at the age of sixty-three. The mantle of responsibility for the family came naturally and comfortably to rest on Bennett's shoulders. His brother Ronald was by then a first officer in the merchant marine, bound for the port of Galveston on the Texas coast. His sister Evelyn, who was thirty-one, was a teacher at the normal school at Fredericton, while sixteen-year-old Mildred was at home with her mother, but soon to prepare for her entrance exams for Mount Allison University at nearby Sackville, New Brunswick. Once his mother and sister were settled into a life without husband and father, Bennett returned west to make verbal war on the compromise Autonomy Bill Sir Clifford Sifton had drafted for Sir Wilfrid Laurier to submit to parliament. That clause stated that the provision for separate schools that had been established for the Territories in 1901, not the system in force in 1875, was to apply in the new provinces.

Even that was too much for Bennett. While the uproar over Sifton's resignation made few waves across Alberta, it set off a powerful reaction among militant Ontario Protestants against the clerical intrusion into Canadian politics. It so happened that by-elections were being fought that spring in the constituencies of North Oxford and London. Both Bennett and Haultain were invited to speak for the Conservative candidates, and they did so with great vigour – but all in vain. The Liberals carried what were normally Liberal seats.

The campaign Bennett undertook in Ontario marked his introduction to the readers of the *Calgary Eye Opener*, Bob Edward's satirical weekly. Bennett would be in and out of that newspaper for the better part of the next decade, whenever Edwards felt the urge to cut him down to size or to take another side-swipe at the CPR. According to Edwards, Bennett 'would be a very clever fellow if he did not know it.'[9]

Edwards, a Scottish immigrant, had tried to found weekly newspapers at several points in Alberta before he moved the *Eye Opener* to Calgary from High River in 1904. Hugh Dempsey has described Edwards as an angry man lashing out at the inequities of Canadian society:[10] 'He was repelled by the hypocrisy of the established churches, the callousness of bureaucrats, the dishonesty of politicians and the rapaciousness of corporate interests... In truth the *Eye Opener* was not a newspaper but Bob Edwards' personal platform for social comment and humor.' Edwards was one of the authentic 'characters' Calgary nurtured during the first decade of the twentieth century. His weekly eventually circulated as far east as Toronto.

In Calgary, Edwards found the CPR a worthy recipient for his vitriol-spiked barbs. When J.S. Dennis, the western superintendent of the CPR, took exception to an article Edwards had published on Dennis and the CPR irrigation promotion in southeastern Alberta, he instructed Bennett to file suit against Edwards for libel. Edwards won the case, but the feud was on. Edwards took a keen delight in publicizing CPR train wrecks, with photographs where possible. In Calgary the company's operations made it particularly vulnerable to unfavourable publicity.

To serve the steadily expanding wholesale warehouses along Ninth Avenue, Tenth Avenue, and Eleventh Avenue, the CPR had built half-mile-long spur tracks in the lanes between Eighth and Ninth avenues and between Tenth and Eleventh avenues. These tracks, along with its double-tracked main line, gave it four strings of trackage running through the heart of downtown Calgary.

Calgarians living south of the tracks had to cross them to get to the retail stores or offices in the business section. If the transcontinental trains were not blocking First Street or Second Street West, yard engines shunting box cars back and forth to the wholesale buildings could block them just as well. When the clanging bell of the yard engine did not move dilatory pedestrians and wagons out of its way, a sharp blast from its whistle would start a stampede of horse-drawn vehicles in all directions. Worst of all, the trains blocked traffic frequently during the early hours of the morning when Calgarians were bound for work. Even when the way was open, pedestrians had to pick their footing carefully around the potholes that developed in the approaches to the right-of-way.

For Calgarians the crossings were at worst a potential hazard to life and limb, at best an ever-present inconvenience. Edwards never allowed the railway-crossing accidents and traffic jambs to go unreported in the *Eye Opener*. And when a week passed without anything untoward happening, that could also make an item. To wit: 'We are happy to report that not a single pedestrian accident or wrecked buggy occurred on the First Street West CPR crossings last week.' Because Bennett was so closely associated with the CPR, he became a natural subject for Edwards's attention.

In the first provincial election that followed in the fall of 1905 the *Eye Opener*, despite Edwards's antagonism towards the CPR, came out in support of Bennett, who was running against W.H. Cushing. Then he undercut his support by publishing a large cartoon of Bennett sitting on a bench between two comely ladies.

BENNETT: 'How happy could I be with either, were t'other dear charmer away.'

Hot air will carry a balloon up a long way, but it won't keep it there.

One was labelled 'CPR' and the other 'Calgary.' The cut-line read: 'How happy could I be with either, were t'other dear charmer away!' Bennett's loss of the election to Cushing was greeted by the *Eye Opener* with another large front-page cartoon. The cartoon focused on a huge balloon falling to earth, with a large hole at the top, out of which the air was escaping. On the underside in a basket was a small man labelled 'Bennett' frantically trying to blow air into the balloon through a tube. Below was the cut-line: 'Hot air will carry a balloon up a long way, but it won't keep it there.'

Edward's most prominent 'ragging' of Bennett, certainly the one longest remembered in Calgary, occurred when the *Eye Opener* republished a couple of derailment pictures it had previously run under the heading 'Two CPR Wrecks.' Then, in an adjacent two columns, it published, apropos of nothing, a large photograph of R.B. Bennett.[11] It was overlined: 'Another CPR Wreck.'

Bennett was by no means a passive recipient of Edwards's barbs. Indeed, quite the reverse was true. He was undoubtedly the moving force behind the decision of the CPR to ban the *Eye Opener* from its passenger trains on the grounds that it was an obscene publication. Bennett also commented to mutual friends that he was going to drive Edwards out of Calgary, whereupon Edwards reported the threat in the *Eye Opener*. Eventually, however, the feud played itself out and Edwards, after supporting Bennett in the 1911 general election, published what amounted to a public apology to Bennett.[12] In the end, they became fast friends. Edwards became a regular at the Bennett table, and Bennett became the drafter of Edwards's will and the executor of his estate.

During the 1905 election campaign, Edwards, surprisingly in view of his bilious view of religion, had supported the Separate Schools provision of the Autonomy Act. For Haultain and Bennett, the education clause was not by any means all that was wrong with the Autonomy Bill. The federal government was refusing to transfer ownership of the land and natural resources to the provinces. It was thus placing the new provinces in an inferior position to every other province in Canada. Both new provinces had looked forward to the revenues they would obtain from land sales and resource development to pay for capital assets and government services. Laurier's rationalized this step by stating that the dominion needed ownership of the land to facilitate settlement of the west with the immigrants it was bringing in from the United States, Britain, and Eastern Europe. Annual grants would be given to the provinces in lieu of revenues from resources. But that was only perpetuating the long-standing grievance of the Territorial government – dependency on Ottawa for the bulk of its income. It would continue to be a festering sore in dominion-provincial relations for another quarter of a century.[13]

For Bennett and for Calgary and southern Alberta, however, even these disabilities were as nothing compared with the action of the Laurier administration in converting the North-West Territories into a Liberal party satrapy in the guise of conferring provincial autonomy. The first step was to appoint Frank Oliver of Edmonton to replace Sir Clifford Sifton as minister of the interior. Then Edmonton and Regina were selected as the provisional capitals of the two provinces until the soon-to-be-elected legislatures chose permanent capitals.[14]

The first initiative in creating the provincial entities was the appointment of a lieutenant-governor for each province. He was empowered to name a provisional premier, who could select a provisional cabinet to set up the machinery for electing the first legislature. When it came to naming the lieutenant-governors of the new provinces, Ottawa chose two lifelong Liberals. A.E. Forget, lieutenant-governor of the Territories since 1897, was named for Saskatchewan and G.H.V. Bulyea was selected for Alberta. Both of them passed over F.W.G. Haultain, who had been the de facto premier for fifteen years, in favour of well-known Liberals as provisional premiers – Walter Scott in Saskatchewan and A.C. Rutherford in Alberta. Scott and Rutherford, in turn, selected only Liberals for their provisional cabinets.

In this situation, Bennett found it impossible to resist the importuning of a Conservative convention that he become the party's provincial leader and a candidate in the Calgary constituency in the first provincial election in 1905. He ran against W.H.

Cushing, a former mayor, president of the Board of Trade, and prominent manufacturer. When the constituencies were ultimately established for Alberta, reputedly with the gerrymandering skill of Frank Oliver, the southern Albertans shouted 'Foul!' More seats were allocated to the Edmonton area than to Calgary, despite the claims of Calgary to a superiority in population. In the Edmonton area, there were a half-dozen pie-shaped ridings surrounding the city, making for easy access for the candidates. In the south the constituencies were cut up in narrow strips stretching from the Rockies to the eastern border, making election campaigning impossibly time consuming. The Liberals, finally, had the help of Oliver's political machine and all the federal and territorial employees in the province. Given such an overwhelming advantage, it was hardly surprising for the Rutherford Liberals to win the election. What was unexpected was the margin of victory − twenty-three Liberals to only two Conservatives. One of those two Conservatives was *not* R.B. Bennett.

It was a mean and nasty election, even given the crudities of frontier politics. The normally Conservative *Calgary Herald* took a sideswipe at Bennett even before the Tory nominating convention. Was it, it inquired, fit and proper for Bennett to stand for nomination in view of his extensive corporation connections? Persons with such connections normally found it difficult to serve two masters, the public interest and the interest of their employers or clients. After Bennett was nominated, the *Herald* swung to his support, but continued its crusade against the corporate menace by switching its aim to the Liberal cabinet ministers. The *Albertan* not only overplayed the publicity it gave to the Liberal party, but kept up a drumbeat of editorial criticism of Bennett and opened its letter columns to derogatory anonymous writers. Bob Edwards, who was against all political parties equally, urged the voters through the *Eye Opener* to ignore party labels and vote for the man. He opted for Bennett over Cushing in Calgary, but asserted that Bennett, as a leader, would want nothing but nonentities and spineless nincompoops as followers. The Conservative candidate in Gleichen fitted those qualifications perfectly, he contended.

For Bennett, the election on 9 November 1905 was an unmixed disaster. There was, in fact, no provincial Conservative party organization worthy of the name. What organization muscle it had was concentrated almost wholly south of Red Deer. Bennett had to try to make up for this lack by spending most of his time in the constituencies. His efforts could by no means overcome the Liberal party advantages, particularly in the north where the Liberal majorities were overwhelming, many in the 300, 400, and 500 vote range. South of Red Deer the Conservatives still lost, but by eminently more respectable margins – in the thirties and forties.

Bennett lost the Calgary seat to Cushing by only twenty-nine votes. He attributed his defeat to two main reasons – that as a leader he had to spend so much time in the country, and that a labour candidate in the field took votes from the Conservatives by attacking Bennett's corporate connections.

Bennett's trenchant attack on the Liberal party's Schools Act stance unquestionably cost him a measure of Catholic support. 'Forever and forever,' he thundered, 'you cannot change the provision that relates to Separate Schools! Is that a fair deal? [Who] are the best judges of educational law, [you] or men who sit in Ottawa? Shall they pass laws for us or shall we pass laws for ourselves?'[15] While the Catholic hierarchy never ceased to oppose the Laurier-Greenway compromise, ordinary Catholics lived easily with the watered-down version of separate schools rights that existed in the Territories. When Bennett and his Conservative followers made these schools an election issue it created a widespread fear that they might lose even their compromise rights. In the predominately Catholic French and German ridings the Liberals went in by landslide majorities.

Bennett's reaction to his defeat, if he had ever been tempted to descend to the patois of the streets, was 'the hell with it!' He had not sought the leadership of the Conservative party when he had been the unanimous choice of the convention that summer. He regarded it as a temporary position he would gladly pass on when a permanent leader emerged from the ranks. He resigned as leader at once to devote all his attention to his legal practice and the corporate interests his opponents had criticized so much during the election campaign.

A year after the 1905 election Bennett wrote to Max Aitken that he had decided to retire from politics and asked for his reaction. That he was serious about retiring can be seen from his absence from the program when Sir Robert Borden, the Conservative leader, made his tour of western Canada in 1907. It was not something Bennett shouted from the housetops; he just stopped participating. It was a decision of which Aitken approved, but he felt constrained to add a codicil – he was sure Bennett's ultimate achievement would be to become prime minister of Canada.

Aitken was by then, at the age of twenty-seven, successfully launched into the most meteoric financial career in Canadian history, from pauper to millionaire in less than half a decade, to multimillionaire in less than ten years. He was eager to take Bennett along. The relationship that developed between Aitken and Bennett was living proof of the aphorism that opposites attract. They shared a visceral passion for the British Empire and the Joseph Chamberlain vision of its future, but nothing else. Where Bennett was aloof, Aitken had mastered the art of making friends. While Bennett's temper was explosive, Aitken seldom angered, and he used his ready smile as an instrument for quiet persuasion. He yielded nothing to Bennett in the size of his ego, but, unlike Bennett, he seldom let it show.

After the Alberta election of 1898, young Aitken sold his interest in the Calgary bowling alley. He returned to the east and stopped off at Montreal, where he picked up an insurance agency for the city of Saint John. He did very well over the next two years selling insurance as well as bonds, but he lost most of his income gambling at poker and dice. In 1902 he met John F. Stairs, the leading financier of Halifax and president of the Union Bank.[16] Stairs took an instant liking to Aitken and set up the Royal Securities Company for him to run. Part of his function was to ferret out profitable small Maritime enterprises that could be put together and turned into bond issuers, all the while keeping his eye peeled for prosperous small banks that Stairs's Union Banks might buy.

Until the turn of the century in North America, individual enterprise was truly individual. Frick, Carnegie, Sears, Simpson, Flavelle, Eaton, Hearst, and Massey were not only recognized names of great businesses, they were names of real flesh and blood men who had built those businesses and owned them. All that changed with the development of security capitalism,[17] epitomized in New York by the organization of the United States Steel Company by the house of Morgan. It was the security capitalism boom that made Aitken a multimillionaire, and helped to do the same for R.B. Bennett.

The Morgan-Carnegie transaction is a classic case study of how the system worked. Morgan paid Carnegie $447 million for his steel mills, substantially more than Carnegie thought the business was worth. Then the bank used it as the foundation on which it erected the steel trust by buying a number of other steel companies and amalgamating them into a single company. To do so, it floated a bond issue of sufficient size to pay for the entire transaction and issued common stock, giving the actual ownership of the enterprise to itself and to favoured groups of bond purchasers. When, through economies of scale and rationalization of production, marketing, and management in a booming economy, the value of the common stock ultimately skyrocketed, everybody got rich, except the bondholders who got only interest on their investment.

From the beginning, Aitken possessed a talent for analysing a company and deciding quickly whether it could be melded into a profitable amalgamation with other companies. When Stairs died in 1904, Aitken was forced to develop an expertise in solving corporate problems, for they were on the threshold of undertaking several important financial transactions. By the time Bennett reached the conclusion he was done with politics, then, in 1907, Aitken was more than eager to have Bennett join him for the ride. Together they put together Calgary Power and the Canada Cement Company. As Aitken wrote later of Bennett: 'He took on the direction of two of my concerns: a hydro electric plant with a widespread distribution system and also a cement works. His business administration was brilliant. The lawyer turned executive astounded me by his grasp of details, sound judgments and swift decisions.'[18]

Fulsome as that praise appears at first glance, it does less than justice to Bennett. Aitken's reference to 'my concerns' is an exaggeration. Both were amalgamations he had put together with Bennett's assistance and, while Aitken emerged with substantial equity holdings in both companies, neither could be described as 'his.' Aitken's forte lay in amalgamating successful businesses so that the profitability of the whole exceeded that of the sum of the parts. In contrast, Bennett's experience on the western frontier was with embryo companies struggling to be born in a financially deficient environment. His experiences with cement plants, electrical utilities, and country grain elevators all belonged in that category.

Because he had arrived in Calgary with his books and $500 in his pocket, Bennett's march along the road to affluence had to begin with very small steps and at a very slow pace. As luck would have it, one of the first investments he made enabled him to lengthen his stride and increase his pace substantially. Yet on the surface it had every appearance of being the sort of long-shot speculation only the most gullible would contemplate. It was the purchase of a defaulted mortgage on a tract of land with a flawed title.

When, in 1888, the Dominion of Canada sold ninety-four acres on the southern edge of Calgary to the Calgary and District Agricultural Association for $2.50 an acre, it placed a caveat on the title. It stipulated that the tract was to be used solely for an agricultural exhibition; if any attempt were made to subdivide it, the title was to revert to the federal Department of Agriculture. The association promptly placed a mortgage of $3000 on the property to provide funds to build a race track and grandstand and to make other improvements. It underestimated the cost of the improvements and had to add another $1000 to its debt.

The exhibition association had been formed a full decade

ahead of its time. The countryside around Calgary was still dominated by ranching rather than farming, which made for a sparsity
of population. All-weather roads were still unknown in Alberta,
where traffic moved over prairie trails at the pace of a walking
horse. The exhibition failed to attract either exhibitors or spectators in sufficient numbers of justify its existence. It went out of
business in 1892, leaving an interest-accumulating mortgage for
$4000 in its wake.

In view of the caveat on the title, how much would a prudent
investor pay for such a defaulted debt? $2500? $1000? $50? No
matter. When the Calgary exhibition was revived at the turn of
the century under the grandiose title of Inter-Western Pacific
Exhibition Company and went looking for the owner of the
exhibition grounds it encountered R.B. Bennett, who had lately
acquired the property from a trust company. Could they use the
grounds again to stage their re-established exhibition? They
could, Bennett replied, for a nominal rental to help pay the taxes.
This time, despite the run-down condition of the grounds, the
exhibition caught on. The directors were encouraged to make it a
permanent Calgary attraction and decided to buy back the property and rehabilitate the buildings and grounds. Would Mr Bennett sell? Indeed he would – for $7000.

The astonished directors, who were mainly friends and clients
of Bennett's, boggled at the price. They tried to haggle, to appeal
to his civic consciousness, to his better nature, to his friendship.
His asking price remained $7000. Eventually the directors per-
suaded the Calgary city council to buy the property, which it did
on 14 February 1901 for $7000.[19] It was that $7000, or what was
left of it after Bennett paid off his mortgage, that become the
foundation on which the Bennett fortune was built, not the
largesse of Max Aitken.

The capitalist economy that was developing in southern
Alberta was more than a continent removed from anything
resembling the security capitalism that Aitken was involved with.
It was capitalism of a sort, but a bootstrap capitalism firmly
anchored to the supplying of fundamental needs of the incoming
settlers by the incoming settlers themselves. Lawyers, even those

lacking ready capital to invest, could get in on the ground floor of newly organized enterprises by accepting shares in lieu of legal fees. In Bennett's case, his CPR connection would certainly have opened avenues of profitable real estate investments for him. Moreover, it was the effort of the CPR to extricate itself from its most vexing problem that provided Bennett with his best investment opportunity.

That problem was the railway's inability to devise a satisfactory system for getting the increasing volumes of grain being produced from the farmyards of the west to the ultimate consumers in the east. At first the CPR encouraged the construction of flat warehouses to take delivery of the grain and load it into boxcars, but this process was so costly the farmers demanded they should load their own box cars directly from their wagons. Because it could take a week to complete that loading the railway resisted, on the grounds that such delays cost it too dearly in tied-up equipment. A solution to its problem developed soon after 1900 when an American invented the vertical grain elevator. Not only could it unload farm wagons in minutes, but it could fill boxcars in an hour instead of a day. Much too busy to build its own elevators, the CPR hit upon a scheme to attract private investors to the field. It offered to supply the land on which to locate the elevators and the spur track on which to spot the boxcars for loading, cost free, to whoever would build elevators at its townsites.

At $6000 for a wooden structure that could hold 30,000 bushels of wheat, the country grain elevator quickly became the soundest investment available in western Canada. With a run of reasonably good crops, the owner of the elevator who could fill and empty his structure two or three times during a crop year could pay for the cost of construction in three or four years. The profits from the first elevator would provide the down-payment on the second elevator in the next town down the line.

It was the grain business that first brought Bennett and John I. McFarland together into what would become the closest of lifelong friendships. McFarland had come west from Ontario to work for a grain company in Winnipeg in 1896. Then he got a job running a grain elevator in Strathcona, south of Edmonton. One elevator on the Calgary and Edmonton Railway south of Edmonton became two, then four, then eight, and McFarland sold out his Calgary and Alberta Elevator Company to the Bawlf Company of Winnipeg and moved to Calgary as its general manager. Bennett, meanwhile, took a somewhat different path into the grain business. He became president of the Globe Elevators Company, which built a large terminal elevator in east Calgary, hard by the Calgary Brewery and a couple of newly constructed flour mills. The company would clean and store the grain for the flour mills, and see to the transshipment of grain to the Pacific coast and Fort William. Once the grain business had brought McFarland and Bennett together, they became joint venturers in each other's deals for the rest of their lives.

In this same period, Bennett's law practice was becoming very busy and his CPR activities were multiplying as well. The railway's land sales were booming as never before and it was launching a gigantic irrigation project east of Calgary. It decided it needed Bennett as a full-time vice-president for irrigation and insisted that he move into the CPR Natural Resources Building, a block and a half southeast of the Clarence Block. Bennett agreed to take on the vice-presidency and to move his office, but he would not give up his law practice. He would manage both – by installing a private phone line between the Clarence Block and his CPR office to keep him instantly accessible to both sets of employees.

John E. Brownlee, later premier of Alberta, was an articled student in the Lougheed and Bennett office in 1908. Part of his responsibility was to operate that special telephone line, a chore that also entailed carrying law books and documents back and forth between the offices.[20] Brownlee's most vivid memories, however, were of the evening hours he spent in the office. He and another student fell into the habit of returning to the law office after supper to pursue their studies. It was a rare occasion when Bennett was not also there at some time during the evening. Mostly he worked alone in his office, but at least once a week he would interest himself in what the students were doing. If this subject interested him he would launch into a dissertation that would keep his young listeners entranced. Then he would bombard them with chapters and verses of sources to be consulted. The one quality that seared itself into the memories of everybody who knew him, Calgary law students and Ottawa politicians alike, was his fabulous memory and his instant recall, not only of the gist of ideas but of the exact wording in precise context.

For Bennett, working a sixteen-hour day, six days a week, was something that came as naturally as breathing. It was something he had begun in the first days of his arrival in Calgary, something he continued long after the CPR appointed him vice-president of its irrigation company. If the demands on his time were such that he could not encompass them within a ten-hour day, and if he had disavowed any further interest in politics, how did it happen that he became a Conservative candidate for the Alberta legislature in the election of 1909?

The factual answer seems to be that he was absent from the city when the Conservatives of Calgary held their nominating convention and George Robinson, his friend, quondam election agent, and campaign manager, placed his name in nomination without his consent. The convention duly voted unanimously to accept him. There was more to his decision not to reject the nomination, however, than the party loyalty that prevented him from embarrassing his friends. In the time that had elapsed since his defeat in 1905, his animus towards the Liberal government in Edmonton had intensified rather than diminished. Not only had it selected Edmonton over Calgary to be the capital of Alberta, but it had dictated that the University of Alberta be located in the town of Strathcona, opposite Edmonton, on the south bank of the Saskatchewan River. For some months thereafter Bennett was involved in trying to put a committee together to organize a rival institution in Calgary. The Alberta government had also adopted one of Bennett's pet projects, later abandoned, of using the provincial credit to subsidize railway construction. In all, it had guaranteed more than $25 million worth of railway bonds for the Canadian Northern, Grand Trunk, Midland Railway, and Alberta and Great Waterways Railway. Most of 1700 miles of construction was to be in the Edmonton area, or to feed into and out of the Edmonton area, thus turning Edmonton into the railway hub of Alberta. This surely was the unkindest cut of all, to both Calgary and the CPR.

Though he campaigned vigorously, the Liberal campaign for 'Rutherford, Reliability and Railway' was too much for the Conservatives, and when the ballots were counted on 22 March 1909 the Liberals had elected thirty-seven members, the Conservatives two, plus one Independent Conservative. There was also one Socialist. This time one of the successful Conservatives *was* R.B. Bennett. He won one of the two Calgary seats. The other Conservatives were George Hoadley of Okotoks and Independent Conservative Edward Michener of Red Deer.

The landslide victory of the Liberals settled nothing for Bennett and, between the election and the first sitting of the House, he concentrated his focus on the Great Waterways Railway promotion. It was indeed a promotion worthy of his attention, perhaps the most fanciful railway promotion in the history of Canadian finance capitalism.

The Great Waterways saga began with the arrival in Winnipeg in 1908 of W.R. Clarke, a Kansas City, Missouri, railway construction contractor, on a safari to spy out the possibilities of setting up a Canadian subsidiary. He discovered a group of Winnipeg promoters who had a charter to build a railway from Edmonton to Fort McMurray. He borrowed the charter and went off to Edmonton to check on its possibilities, and whether such a railway would qualify for government grants or bond guarantees. It would indeed. Clarke, however, was advised by the government not to buy the Winnipeg-owned charter. The Alberta legislature would incorporate a provincial company for him, the Great Waterways Railway Company.

With the Alberta government's $7.4 million guarantee in hand, Clarke went off to New York to arrange for J.P. Morgan and Company to float a bond issue for him in England. It was the terms of that bond issue that got Albertans, egged on by Bennett in a couple of speeches, to take a second look at the Great Waterways project. The fifty-year first-mortgage 5 per cent bonds were sold for 110 per cent of par. The *Financial Post* and the

Financial Times expressed puzzlement at these figures when Alberta government 4 per cent bonds were selling for 99 per cent in London. The debate over the terms of the bond issue, along with criticism of the high cost of the Great Waterways contract, kept the railway before the public between the election in March 1909 and the first session of the new assembly in February 1910. Other members of the legislature, including the Honourable W.H. Cushing of Calgary, the minister of public works, and J.R. Boyle, the Liberal member for Edmonton, began pawing around in the Great Waterways financing, particularly when it was revealed that the cost of construction would be a third higher than the costs of any other railway.

Until the Great Waterways Railway problems surfaced, political life for Premier Rutherford and his four-man inner cabinet had been a salubrious voyage on the sea of tranquillity. From their temporary home in an annex to the Terrace Block, they could gaze out to the steadily rising stone and marble Legislative Building with warming pride. The natives were certainly well disposed towards most of their endeavours. Then, just before the session began in 1910, the sea of tranquillity was hit by a tidal wave.

First, rumours spread across Edmonton that Cushing was outraged over the Great Waterways deal, which was allegedly completed by Rutherford and Attorney-General C.W. Cross without consulting him.[21] Then it was reported that Cushing had resigned from the cabinet and that several members of the legislature would demand a revision of the contract. When the legislature opened, a storm of opposition to the Waterways contract developed, Cushing resigned, and J.R. Boyle blasted the administration in a two-hour speech. Out in the countryside, the newspapers were taking the public pulse and finding it running strongly against the contract. In Calgary, the executive of the Liberal party went into emergency session and unanimously pledged its support to Cushing.

In late February Clarke arrived in Edmonton with a compromise proposal to allay criticism of the company's lack of financial responsibility. The company would guarantee the government that, until it had finished building the road, it would leave $1 million of the loan in the hands of the bank to protect the government against loss. But still the opposition continued and, on 2 March 1910, Bennett arose to make his long-anticipated contribution to the debate.[22]

There was never any doubt of Bennett's position. The question in the public mind was whether his eloquent marshalling of the critical facts would be enough to bring down a government so recently re-elected with such an overwhelming majority? Bennett did not begin to speak until late in the afternoon and was forced to interrupt his oration after about an hour when the House adjourned for supper.

Word that Bennett was speaking spread quickly around Edmonton and, by seven o'clock, a large crowd had gathered outside the Terrace Building annex. When it became obvious that there were twice as many spectators on hand as there were chairs in the assembly room, the door was broken in and the crowd poured into the room. When Bennett appeared at the entrance to the room to wend his way to his seat, the spectators jumped to their feet to give him a standing ovation. Of the speech itself, the *Edmonton Journal* reported in the lead paragraphs of its five-column report:

Yesterday's sittings of the Legislature were the most sensational in the history of the young province of Alberta. Never in its four and a half year life has such interest attended a debate on the political questions of the day. Never before had the members of the legislature and those who crowded into every nook of the building witnessed such a display of forensic eloquence as was given in the afternoon and evening session.

The long looked for speech of R.B. Bennett on the Great Waterways agreement marked a new era in the local legislature. For in the splendor of the diction and the physical endurance of the orator it established a high water mark for Parliamentary debate in Alberta. Exclusive of the two-hour adjournment he addressed the house for more than five hours in a flow of eloquence that was fully sustained from start to finish. . . . He held his listeners spellbound from start to finish.

Not only did Bennett draw upon the knowledge of railway

construction and operation he had gained as solicitor for the CPR, but he had taken the trouble to visit the construction site and see for himself what was going on. And what was wrong with what was going on were chapter and verse of his speech. The way the Waterways project was being financed provided him with the text for a detailed history of railway financing in Canada and the United States. The way in which the law partner of the attorney-general had been retained by Clarke as counsel for the railway became the text for a lecture of legal ethics and conflict of interest. The arithmetic of the financing led him to the conclusion that Clarke had skimmed at least a $300,000 profit from the sale of the government guaranteed bonds alone. Even greater profits would be extracted from the artificially exaggerated mileage of the contract, paying $20,000 a mile for 350 contract miles compared with only 275 actual miles.

He was particularly scathing in his criticism of the picayune financing of the Clarke enterprise – undertaking a $7.4 million construction contract with only $50,000 capital. As a royal commission would later discover, that capitalization was even flimsier than Bennett suspected. Clarke had borrowed $50,000 from the Merchants Bank and used it to buy $50,000 worth of stock in Great Waterways. This only-on-paper corporation then deposited the $50,000 in the Merchants Bank in a newly opened account. The inducement Clarke had offered the bank to get the loan was double-edged: the railway would leave the $50,000 on deposit in the bank, thus protecting the bank from loss; then, when it got into the railway business, it would give all its banking business to the Merchants Bank.

Bennett was scathing in his criticism of the government for taking Clarke on trust, for its failure to check his bona fides and background adequately, and for neglecting to have government engineers check his engineering. Then he focused attention on the unfavourable settlement potential of the bush and muskeg country through which the line was to be built. It would never be able to support enough people to generate sufficient traffic to pay its operating expenses, let alone the interest on its debt.

Boyle, the 'traitorous' Liberal member for Edmonton, had

made some of the same points in his speech the previous day. The difference was in Bennett's mastery of the subject, the elegance of his language, his voice control hour after hour, his lack of reliance on notes, and the cutting edge of ridicule he used so effectively.

The Bennett performance was undoubtedly everything the newspaper accounts said it was. And while it helped to persuade ten government supporters to vote against the railway, the contract still carried by twenty-three votes to fifteen. The huge Liberal majority was too great to overcome. But, as correspondents later wondered, did Bennett's super performance perhaps make the members suspicious of his cleverness. Was he not simply too good to be true? There was one other factor that may have dissuaded some of the wavering Liberals from voting against the contract. In his peroration Bennett fell into a trap even freshmen debaters know enough to avoid. He threw in an irrelevancy that enabled his opponents to distract attention from the real issue being discussed.

The main target of all the critics of the project was C.W. Cross, who was most prominent in every phase of the Great Waterways controversy. Bennett traced many of the seemingly inexplicable aspects of the negotiations with Clarke to the office of the attorney-general. Then, almost as an aside, he gave voice to a street rumour that Cross had obtained a $12,000 contribution to his recent election campaign expenses from a telephone company negotiating a contract with the government.

That accusation threw the House into an uproar. Cross was on his feet to deny the charge and challenged Bennett to reveal the source of his information. Eventually Bennett pointed to a spectator sitting outside the railing who, he said, had given the information to Cushing. Instead of ending on a high note that would have roused his listeners to a frenzy of support, Bennett's speech ended in a minor flurry of cross-floor bickering between Bennett and Cross and back-bench hecklers. And that was the way the Great Waterways debate ended – it petered out, not with a roar but a whimper.

The government appointed a three-man judicial inquiry to discover whether any members of the government had been interested personally in the project. The majority report of the commissioners found nobody guilty of anything more than ineptitude and incompetence. Clarke, refusing to appear before the commission, retreated to Missouri and was never heard of again. Premier Rutherford, Cross, and two other cabinet members resigned and A.L. Sifton was persuaded to leave the Alberta Supreme Court to become leader of the Liberal party and premier. The Great Waterways Railway defaulted on its bonds and the province had to make good on its interest guarantee to the bondholders.

Once in office, the Sifton administration cancelled the contract with Great Waterways and had the legislature approve taking what was left of the $7.4 million covered by the bond issue into the general revenues of the province. That action brought the Liberal government back into head-to-head confrontation with Bennett.

The government's reasoning was quite straightforward: the railway was able to borrow the money only because of the government guarantee. The company went out of business when the contract was cancelled following default on its interest-paying commitment. Since the government was now responsible for both interest and principal, it was entitled to have the use of the money until repayment was due. The Royal Bank, where most of the money was on deposit in Montreal at 3½ per cent interest, thought otherwise. It was accountable to the bondholders who had invested the money for a specific purpose – the construction of a railway. If the purpose of the investment was not achieved, would they not be legally entitled to get their money back? Bennett's advice was that the bank should hold the money for the bondholders and refuse to turn it over to the government. The government sued the Royal Bank and the issue wound its way through the courts for the next couple of years (see chapter 4).

In the meantime, Bennett had been deeply involved, for several years, in Max Aitken's Calgary Power and Canada Cement promotions[23] – not because Aitken had put him into either gratuitously, but because Bennett had been involved with the City of Calgary's power problems, and with the cement industry, before Aitken had heard of either.

At the time of Bennett's arrival in Calgary, electric utilities in any real sense had not yet been invented. Toronto, New York, and London were still lighting their streets with gas. Calgary was far ahead of the times because, as early as 1889, it had several lights on street corners, powered by electricity supplied by the Eau Claire sawmill on the adjacent Bow River. After 1900, when the use of electricity was expanding, the city was toying with the notion of installing electric streetcars. It established a utilities committee to have charge of water and sewer mains and to control the erection of power poles. In 1905 it decided to get into the electrical distribution business, and the committee began to look around for power suppliers.

Bennett was solicitor for the Alberta Portland Cement Company, which Toronto and Owen Sound interests were building in east Calgary. In addition to its $300,000 cement plant and steam-powered electrical generator, it had acquired a hydroelectric power site on the Bow River thirty miles above Calgary on which it ultimately planned to develop a power plant capable of generating 10,000 horse-power of electrical energy. When it completed its cement plant in 1906 it moved immediately to get into the electrical business as well. Bennett took its offer to the Civic Utilities Committee. Meanwhile, a group of local promoters incorporated the Calgary Power and Transmission Company to take over the Eau Claire generating plant. It undercut the price quoted by the cement company and got the contract.

That set Bennett off on one of the loudest of his public shouting matches at the city council. He lashed out at the aldermen, accusing them of leaking his company's bid to the opposition. He took on the owners of the new company, accusing them of promoting the company on a shoestring and bribing people with discounted stock to induce them to become company directors. He contrasted this with the $300,000 investment by his clients, who were also committed to develop hydroelectric power to guarantee the future needs of Calgary. The chairman of the Utilities Committee took the floor to reply in kind. He called Bennett a windbag and threatened to push him into the street and punch him in the head.[24] Physical contact was avoided, but the argument over the power deal was on and off the front pages of Calgary newspapers for many weeks during 1907. The ultimate solution of the Calgary power controversy was the simple one. The city bought power from both companies at low prices set by the competition between the two. It was not long before the backers of the Calgary Power and Transmission Company became disenchanted with their investment and went looking for somebody to buy them out. They found Max Aitken, who bought the company.

Whether Bennett negotiated Aitken's purchase of the Calgary company is not a matter of record, but he was certainly involved in Aitken's purchase of the Alberta Portland Cement Company's electrical generating facilities. It was Bennett who notified Aitken that the facilities were coming onto the market and who conducted the negotiations that consummated the sale.

Aitken's interest in the Calgary electrical plants undoubtedly arose from the fact that he had made money on several occasions by taking over West Indies utilities and recasting them into profitable enterprises. The Calgary Power promotion differed from the West Indies counterpart in one important aspect – Aitken used his own money in Calgary. In other operations his modus operandi was to obtain options to sell from the owners of the individual companies and then to sell the options to the new company he incorporated to take them over. He would thus profit in three ways – on the sale of the options, on the sale of the bonds and preferred stock in the new company to investors through his Royal Securities Company, and on the capital appreciation of the common stock of the new company he got free, or purchased at a substantial discount.

The Calgary Power Company Aitken and Bennett put together in 1909 became one of the great Alberta success stories, and Bennett served as its president during the decade of its greatest growth. The secret of its early success was the long-term contract Bennett negotiated with the City of Calgary to supply all its electric needs. With this contract in hand, Calgary Power was able to raise the capital it needed to embark immediately on the Horseshoe Falls hydro dam on the Bow River, followed by the even larger Kananaskis Falls plant two years later.

The Calgary Power promotion was the essence of cut-and-dried simplicity, in contrast with the saga of Canada Cement. Bennett could not have been called a star player in the Canada Cement drama, but he was far from being a bit-player either, and in the early stages of the action he played a role of considerable importance.

The Rocky Mountain Cement Company of Blairmore, Alberta, was not included in the original group of companies that made up Canada Cement. Bennett was the titular head of the company and W.J. Budd, a Calgary businessman, was its general manager. The story of the ultimate acquisition of Rocky Mountain by Canada Cement sheds some light on some of the interesting manoeuvres of the incubating years of Canadian finance capitalism.[25] It began in the fall of 1909 when Bennett opened negotiations with Budd with the intention of buying out Budd's interest in the troubled company and becoming majority owner of the company's shares. Bennett got an option on Budd's shares and went to Montreal to discuss a possible sale of the company to Aitken. In the meantime, B.V. Bravender, the western manager of Aitken's Royal Securities Company, went to Budd and persuaded him to renege on his deal with Bennett – that he could get Budd twice as much from Canada Cement as Bennett had offered and they would split the difference. When Bennett got back to Calgary he found a letter from Budd awaiting him, cancelling his offer to sell to him. Bennett wrote to Aitken on 31 January 1910, bitterly denouncing the action of his western manager:

I am disgusted about this whole matter. I am coming to the conclusion that in business, honesty is not an important asset. I left Calgary having arranged with Budd to acquire control of the property on terms mentioned – in my memo to Mr. Drury. I arrived home this morning and I find a letter from Mr. Budd as follows: 'All negotiations off. Talk to Bravender and you will have a satisfactory reason . . .' I have Budd's letter offering me his stock on conditions I mentioned when in Montreal. If you authorize me to do so I propose to enforce my rights. I have told Mr. Bravender perfectly plainly that I do not think you are the kind of man who would permit yourself to be held up by Mr. Budd, that you are not paying $200,000 for water and for $400,000 you could put in a plant in Blairmore with double the output of the present mill. I am very much disappointed. I have honestly endeavoured in your interest to obtain the possession of a valuable property at the best possible price, declining to consider a commission or a division of the profits, and I find your representative in this province has practically made my efforts unavailing. I want you to consider this letter absolutely and strictly personal and to burn it as soon as you have read it, but I feel it is my bounded duty to place before you the facts so that you may understand exactly where we are at.[26]

How this aspect of the deal ended is not known, but it was not long before Bennett persuaded the Rocky Mountain directors to fire Budd. Rocky Mountain was, at best, a fringe operation with an undersized plant and limited market in the Crowsnest Valley, but the ultimate acquisition of the company by Bennett and the sale to Canada Cement illustrate the agility of Aitken's promotional mind. When Rocky Mountain was having trouble paying for some necessary repairs to the plant, Aitken suggested to Bennett that he should default on the bond interest and put the company into receivership and then buy it back at a substantial discount at the bankruptcy sale. Bennett rejected that proposal. It was then that Aitken came up with the scheme that was eventually adopted.

In the spring of 1910, while Bennett was still involved in the dispute with Budd, he discussed the problems of the Blairmore plant with Frank Jones, an outstanding Nova Scotia engineer and general manager of Canada Cement. Bennett's tentative conclusion was that the way to turn Rocky Mountain into a profitable investment would be to double the plant's capacity and extend its market area. Unhappily for the cash-strapped company, such expansion was financially impossible. When Jones reported his conversation with Bennett to Aitken in Montreal, he read more into Bennett's brainstorming about expansion than was justified.

He told Aitken that the expansion Bennett was planning would interfere materially with Canada Cement's future prospects. That being the case, Canada Cement should entertain plans to buy up the Rocky Mountain plant.

Aitken called in V.M. Drury, his brother-in-law and general manager of his Royal Securities Corporation, and instructed him on the contents of a letter he was to write to Bennett. After telling Bennett of Jones's conversation with Aitken, Drury wrote, 'It would be wise to write a letter to Mr. Aitken, which he could show Mr. Jones, in which you set forth the proposed plan of expansion.'[27] In the financial world of 1910, it was not thought unethical for Aitken not to disclose to Jones his interest in Rocky Mountain. The extra cost to Canada Cement of the Rocky Mountain shares would make little change to the multimillion dollar capitalization of the Cement Company, but the trumped-up competitive threat of Rocky Mountain Cement to Canada Cement's Alberta operation might double the multi-thousand dollar profits Aitken and Bennett would gain from the Rocky Mountain shares. On 14 April 1911 Aitken wrote to Bennett confirming that arrangements were now complete for him to exchange his shares in Rocky Mountain Cement for shares in Canada Cement.

The original idea of putting a cement conglomerate together came not from Aitken but from the son of the legendary Sir Sandford Fleming, the eminent pioneer railway builder, chief engineer, and surveyor for the CPR, and the inventor of standard time.[28] The Flemings and associates owned three cement plants and, in April 1909, they approached Aitken to inquire about the feasibility of putting a cement amalgamation together, with their companies as the key participants. Aitken jumped at the idea, and not only for the profit potential of such a promotion. Through Fleming he would get his foot in the door of the CPR-cum-Liberal-party establishment. The project was made doubly attractive when it was endorsed by Sir Edward Clouston, general manager of the Bank of Montreal. He promised to provide Aitken with the financial support he would need if he investigated the proposal and decided to proceed.

The Canada Cement Company Limited was incorporated by Aitken by a private act of parliament. The next step was to do a financial appraisal of the Fleming companies, two of which were in Ontario and one in Exshaw, Alberta. Aitken hired C.H. Cahan, a Montreal lawyer and later prominent Conservative party politician, to make the investigation. When Cahan came back from Alberta with his assessment of the plant, it was disturbing news for Aitken.

The Exshaw plant was a financial disaster and had been from its inception in 1906. One property, which had been purchased for $40,000, was valued at over $1 million when optioned to the cement company. In operation the company had consistently lost money; the Flemings borrowed $100,000 on their personal guarantee from the Bank of Montreal to pay bond interest. Later, when the bank refused to lend them more, they got a loan of $200,000 from the CPR. When Aitken received Cahan's report, he smelled a rat. The Flemings were using him to bail them out of this bad investment. Aitken, at that point, could have backed out of the deal, but that would have cost him a lot of money. He had already hired Frank Jones as general manager at a promised salary of $50,000 a year. He decided to proceed with the promotion, but to bring in enough other cement plants to enable their owners, as directors of the new company, to swamp the Fleming interests. In quick order he had options to sell signed by thirteen companies.

The board of directors of Canada Cement included several prominent industrialists and bankers, along with a representative of each of the thirteen optioned companies. The board was presented with the balance sheets and other financial information for each of the plants on which options to purchase had been obtained by Aitken. The board agreed unanimously to exercise all the options except the one covering the Fleming Alberta plant, even though Sir Sandford Fleming, who was then in his eighty-third year, had agreed to become president of the new company. Fleming was outraged.

Aitken stepped in at once to make peace. He persuaded the board to offer Fleming a compromise, and a much lower price for his Exshaw plant. If he would sign a letter acknowledging he was satisfied he had received a fair price for his property, he would receive a $50,000 cash payment. Fleming signed, but within a matter of weeks he wrote to Senator Edwards, who had succeeded him as president of the company, demanding an investigation into an alleged misappropriation by Aitken of 1.35 million shares of the $100 par company common stock. Some of this stock had been issued to the owners of the companies and some had been sold to Aitken and to the public at $30 a share. The directors offered Fleming the right to name a couple of investigators to make an impartial investigation of his charges, but they dismissed the complaint as groundless. Nevertheless, the following year, Fleming, in a letter to Prime Minister Sir Wilfrid Laurier, repeated his complaint about Aitken and asked for a parliamentary inquiry. The government, then deeply engaged in the debate over reciprocity with the United States, never did get around to Fleming's charges. Bennett became involved peripherally in the Fleming-Aitken controversy when Fleming sent copies of his letter to Laurier to the newspapers. The outraged Aitken wanted to sue Fleming for libel, but Bennett advised against it. Then, after Laurier's defeat, Fleming appealed to Borden. Bennett intervened to assure the prime minister that Fleming's charges were groundless.[29] The charges were still floating around when Fleming died in 1913.

CHAPTER FOUR

Member of Parliament

There would be more exalted episodes in Bennett's life in Canadian politics than the 1911 federal election, but he had never before been as totally involved as he was in that campaign. He was a committed Calgarian and a committed Albertan and, as such, had been involved in local issues in his previous runs for office in the Territorial Assembly and the Alberta legislature. But he also regarded himself as 'every bit as much a Britisher as any Englishman born within the sound of Bow Bells.' Indeed, as he would write to Max Aitken at about that time, he wondered whether he might ultimately cap his political career by following Aitken's example and seeking a seat in the Mother of Parliaments. Certainly he was committed to Aitken's Empire Free Trade crusade and to Chamberlain's vision of a British Empire welded together by the common tariff of its dominions.[1]

Two years before the 1911 election, Aitken had completed his mergers of the cement companies, several eastern steel companies, and two Calgary power companies and had moved to England with his family on an extended bond-selling excursion. Fate intervened in the form of a financially cemented friendship with Bonar Law, the Canadian-born leader of the British Conservative party, and Aitken was elected to parliament by one of that party's pocket boroughs. Thereafter, he seldom returned to Canada, save for short business trips. He rose, almost instantly, to the leadership of the British Empire Free Trade movement when Joseph Chamberlain became an invalid. The discussion between

Aitken and Bennett over branching out into Canada had reached a point where Aitken, at Bennett's suggestion, had tried to buy the *Calgary Herald* to give the movement a Canadian voice.[2] That deal was never consummated, but the depths of Bennett's own feelings are revealed in one of his letters to Aitken in November 1910:

If the empire is to endure, the self-governing nations which compose it must in some way be federated. Unless there is a recognition of common interests, common traditions, and above all common responsibilities and obligations, and too within the lifetime of this generation, independence is inevitable not of Canada alone but of all the nations that make up the Empire...I believe that Canada awaits the coming of a man with a vision, a statesman with a revelation, one who sees our destiny and who will arouse the latent patriotism and pride of our race and by appealing to all that is best within us lead us to an Imperial Federation where among the nations that comprise the union Canada must take a foremost place and in time direct the larger destinies of our world-wide Empire.

The passage is vintage Bennett oratory transcribed to paper: the ebullient phrases piled on top of each other, the easy flowing thought – it is all there. By sheer happenstance, the Laurier Liberal government would provide R.B. Bennett with a federal election issue in which he would, in the words of the *Albertan*, 'wrap himself in the Union Jack to beat back the American invaders.' In short, he would never have another election campaign into which he would be able to throw himself with a deeper emotional commitment. It all came to pass because the Liberals negotiated a trade agreement with the United States and sought to coast back into office on the reciprocity issue of the 1911 general election.

At first when Bennett agreed to accept the Conservative nomination, it looked as if he was enlisting in a cause that was irretrievably lost. The farmers in the Calgary area, as elsewhere in Alberta, embraced the reciprocity agreement with joyous hosannas. Duty-free farm machinery had been the holy grail of agrarian leaders since they first settled the west, and duty-free access to the American market would add 10 per cent to the prices they got for everything they grew. How could any Conservative candidate hope to defeat any Liberal candidate who offered such benefits?

In the beginning, however, it is doubtful if winning or losing bulked large in Bennett's thinking. Running for parliament provided him with an escape hatch, a graceful way of getting out of provincial politics. The Conservative party, of which he was the nominal leader, did not exist as a viable organization. In an era in which political patronage counted for everything, the Conservatives could offer little inducement for party workers. Even if Bennett had been an organizing genius, which he definitely was not, putting an effective party together in Alberta without patronage was impossible.

More than that, Bennett realized there was no future for him as an opposition member of the Alberta legislature. He had shot his bolt in the Great Waterways Railway scandal. While he had shaken the Liberal government to its foundations, he had not succeeded in toppling it. Under new management it had pulled itself together and was running the province as it saw fit. Ahead of him loomed three more years of listening to the twaddle of minds he scorned. The fortuitous arrival of the federal election two years ahead of schedule was a reprieve from the cloying atmosphere of the legislature.

As the Liberals were negotiating a free trade agreement with Washington, they had good reason for believing they were onto something good, politically. Central Canada had also been enjoying an unprecedented boom over the previous decade. Investment capital was pouring in from England and from the United States to double the value of investments from both sources between 1900 to 1910. A rapid expansion of industry and commerce was draining the population from the farming areas to the cities. The annual number of building permits in Montreal increased eight-fold, and in Toronto five-fold, over the decade. Bank deposits almost trebled. Freight traffic through the Welland Canal trebled, exports increased from $180 million a year to $300 million, and imports rose from $172 million to $370 million. It was Laurier's attempt to expand central Canada's foreign trade that set events in motion that eventually led to the reciprocity agreement.[3]

Until 1907 Canada operated a two-tier import duty system. There was a general tariff and a British preference tariff, which called for lower rates of duty. In 1907 Canada set out to negotiate an intermediate rate with a number of other countries on a quid pro quo basis. In return for being granted lower tariffs on Canadian exports, Canada granted lower rates on duty on some French, Italian, and Japanese goods. In 1909 the United States took cognizance of these Canadian concessions and enacted the Payne–Aldrich Tariff. It provided for the levying of an additional customs duty surcharge of 25 per cent on the goods of all countries that discriminated against the United States. It was deemed, in Washington, that Canada's British preference rates and intermediate rates both discriminated against the United States.

The Payne–Aldrich Tariff threatened to disrupt the thriving trade that was developing between Canada and the United States. The Canadian government had potent reasons to accept when the Taft administration invited it to begin negotiations to bring the United Stated under its favoured-nation custom rates and thus exempt Canada from Payne–Aldrich. Negotiations took a couple of years but, in January 1911, the two countries announced they had agreed to a reciprocal trade agreement. The agreement was narrow in scope. It reduced the duties on farm implements and on several classes of manufactures, and provided for free trade in both directions of agricultural products.

When the terms of the agreement were unveiled in Canada, the first reaction was almost unanimously favourable, particularly on the part of farmers' organizations. In Saskatchewan even F.W.G. Haultain, the Conservative leader, joined in the unanimous vote of the Saskatchewan Legislative Assembly in endorsement of the pact. The Conservative party of R.L. Borden was thunderstruck by the agreement – for one of the main planks in its 1908 campaign had been a promise to negotiate just such free entry into the American market for Canadian agricultural products. How, now, could Borden logically oppose the treaty? Worse, how could he prevent the Laurier Liberals from calling an election with the treaty as the issue and coasting back into office for another term?[4]

The answer came not from the Conservative party or its leader but from a group of British-to-the-core Ontario Liberal business leaders. They issued a manifesto on 20 February against reciprocity because, they said, it would further weaken Canada's ties with Britain and make it more difficult to resist political union with the United States.

There followed a whole series of domino reactions to the Toronto protest. The Toronto Board of Trade called an emergency general meeting to oppose the agreement. Sir William Van Horne launched the CPR on a campaign against it. Sir Edmund Walker, president of the Canadian Bank of Commerce, described the struggle triggered by the agreement as one between Canada's 'British Connection' and 'continentalism.'

Sir Clifford Sifton, the former Liberal minister of the interior, moved into the backrooms of the Ontario Conservatives and worked full time to stir up the opposition of Ontario business leaders. Henri Bourassa, the French dissident leader in Quebec, joined the opposition. So did many Ontario and Quebec labour groups, who saw their new jobs threatened by the pact. With the passage of time, only the farmers, ranchers, and fishermen kept the free trade faith.

Canadians had long been given to looking back over their shoulders for the resurgence of 'Manifest Destiny' – the doctrine that held that Americans were chosen by God to occupy the entire North American continent. It was a doctrine that played a part in the war of 1812, the obliteration of the Indians, the annexation of Texas, the Mexican war, and the annexation of California and Oregon. It had only recently resurfaced in the Spanish-American war and the annexation of Hawaii and Puerto Rico. Much closer to home, there were the Maine boundary dispute, the Alaska boundary dispute, and the San Juan Island dispute, all calculated to rattle Canadian teeth.

When the Sifton-CPR immigrant enticers were working so successfully in the United States, doubts were raised in eastern Canada over the wisdom of this policy. Eastern Canadians were concerned that legions of Americans settling in western Canada might become spearheads of a campaign to annex western Canada to the United States.

The annexation threat became the issue of the 1911 election, but not so much because of initiatives in Canada. It was American politicians and newspapers that kept the annexation question alive.[5] President Taft publicly described Canada as being then at 'the parting of the ways.' Champ Clark, the speaker of the House of Representatives, stated, 'I hope to see the day when the American flag will float over every square foot of British North American possessions clear up to the north pole.' On a later occasion, Clark said the United States was prepared to annex Canada. The United States newspapers broke out in a rash of pro-annexation editorials, and an ominous note was added when the Hearst newspapers joined in the chorus. It was William Randolph Hearst whose thundering against Spain led to the Spanish American War and the American invasion of Cuba. Hearst's support of the Reciprocity Agreement certainly helped stiffen Canadian opposition to it. The process was further helped when eastern Tories charged that the Liberals were providing Hearst's Buffalo paper with advance copies of Laurier's speeches, so papers containing extended summaries could be circulated quickly throughout Ontario.

Never before had Americans in the northern United States paid so much attention to a Canadian election. In Buffalo, people foresaw the entire Canadian grain crop moving into export markets through Buffalo to New York. Minneapolis expected the wheat crop would be marketed through Minneapolis and moved to market over Jim Hill's Northern Pacific Railway. Chicago looked favourably on the prospect of becoming the banking centre of all Canada and reducing Toronto and Montreal to financial backwaters. Even Spokane, a somnolent back-country town in Washington, had visions of becoming the supply centre for Alberta and the British Columbia interior. All these strands were emotionally embroidered into Bennett's speeches.[6] But it was some never-identified Toronto phrase maker who came up the the slogan that became the war cry of the Conservatives: 'No truck nor trade with the Yankees!'

It was a slogan that expressed Bennett's own sentiments when he opened his campaign for parliament in late August. In every speech he emphasized the wisdom of actively trying to increase trade, particularly Alberta exports, with the United Kingdom. Indeed, his anti-American bias and dedication to everything British had only recently been demonstrated in a minor hassle over a local residential real estate subdivision.

The primary focus of the joint campaign of the Canadian government and the CPR to attract immigrants from the United States was on the farming population, but it also attracted substantial numbers of American real estate agents, merchants, and businessmen to Calgary. As the central area of the city filled up with business and commercial construction, residential settlement began to spill over the southern boundary of the city at Seventeenth Avenue to the lower reaches of what was known as 'American Hill' – so called because of the number of well-to-do Americans who had settled on its slopes.[7] The steep incline to the top of this tableland, however, retarded hillside settlement until the automobile age had sufficiently matured to facilitate comfortable access. Eventually, around 1908, a road was put through and the CPR, which owned the entire 320-acre hill, began to think about turning it into a new subdivision.

Into that planning picture strode Barney Toole, a friend of R.B. Bennett and, until recently, a CPR staff real estate salesman. Toole had left the CPR to found a private firm of realtors who would concentrate on finding buyers for the large estate lots the railway was going to have for sale on the hill. Toole was a south of Ireland Anglican, of whom there were no more dedicated British subjects extant. Having a CPR subdivision called 'American Hill' violated every British bone in his body, and he hastened to call the outrage to the attention of any of his business acquaintances who would listen, including those who gathered around the Bennett table in the Alberta Hotel. Bennett passed along Toole's protest with his own endorsement to J. Lonsdale Doupe, the CPR land commissioner in Winnipeg. He too agreed a more fitting title must be chosen for the new subdivision.[8]

Recalling the elegance of Montreal's most prestigious residential area, Doupe had no difficulty finding an improvement on 'American Hill.' He designated it 'Mount Royal.' Then he took a giant step towards eradicating every trace of American influence. He gave all the streets Canadian names, even French-Canadian names, including Montcalm, Verchères, Vaudreuil, Lévis, Quebec, Frontenac, Montreal, in addition to Wolfe, Durham, and Sydenham. To Doupe, giving the new streets French names was the cream of the jest. 'There,' he chortled, 'let them damn Yankees try to pronounce those names when they tell their friends where they live!'

The episode is indicative of several facts about Calgary. Among its predominant British-Canadian majority there was some latent anti-Americanism that gave its population a built-in inclination to oppose reciprocity. Calgarians were also easily disposed to identify reciprocity with annexation, and they were worried by the connection. All these factors were grist for Bennett's campaign, once he shifted it into high gear. It was a short campaign, lasting less than a month, but it was the bitterest campaign in Alberta history, on more counts than one.

Readers of the *Calgary Herald* might have assumed there was only one candidate in the race − R.B. Bennett. It ran front-page boxed editorials supporting his stand, and advertised his meetings with front-page streamer headlines. It ignored his opponent and his opponent's meetings, even though I.S.G. Van Wart was one of Calgary's most successful pioneer businessmen and president of the Calgary Industrial Exhibition Company, forerunner of the Calgary Stampede. The *Albertan*, in contrast, ignored Bennett's meetings and kept up a drumbeat of personal attacks on the Conservative candidate.

No longer content to let the competing candidates conduct their own campaigns, both the *Herald* and the *Albertan* opened space daily on their front pages for blistering editorials. The *Herald* ran a news story noting that the Liberal candidate, not having made a speech in a week, was rumoured to be dropping out of the race. Van Wart's denial, couched in a bitter personal attack on the editor of the *Herald*, naturally got two-column front-page attention in the *Albertan*. For its part, the *Albertan* called Bennett the 'wind instrument' and criticized his lack of enlistment in the Boer War when the empire was pleading for volunteers.

As the campaign opened in southern Alberta, Bennett was the taken-for-granted underdog. Van Wart was not only a popular and successful businessman, but he had the active support of every farm leader in the south country, including Henry Wise Wood, who came to Calgary to participate actively in his campaign. Alberta farmers had imbibed the free trade gospel from birth, particularly when it came to farm equipment and machinery, and there were enough farmers around the Calgary constituency to make their opinions count. One of the difficulties faced by the Liberal camp, however, was Van Wart's fumbling platform style. He was no match for the likes of R.B. Bennett. As a result, the Liberals tended to rely on others to carry the oratorical load for their candidate.

Bennett, however, had long been the kind of speaker that drew a crowd, the kind of speaker a crowd warmed to. In the 1911 campaign he reached the height of his power. During the final week of the campaign he spoke to two or more meetings each night, meetings that jammed church halls and community halls and occasionally filled neighbourhood parks and skating rinks.

Elsewhere in Canada, election campaigns were being waged over the reciprocity issue exclusively, but in Calgary the Liberals also concentrated on the personality and character of R.B. Bennett, in particular, and on corporation lawyers in general. Early in the campaign, Bennett was denounced for having sought an injunction from the courts to keep the Canadian Northern Railway and the Grand Trunk Pacific from entering Calgary. He was accused of having led a drive in the North-West Assembly to repeal an ordinance limiting labour in coal mines to eight hours a day, and of sponsoring a bill to imprison poor people for debt. For the last half of the campaign, Bennett had to devote part of his speeches to his own defence, including a frequently tedious explanation of how corporation lawyers were required by their profession to represent their clients' interests. He explained that the repeal of the eight-hour ordinance was at the request of the miners themselves and had been supported by twenty-two members of the assembly. His debtor motion was to enable poor people to pay their fines by instalments to keep them out of jail, not put them in jail. As to his being accused of antagonism towards the working class, he pridefully recalled his strong support of the union during the Calgary carpenters' strike, and the fact that he had introduced the first Workmen's Compensation Act in Canada into the North-West Assembly. Naturally, it being that kind of campaign, he coupled his own defence with personal attacks on his opponent's anti-labour record, particularly his membership in a recently exposed combine that artificially raised prices to Calgary consumers.

Bennett's crowd-rousing talents did not lie in his ability to mount defences, answer charges, and justify himself. They lay in attack, and it was attack on the reciprocity agreement that brought out the crowds to his meetings. In this election, Bennett attracted more hecklers than he had ever experienced before, but for the most part he was able to turn them to his advantage. Bennett's collisions with ranchers anticipating an extra dime a pound for their steers and with farmers wanting to pay 10 per cent less for their machinery made good theatre, brought the crowds to his meetings, and brought them back, again and again, as the campaign reached for its climax.

In his handling of hecklers, Bennett was the corporation lawyer burying an opponent in a rockslide of statistical argument. But when he turned to the sacred duty of safeguarding the British connection, he was the fourth-generation heir to the British colonists who had fled Connecticut for New Brunswick a decade before the American Revolution forced United Empire Loyalists to follow suit. The deeper he wound into his patriotic theme, the stronger became the audience reaction. Calgary, the most American-tinted of all the western cities, reacted most strongly to the spectre of American annexation. It was a reaction that intensified as the campaign reached its climax − at a rally that filled the

Sherman Rink two days before the election. But it was the public reaction on election night that was the true measure of Bennett's impact on Calgary.

The *Calgary Herald* had erected a bulletin board in front of its building to post the national and local results as the polls closed at five o'clock. By six o'clock there was a crowd of at least one thousand blocking traffic through the Centre Street-Seventh Avenue intersection. Bennett's victory trend was apparent very early and the cheers grew louder as additional polls were added to the total. Not only did he sweep every Calgary poll, winning the seat by a 2500 majority, but he won in Strathmore and Banff and in a number of country polls as well. When he eventually turned up at the *Herald* for his post-election interview, the large second-floor editorial office window was opened for him to speak to the crowd in the street. He was ecstatic when he pointed out how substantially he had won even in Riverside, the German-Canadian ward, and in the Ukrainian poll as well.

The weather meanwhile was turning nasty with mixed snow and rain, so Bennett invited the crowd to join him in a victory celebration in the Sherman Rink. As the Bennett group was leaving the *Herald*, someone liberated one of the office chairs and, when they reached the street, hoisted it to their shoulders, with Bennett in it, and set off on the ten-block walk to the rink. En route they put him down to walk for awhile, then lifted him again as an impromptu band joined the noisy procession. At the rink, the crowd nudged the roller skaters off the floor for a couple of hours of political speechifying.[9]

Richard Bennett would have been less than human not to have been profoundly moved by the outpouring of emotion on that election night. The euphoria his victory engendered in him still seems have been there two months later when he was selected to move the Address in Reply to the Speech from the Throne on 20 November 1911.[10] It was more than a set speech for a ceremonial occasion. It was an eloquent spelling out of Bennett's political credo, beginning with his devotion to the institution of the British monarchy.

An extended reference to that institution was of course dictated by the fact that the new governor general, the Duke of Connaught, was Prince Arthur, the third and last surviving son of Queen Victoria. Bennett made the most of the fact that the duke was the first prince of the blood to open a parliament of a British dominion. After praising the duke's late brother, King Edward VII, he extolled Connaught's own empire-uniting work as an army officer in Egypt, India, and elsewhere. Bennett even recalled that Prince Arthur, at the onset of his military career, had volunteered for service to 'protect our own country from foreign invasion.' (The reference here could only have been to the ill-starred Fenian Raids from the United States across the Quebec-Ontario borders in 1869–70.) That reference gave him an opening to veer at once into a detailed replay of the lately concluded election campaign:

To many of us it seems but fitting that a member of the Royal Family should open a new Parliament with a new government with a clear mandate from the people on a great issue, indicating in no uncertain terms a settled conviction that the Canadian people would consider no trade proposals that menaced or threatened the ties that bind them to the British Empire or render more difficult the realization of the hopes that live in all of us for the commercial and organic union of that empire.

Turning to his own Calgary constituency, he emphasized the patriotic problem that was created by the large numbers of American immigrants who had settled there:

When they learned through the American Press that their former political parties showed unanimity in favor of these [reciprocity agreements] and when American public men preaching that the consequence of this agreement would be the absorption of Western Canada at least by the great republic, it was a little wonder that these people allied themselves with those in favor of the reciprocity pact. But it is a pleasure for me to say on behalf of these new settlers that as soon as they discovered that the Canadian people were not in favor of the agreement they responded to the prevailing sentiment and now propose to devote their time and energy to the upbuilding of this great country. That is, I think, a cause for congratulation and rejoicing.

After congratulating the government for the assistance it promised in the Speech from the Throne to western agriculture, Bennett returned to the role he had played as a social reformer in the Territorial Assembly when he had been the first to introduce the idea of a workmen's compensation act. This time he urged the establishment of a national department of public health. He called attention to American studies that indicated most accidents occur towards the close of longer days' work when 'vital forces are low, and too many railway accidents have been directly attributable to the employees remaining too long on duty. Too often it has been found that child labour and the work [undertaken] by married women has involved the loss of vital force in succeeding generations, which would one day hold us in judgment for the manner in which we have fulfilled the trust imposed upon us.'

In the economic field, he urged the government to undertake the construction of terminal grain elevators at Fort William, Vancouver, and Prince Rupert to speed the movement of western grain into the markets of the world. And he called parliament's attention, for the first time, to the implications for Canadian trade of the scheduled opening of the Panama Canal in 1915. With two useful warm-water ports on the Pacific coast, Canadian exports of grain could be freed from the icy grip of Lake Superior winters and have year-round access to Liverpool and London. Experimental shipments already had been made from the West Coast around Cape Horn to Liverpool. While the voyage had taken longer than by rail and lake via Montreal, the cost from anywhere west of Moose Jaw had worked out about the same. Once the canal was opened, the journey to Europe could be cut in half and substantial exports be achieved all year round. But, Bennett cautioned, these terminal elevators would have to be operated at levels of charges to the producers they could afford to pay.

He had another agency crying to be born. This was an investors' protection agency that would take control of the security business. Canada, he said, was just entering the period of security financing that the United States had gone through twenty years before. There greed and fraudulent practices of securities dealers had created such a scandal among investors that the great anti-trust crusade was launched and had such unfortunate side effects.

When businessmen formed themselves into corporations they limited their liabilities to the amount of capital they subscribed; so, Bennett argued, the government had the power to impose limitations on the shares they could issue. Some railway and public utility companies flooded the country with watered stock of no intrinsic value, and users of these facilities were saddled with excessive enhancement of charges for services to pay the exorbitant dividend on this stock. There was an imperative need for a regulatory agency to limit the volume of securities to be issued and to insure that the public could determine the real value of the securities they are buying.

Clearly Bennett, at his initiation into federal politics, was no laissez-faire economic royalist. He had retreated not an inch from the strong stand in support of trade unions he had taken ten years before. He had been one of the first to advocate government intervention at the work benches of the land to impose workmen's compensation for on-the-job accidental injury. He favoured government intrusion into the capitalist economy to own and operate terminal grain elevators. He supported the use of government subsidies to generate railway construction in western Canada. In his economic thinking he was the consummate pragmatist who, but for the depths of his British imperialist passion, might well have drifted into the gambit of the social gospellers of his era.

The centrepiece of Bennett's platter of proposals was a tariff commission to employ a panel of experts to take over responsibility for determining 'scientifically' the rates of duty to be applied to protect Canadian manufacture of those products that could be made economically. The markets for those products Canada could not make, economically, should be allocated to 'the motherland and the overseas Dominions.' The level of duties to be levied here, too, would be set scientifically so that Canadian consumers would be protected:

It is important if we are to bring about the commercial and organic union of the British Empire, of which I am sure we all have an abiding hope, we must do it by commercial means. The genius of Pitt, the genius of Chamberlain, the genius of other great English statesmen have foreseen the extraordinary possibilities of uniting the overseas Dominions and the mother country to commercial ties and commercial bonds. It is essential that we in Canada, as the greatest partner, should extend our trade so far as possible among the British Dominions and the Motherland.

Was Bennett, in that speech, firing off the first volley of a charge that would launch him on a career as leader of the Canadian crusade for Empire Free Trade? Was the 'statesman with a revelation' he had described in his letter to Max Aitken, 'the man with the vision' who would emerge to 'lead us to an Imperial Federation,' Richard Bedford Bennett, who was now making his maiden speech in the House of Commons? Certainly his speech was not the pedestrian kind of thing ordinary politicians threw together for the moving of the Address in Reply to the Speech from the Throne.

If that were Bennett's intention, he struck out. The response of the House of Commons was perfunctory, at best, perhaps because the ambience of the House on the occasion of his speech was against him. It was Sir Wilfrid Laurier's seventieth birthday and his desk was piled high with roses; together with the felicitous speeches, they gave the place a festive air. Then Borden and Laurier chose to refight the election campaign in aggressive major speeches. While Bennett had contributed one of the six hours of speech-making that day, he got only two paragraphs of attention in the three columns the *Ottawa Journal* devoted to reporting the session.

Whether the lack of response to his speech had anything to do with it or not, Bennett's disillusionment with the life of a back-bench member of parliament was one of history's quickest and most complete. Less than three weeks later, on 9 December, he wrote to Max Aitken:

I am sick of it here. There is little or *nothing to do* and what there is to do is that of a party hack or departmental clerk or messenger. I will probably leave here. There must be more doing that counts than is at present apparent.[11]

Bennett's description of the life of a private member of parliament was the literal truth: they really did have nothing to do. The cabinet ministers had no time for them; for their first six months they would be too busy learning their own responsibilities to have time to chit-chat with back-benchers. The private members could sit in the House and listen to speeches and interject an occasional interruption. They could spend their time on private business, if they could find any to do. They could become involved in the bridge games that flourished in the smoking room next to the library. They could stretch out on the couch, with which all members' rooms were equipped, and sleep.

And here was R.B. Bennett, who had been working a ten- to sixteen-hour day, six days a week, for almost ten years. After a full day as the CPR vice-president, irrigation, he could be found most evenings in the office of Lougheed and Bennett, wrestling with a succession of problems of vexing complexity. Suddenly, he had no reason to get out of bed in the morning. Here he was idly wandering the House of Commons corridors and $10,000 a year poorer for doing so, having resigned his CPR retainer the day after his election.

Nevertheless, it should have taken more than a couple of weeks for the glamour that was normally attached to being a member of parliament to wear thin. Something more than mere physical inactivity must have been accentuating the sorriness Bennett was feeling for himself. The likeliest explanation, of course, for the depth of his choler was his having been passed over for a cabinet appointment. Certainly his sensational victory in Calgary, as the only Conservative elected in Saskatchewan or Alberta, qualified him as a candidate. Immediately after the election, speculative dispatches from the Ottawa Press Gallery advanced his name as the likely choice for solicitor-general. These stories could hardly have pleased Bennett, for the office was then largely ceremonial, and he would have felt he was worthy of some more exalted position.

Bennett would have been aware, of course, that Borden had a very serious problem with two claimants from a single law office in Calgary, an unheard-of situation. Lougheed, with twenty-two years of service in the Senate behind him, had to be appointed government leader in the Senate. But if Borden really wanted Bennett in his cabinet he could have found a way of justifying it.

One of the incidental advantages that Bennett gained from his membership in the House of Commons was the easy access it provided to the meetings of the board of directors of the E.B. Eddy Company across the Ottawa River. The affairs of the Eddy Company, along with those of Jennie Shirreff Eddy, had been moving steadily upward on Bennett's agenda. They included the interminable negotiations he had been carrying on with the government of Quebec over the succession duties on the Eddy estate. Indeed, it had been what Mrs Eddy and her lawyer T.P. Foran regarded as the 'outrageous' demand of the Quebec government that brought Bennett into the Eddy company situation in the first place in 1908. They needed somebody with Bennett's financial expertise to take charge of negotiations with Quebec.[12]

The E.B. Eddy Company began in a rented room in the J.R. Booth sash and door factory in Hull in 1851. By the time Bennett became involved, it encompassed twenty buildings that stretched for two miles along the north shore of the Ottawa River from Chaudière Falls to the mouth of the Gatineau River. It was a fitting monument to one of Canada's super self-made men of the Victorian age. E.B. Eddy was just twenty-four years old when he completed moving his minuscule phosphorous match-making business from Bristol, Vermont, to Hull. Then, while his first wife 'kept the store' – supervising the crew of women and girls who hand-made the phosphorous matches and cardboard containers – Eddy took to the road peddling his matches. He discovered that markets existed for all manner of other wood products – pails, washboards, clothes pins, toothpicks. Within a decade Eddy was into the manufacturing and marketing of all these products, along with the operation of sawmills and paper mills to supply needed materials.

By 1865, if an object was made of wood, the odds were that Eddy was making and marketing it throughout the British colonies and into the adjacent United States. To backstop these operations Eddy had accumulated huge timber limits adjacent to the headwaters of the Gatineau and the Ottawa rivers, timber limits that would ultimately exceed 1900 square miles in extent. The Eddy name was now, or was about to be, included with the Booths, Bronsons, and Edwards when 'the Ottawa lumber barons' came up for discussion. He might, indeed, have belonged from the beginning if it had not been for a recurring disaster – fire. There were no fewer than twenty-seven fires at the Eddy property from the first in 1854 to the great fire of 1900.[13]

It was the fire of 1885 that led indirectly to the incorporation of Eddy's holdings into the E.B. Eddy Company Limited. The insurance coverage of the plant at the time proved insufficient to cover the rebuilding costs, so a $300,000 company was incorporated and three of Eddy's key employees and his solicitor became shareholders. Eddy retained three-quarters of the 3000, $100 par shares; G.H. Millen, the general superintendent of the company, owned 201 shares; W.H. Rowley, the secretary, owned 226; S.S. Cushman had 153 shares; and J.J. Gormully, the solicitor, had 166 shares. All were directors of the company.

It was also a fire, this one in 1900, that led indirectly to the Eddy company becoming a pioneer of the Canadian newsprint industry. By the turn of the century great strides had been made in the technique of substituting wood pulp for rags in the manufacture of paper. Concurrently with that was the development of hydroelectric power, which supplied an abundance of the cheap power needed to operate the heavy grinding equipment that converted wood logs into fluid for newsprint manufacture. The fire of 1900 cleared off the entire Eddy riverbank and made room for the power plant, pulp mill, paper mills, and storage space for the huge piles of logs essential for paper making.

Following Eddy's death on 10 February 1906, the publication

of his will revealed how obsessed he had become with the idea of perpetuating the E.B. Eddy name and the E.B. Eddy Company.[14] His only surviving direct descendant was Ezra Eddy Bessy, the juvenile son of a deceased daughter. He left young Bessy one-eighth of his estate, provided that upon reaching the age of twenty-one years he formally changed his name to Ezra Butler Eddy. Otherwise the grandson would receive but a minor bequest.

Perpetuating the E.B. Eddy Company was more complicated. The first step was to bring his widow on side. Here he converted to writing what he had been telling Jennie Shirreff Eddy for years: 'The greatest desire of my heart is that the business be continued after my death.' To achieve this he believed that his widow should abandon all the rights she enjoyed under the Quebec Dowager Act. If she agreed, he would vest his majority control in the Eddy company in a ten-year trust. At the end of that period, she would receive five-eighths of Eddy's shareholding in the company and accumulated assets of the trust. He also left 200 shares each in trust for Millen, Rowley, and Gormully, and 150 shares to Cushman. Thus, at the end of ten years, their combined shareholdings would total 1491 shares, while Mrs Eddy and the grandson would hold 1509.

The bequests to his former associates were conditional upon two caveats: they must serve as his executors for the term of the trust without any additional payment for services rendered; and they must remain in the employment of the companies in their current capacities, for which they would be limited to their current compensations. Then Eddy reached even further out of the grave to circumscribe the actions of the four, who remained directors of the company. The company had negotiated a $3 million bank loan with which to fund its expansion into the pulpwood and newsprint business. Until they managed to work that bank loan down to $300,000, a limit of 6 per cent was placed on the annual dividend that could be declared on Eddy company common shares.

During the last years of his life, while E.B. Eddy was concentrating on drafting a will that would perpetuate the existence of

E.B. Eddy Company Limited, he seemed to be unaware of, or chose to ignore, the existence of the Quebec Succession Duties Act.[15] It provided for the taxing on a graduated scale of estates within the province. Rates of taxation on bequests to relatives ranged from 1 per cent for minimal values to 5 per cent on those over $200,000. If the amount exceeded $800,000, an additional 3 per cent surtax was imposed. If the bequest was to a stranger, the minimum rate was 10 per cent plus a surtax of 5 per cent if it exceeded $450,000.

It took the Quebec government several months to complete its evaluation of the Eddy estate for succession duties purposes. When it submitted an assessment to the estate for $700,000, the executors and Mrs Eddy were outraged. The bulk of the estate consisted of shares in the E.B. Eddy Company, as well as the residential property in Hull and enough cash to fund several small bequests to relatives and to establish a trust to pay his widow $8000 a year for the term of the trust. It did not matter whether the assessment became the liability of the estate or the legatees – in the main, they were the same people – because there was no money available in the estate to pay the death duties. None of the legatees – his four associates, Jennie Eddy, and the grandson – had the cash required either. For them to have collectively sold sufficient shares in the Eddy company to pay the death taxation would have defeated the purpose of the trust.

Small wonder that Jennie Shirreff Eddy went looking for her old friend, R.B. Bennett, to assist in the negotiations with Quebec. He found the Quebec negotiators unwilling to consider any reduction in the assessment, though they did agree to allow the asset-rich, cash-poor estate to settle on an instalment plan of sorts extending over a period of five years. Underlying the intransigence of the Quebec officials, Bennett and Foran thought they detected a deep resentment towards the Eddy will itself. As Hull's largest employer, richest resident, and most prominent citizen, Eddy was expected to include in his will some handsome bequests to Hull's many Roman Catholic charitable organizations, hospitals, and religious institutions. He left them nothing! Instead, his petty largesse went exclusively to Protestant organizations on the other side of the river in Ottawa: the Protestant Ottawa General Hospital, $5000; the Protestant Ottawa Old Folks Home, $1000; the Ottawa Protestant Orphanage, $1000.[16]

Nor did the resentment of Quebec officials end, as far as Bennett was concerned, with the final settlement of the E.B. Eddy succession duties problem. Over a decade later, Bennett was having difficulty finding the money with which to honour a Jennie Eddy bequest to Dalhousie University. He wrote to President Mackenzie, blaming his problems on the excessive succession duties levied by Quebec on her estate.[17]

It may well have been that it was the urgent need for cash to pay the E.B. Eddy succession duties that led the Eddy directors–cum–trustees to ignore the injunctions in the will against increasing either their salaries or the dividends on their shares. Eddy died just as the newsprint industry was poised on the brink of profitable expansion. The Eddy company earning rose from $301,000 in 1906 to $399,000 in 1907 and $416,000 in 1908. The dividend rate was raised to 9 per cent in 1906 to 14 per cent in 1907 to 50 per cent in 1910.[18] There is an unsigned draft of an agreement in the Bennett correspondence that reveals the trustees had been over-rewarded by a total of $215,651 during the life of the trust, which they agreed to repay so their inherited shares would be transferred to them.[19]

As the Eddy company passed the half-way point of the ten-year trust, the minority shareholders began thinking about the possibilities, and the wisdom, of cashing in their inheritance, either through the sale of their minority interest or by including Mrs Eddy and dealing for the entire company. When Bennett became privy to the decision of the others to go looking for buyers, he wrote to Aitken in Montreal on 18 March 1911: 'As soon as I am finished with the Court of Appeal in Edmonton I am coming east and should arrive by March 31. You may have heard about the Eddy business in Hull. Mrs. Eddy has asked me to try to look after her interests and I am not at all satisfied to have Blaylock have anything to do with this in view of his reputation here. I would like to discuss the matter with you and if you can see an opportunity to prevent anything being done until I see you I'd appreciate it. Please destroy this letter.'[20]

Aitken replied by telegram on 23 March: 'Re Eddy. Six million much more than the property is worth. We have already refused it on our own account.' Another six weeks passed and then, on 18 May, Bennett wrote to Aitken, who had returned to London: 'Rowley went to England re Eddy's. He and his friends suspect that I am trying to prevent a sale being made except through you. They think I would try to hand the business over to you, however favorable an offer might be made by others. I told them they had an entirely mistaken idea as to your wanting the business, that the only statement you had made was that "if six millions of dollars can be obtained for it, it was an exceedingly large price and that we should not hesitate in giving Mr. Blaylock and his friends all the opportunity in the world to dispose of it for that sum." '[21]

Despite Aitken's low opinion of the worth of the Eddy company, his Royal Securities office in Montreal kept working on a deal to buy the company after the directors abandoned their effort to find a buyer in England. By midsummer it had worked one out, and Aitken cabled Bennett he would appreciate any help he could provide by supporting their offer with Mrs Eddy. Bennett by this time was deeply involved in the federal election campaign of 1911 and appears to have taken no action, other than to provide Aitken and his company with a copy of the Eddy will. Negotiations between Royal Securities and Rowley nevertheless continued and, by mid-September, Aitken again cabled Bennett. A deal had been completed with Rowley on behalf of all the other shareholders and all that was needed was for Bennett to persuade Mrs Eddy.

There is no evidence in the Beaverbrook Papers that Bennett, when he had time to look into the proposition being put forward by Aitken, was prepared to recommend it to Mrs Eddy. If he was, and did recommend it, Mrs Eddy was too deeply committed to carrying out her husband's wishes for the survival of his company to consider the offer. The Eddy company disappeared from the

Bennett-Aitken agenda and the situation reverted to the status quo ante, until February 1913.

By this time, Bennett had also become a legal-financial adviser to the grandson, Ezra Butler Bessy. He came of age in 1911, changed his name from Bessy to Eddy, and negotiated a loan of $50,000 with the Prudential Trust Company of Montreal, using his entitlement in the estate as collateral. He promptly blew the money in a series of bad investments and, as Bennett wrote to Aitken, now needed $150,000 to pay off accumulated debts and to live on until his inheritance became available in three-and-a-half years. Would Aitken be interested in lending Eddy the money, at 8 per cent interest payable $36,000 in advance as a deduction from the $150,000? As an incentive, Bennett suggested that Eddy sign an option to sell his shares at the same price Mrs Eddy would agree to sell hers.

Aitken, who was enjoying poor health in March 1913, could work up no interest in the Eddy loan but did refer it to an associate. Aitken, moreover, was unimpressed by the Eddy company as an efficiently run business and suggested that the loan be conditional on Mrs Eddy's guarantee she would undertake a reorganization of the company. Without such a guarantee, he recommended against the loan.[22] That was the end of the negotiations with Aitken on behalf of young Eddy. Eventually Bennett arranged a bank loan for Mrs Eddy to enable her to accommodate the young man in return for an option to buy his 250 shares, when the trust expired in 1916, for $800 a share.[23] These shares, with the shares she received under the will, gave Jennie Eddy a total of 1509 shares − majority control of the company.

The parliamentary session of 1912 was over on 1 April, so Bennett was free until the following November to do what he had been doing best with Max Aitken for three years − laying the foundation for getting rich. Indeed, he did not let his membership in the House of Commons interfere with that process. Their Calgary Power Company was running into problems maintaining a regular water flow through its hydro plant on the Bow River and Bennett summoned the plant manager to Ottawa to negotiate the construction of additional water storage basins with the federal authorities. Unlike Aitken's power company amalgamations in the West Indies, where the parts fitted together quickly and neatly into profitable wholes, the development of Calgary Power had been full of frustrations. After Bennett assumed the presidency of the company, he became dissatisfied with the performance of the general manager and eventually fired him. That led to a law suit that dragged slowly through the courts. The difficulties with Calgary Power, however, did not in any way diminish Aitken's enthusiasm for putting Canadian companies together. Indeed, he reminded Bennett periodically to be on the lookout for opportunities to undertake further amalgamations.

Curiously enough, while Bennett was intimately acquainted with the grain trade through his association with John I. McFarland and as solicitor for several companies, the idea of putting the Alberta Pacific Grain Company together originated with Nicholas Bawlf, a Winnipeg grain dealer, rather than Bennett.

On one of Aitken's irregular trips to Canada, he and Bennett were sitting in a CPR parlour-car en route from Montreal to Calgary when Bawlf suggested making his recently formed company, the Alberta Grain Company, the vehicle for amalgamating several companies. Bawlf had bought McFarland's Calgary and Alberta Grain Company and hired McFarland as his general manager. The renamed Alberta Grain Company had thirty-four elevators. Within a matter of days, Bennett had obtained options to purchase a half-dozen other companies that owned seventy-seven elevators, loading facilities in Vancouver, terminal elevators in Calgary, Red Deer, and Fort Macleod, and a flour mill in Calgary. The Alberta Pacific Grain Company was incorporated on 21 September 1912 with capitalization of $3 million in $100 par value common stock and $3 million in bonds.[24]

Putting the Alberta Pacific Grain Company together took Bennett more than a year. The process involved prolonged negotiations with interests in Vancouver, Calgary, and Winnipeg and the pursuit of prospective participants who could not be persuaded to join. There were even trips to London to keep Aitken persuaded that the grain business was capable of earning the kind of profits Bennett claimed it could.

The Alberta Pacific Grain Company turned out to be the best investment Bennett would ever make, and by long odds. It was put together at the same time as the Lougheed and Bennett law firm was threatening to blow apart at the seams. Until 1909, Bennett's career in law had been about on par with that of most intelligent young lawyers on the make. He had dabbled in politics to get himself better known, taking whatever briefs came along, from minor by-law infractions to one quasi capital case, with the usual disputes over money thrown in for good measure. When he became solicitor for the CPR and moved into the CPR office, he was simply keeping his eye focused on the main chance and largely abandoned his interest in politics. Meanwhile, Lougheed and Bennett kept expanding until it was occupying all the second floor of the Clarence Building. It had become Lougheed, Bennett, Taylor, Allison and McLaws. Bennett was so driven for time by then that he had to leave the daily operations of the office to W.T. Taylor and W.H. McLaws. They ran it without consultation with Bennett, even hiring students and other lawyers without bothering to notify him.

During the 1905–10 interval, Bennett acted for the firm before the Court of Appeal on a few cases a year, winning about as many as he lost. Busy as he was, it made no sense at all for him to be a member of the legislature, a fact he must soon have realized. The decision to abandon the legislature for exile to Ottawa, whatever the rationale, was obviously an aberrant one. Then, simultaneously with his complaint to Aitken about his disillusionment with parliament, came the aborted break-up with Lougheed in 1912.

From 1905 onward, Lougheed had been a partner in name only in the legal business of the partnership. Because of his non-participation, his share of the net income was set at $3000 a year, against which the salary of his son was charged. After the $3000 was deducted, Bennett's share of the net income was set at 40 per cent, Allison and Taylor took 22 per cent each, and McLaws, a recent graduate, received 15 per cent. When Taylor left in 1909, J.E.A. McLeod replaced him.

Lougheed and Bennett, however, was more than a law office. It acted for a number of mortgage and loan companies in making financial arrangements with borrowers. Placing insurance was also a lucrative offshoot of the money-lending business. Lougheed was primarily concerned with the management of his investment portfolio and the development of his multiplicity of real estate holdings in Calgary, which by now included some office buildings and a theatre. In April 1911 Lougheed formed the brokerage firm of Lougheed and Taylor, with the result that some of the mortgage, insurance, and financial business that had been done by Lougheed and Bennett moved to the new company.

The by-now notorious hair-trigger temper of Richard Bedford Bennett reacted as expected. In his own words, he was 'dissatisfied with the action' and made his feelings known to Lougheed and to everyone else who would listen. Lougheed responded with this letter:

For some time now I have been under the impression, owing to what has been communicated to me, and from our personal relations, that you would prefer that I should take the initial step toward . . . [dissolution of] our legal partnership. Furthermore there seems to be considerable dissatisfaction in the minds of the other members of the firm as to the present situation, and I have considered it better that we should wind up our affairs, thus making all interested free to make up a new deal. My son Clarence is about to be married and I am desirous of his becoming interested along with myself in a new business so that he will feel that there is some weight of responsibility on his shoulders. I shall in all probability make some arrangements for an eastern practitioner to join me. I am sending a copy of this letter to Allison and McLaws notifying them of my desire for a dissolution so that they may feel free to act as they choose. Owing to the fact that I cannot be here to contribute in any way toward winding up our affairs I would be quite willing that Allison and McLaws should take the necessary steps toward winding up the business.[25]

It would be hard to image a simpler, more straightforward letter. What resulted from it was anything but simple or straight-forward. Negotiations took place, but not to dissolve the partner-ship, as Lougheed had asked. Instead the partnership was contin-ued as before, except that Allison retired and was replaced by L.M. Roberts. Bennett, because he was so involved with the CPR Irrigation Department, retired from active participation in the law practice in favour of becoming counsel for the firm.[26] The partnership was to guarantee him $15,000 a year on top of what he picked up from the CPR and, later, his parliamentary indem-nity. McLaws would continue to run the office, and he and the other lawyers would have a profit-sharing arrangement. Nobody got around to explaining what was going on to Lougheed – an ironic twist in a firm of high-powered lawyers who lived by 'putting it in writing,' 'spelling out the details so that everyone understands what they are signing,' and 'signing on the dotted line before witnesses.'

In December 1911, when more insurance companies notified the Lougheed and Bennett office they would be moving their business to Lougheed and Taylor, Bennett wrote Lougheed in Ottawa protesting vigorously. Lougheed replied by telegraph: 'Answering your letter sixteenth . . . [our] firm was dissolved last summer and a new firm of McLaws and myself formed with you acting as counsel for new firm. It only remains to wind up old firm previous to June first. Your letter states your election to Parliament destroys counsel arrangement. McLaws and I there-fore according to your desire agreed to its termination and, present firm of McLaws and myself will continue as since June first last. When you return McLaws is authorized to act for me in winding up old business.' Yet the Lougheed and Bennett partner-ship was not wound up, McLaws and Roberts continued at the helm, and the partnership guaranteed and paid Bennett $15,000 a year as counsel until 1917.

At the same time, Bennett was involved in several cross-wired arguments with Aitken over money that would ordinarily have blown a friendship apart. After the Calgary Power promotion was completed, Bennett wrote to Aitken on 12 January 1912 that he had not been well used. He had discovered that while he ended up with 138 shares, Aitken and others had got 275 shares. He admitted he was paid a 'very large fee' at the end of 1910, but had to account to his office for the legal segment of the amount. Not only had he spent a great deal of time and effort negotiating successfully with the City of Calgary, but his substantial influence with the Department of the Interior was exercised in the interest of the company.[27]

Aitken was deeply disturbed by the letter, but replied in a most conciliatory tone. Bennett, he said, did not underwrite as much of the bond issue as the others, hence he received a smaller bonus in common stock. In the beginning he had not viewed Bennett as anything but a legal adviser and had never expected him to undertake to run the company. Moreover, Bennett's expanded activities had taken place since the completion of the underwriting and could not qualify him for shares that were tied to the underwriting. However, because Aitken realized the value of the work Bennett was doing he was working out a scheme under which Bennett would be allotted additional shares over the coming years: 'I was under the impression you were particularly pleased with the way in which I had treated you from a financial point of view ... I am greatly disturbed by your letter.'[28]

In connection with subsequent promotions, Bennett dealt mainly with V.W. Drury or I.W. Killam at Royal Securities in Montreal. He had several arguments with them, which ultimately reached Aitken for solution. One such, in connection with the Alberta Pacific Grain promotion, brought an angry response from Bennett when Aitken tried to assuage his feelings by asking if $90,000 profit on one transaction would satisfy him. Bennett replied: 'Obviously my self-respect will not permit me to accept from you as a gratuity that which I am entitled to as a right. You wrote you have tried very hard to make my name big in the financial world. I am more concerned with having a good name and big assets than having a big name and small assets.'

It would, of course, have been impossible for Aitken and Bennett to commit to paper the precise details of all the arrangements that had to be made to put their deals together. Many of the details were worked out across the table when they met in London or in Canada or on the fly. Many were highly tentative, with several possible amendments. But the tenor of Bennett's letters to Aitken was more that of strangers negotiating at arm's length than of friends from boyhood. The periodic temper tantrums on Bennett's part were particularly puzzling in view of the efforts Aitken made to enrich Bennett. In 1909, at the birth of Canada Cement, Aitken cut Bennett in for a $100,000 ground-floor investment. Similarly, Bennett's firm did a great deal of formal legal work for the various companies the two were involved with and earned fees running high into the thousands of dollars. In 1910 Calgary Power's bill exceeded $8000. The only conclusion the historian can draw from Bennett's reaction to these real or fancied grievances is that he had a built-in reluctance to being beholden to anybody for anything.

Bennett's reference to the way he had turned his influence with the Department of the Interior to the benefit of Calgary Power provided a revealing insight into the ethical standards that prevailed in the early days of Canadian finance capitalism, to say nothing of Canadian politics. Bennett and Aitken were impeccably honest and there was nothing crooked in any of the concerns they promoted. All went on to earn substantial dividends for their shareholders and, for those who bought the common shares they sold, substantial opportunities for capital gains.

There were times when Bennett acquiesced in Aitken's schemes only after a bitter wrestling match with his conscience. He lived strictly by St Matthew's injunction that no man can serve two masters. That complicated his relationship with Aitken and, on one occasion, Aitken reacted critically: 'I can seldom get you to write me any letters containing positive information. Your letter of October 30 re the flour mill seems out of the ordinary. Do you recommend purchase? Future prospects?'[29] To which Bennett replied: 'Your generalization is hardly warranted. I have learned to be extremely careful in the statements I make in connection with financial matters ... [In the milling case] I tried to give you only information that is strictly accurate. You must remember it is not easy to obtain from a close corporation the particulars of its business, especially when you are acting as its solicitor and must not divulge private information that you receive in the transaction of its business.'[30]

This was a moral dilemma that troubled Bennett frequently in his relationship with Aitken. Aitken kept nudging Bennett to recommend enterprises to him that he might buy and expand. He was the solicitor for A.E. Cross, W.R. Hull, and Pat Burns, all of whom were into many endeavours. When he began to examine a company for Aitken, he had to be very sure how his legal clients related to the company under investigation. His position was frequently complicated by the fact that Aitken was always eager to cut Bennett in 'for a piece of the action.' There was one occasion when Cross and a couple of associates were having Aitken, at Bennett's behest, put a financing together for Calgary Brewery. A difference of opinion developed between Cross and Aitken over a technical aspect of the financing, and Aitken tried to persuade Bennett to press Cross to take a certain action. Cross, however, had reached a point where he was usually willing to take Bennett's advice, sight unseen, and Bennett backed away from doing as Aitken requested.

In the general area of turning confidential inside information to their own use, Bennett and Aitken had no more qualms than other company directors of the era, who did it automatically. It went even farther, they regarded it as perfectly acceptable to channel the activities of companies they controlled in a direction that would yield them financial gain. Their control of the fledging Calgary Power Company was a case in point.

Calgary Power was one of the smallest of Aitken's small potatoes. Capitalized at $3 million in $100 par common shares, it was authorized to issue $3 million in thirty-year, 5 per cent first-mortgage gold bonds. Aitken undertook to market the bonds at 90 per cent net to the company and took the common shares to be distributed as free bonus to the bond purchasers or to be held for future sale. There was about an eighteen-month hiatus between the incorporation of the company and the marketing of the bonds. During that time Royal Securities made periodic advances to the new company to pay for the construction of its power plants and distribution facilities. By the time Calgary Power bonds went on sale in 1912, the financial universe was still unfolding as it should, but some of the gloss was beginning to fade from the decade-long boom. The western provinces and their municipalities were finding resistance to their capital demands and corporation bonds were becoming harder to sell in Montreal and London.

Aitken wrote to Bennett in 1913 saying it was imperative that consideration be given to declaring a dividend on Calgary Power common stock.[31] This would add to the attraction of the bonds, make them easier to sell, and earn Royal Securities its commissions, to say nothing of freeing the capital then frozen in unsold bonds. It would also add to the intrinsic attractiveness of the common shares themselves and enable Aitken to brag that his five-year plan was to have Calgary Power common shares selling at par — $100 each — by 1917. At the same time he urged Bennett to get the Alberta Pacific Grain common stock onto a regular dividend basis so they could 'boom' the price of that company's preferred stock.[32] Fortunately, the grain company was a superb profit maker from the day of its birth. There was no possible conflict of interest in advising Alberta Pacific to pay common-stock dividend, but there might have been in the case of Calgary Power — if the company could have made better use of its earnings to finance needed capital construction. The point, however, is academic in the context of the times.

Why Alberta Pacific Grain should have signalled the end of R.B. Bennett's career in financial entrepreneurship is beyond easy explanation. Certainly he was getting the hang of it. Perhaps he had run out of suitable vehicles for the Aitken-Bennett treatment. He hinted at that in reply to a letter from Aitken asking him to look for likely prospects for promotion. Certainly his successes had enriched him well beyond the dreams of avarice. Perhaps that was the explanation. He had reached a stage of life where his future financial security was assured, where he no longer had to allow making a living a consideration in his career decisions. Should he choose, he could put the law behind him and devote the rest of his life to a career in politics. Not the crass-picayune politics of Ottawa and Edmonton, but the soul-satisfying politics of British Empire revivication, of becoming involved in a movement to lead the British Empire to a higher level of existence as a federation of truly self-governing dominions.

Bennett had already hinted at moving from Canada to England to follow Max Aitken into British politics. Aitken's advice, over the years, however, had been contradictory. He had urged Bennett to give up law and devote himself to business, and also to become the national leader of an Empire Free Trade party in Canada. In the summer of 1912 Bennett spent a working vacation in England with Aitken. There he met everybody, from Bonar Law to Rudyard Kipling, who was anybody in the Empire Free Trade movement, and even made a speech on the subject to a political rally in Aitken's constituency. Though the rally was rained on, Aitken rated the speech a success. Later that year, Bennett returned to London to make his presentation to the Privy Council law lords on the Great Waterways Railway case, in the dispute between the Alberta government and the Royal Bank over who should possess the remaining $6 million W.R. Clarke had raised from British bondholders for the railway. The bonds had been guaranteed by the Province of Alberta. When the company defaulted on its interest payment, Alberta became liable. After paying the interest Alberta demanded that the bank pay over the balance of the principal to it.

The bank, on Bennett's advice, refused, holding that it was trustee for people who had subscribed money for the construction of a railway, not, as Alberta proposed, to be used for the general purpose of the government of Alberta. The government sued and won in the Alberta Supreme Court. On Bennett's advice, the bank sought leave to appeal to the Privy Council and leave was granted – the first appeal from Alberta to reach that august body. For a forty-two-year-old barrister from Calgary, whose emotional attachment to the British Empire was almost childlike in its intensity, walking down Downing Street past Number 10 to the Privy Council Building must have been a vibrantly warming experience – particularly since his briefcase contained the factum he had drafted for presentation to the law lords of the Privy Council: Lord Macnaghten, Lord Moulton, Lord Atkinson, and the Lord Chancellor, Lord Haldane of Clone.

The case was heard on 10 December 1912 and the decision was handed down on 31 January 1913: the bondholders, having subscribed their money for the purpose that had failed, were entitled to recover their money from the bank at its head office in Montreal; this was a civil right existing and enforceable outside the province, and the province of Alberta could not validly legislate in derogation of that right. The appeal was allowed and the Alberta government was ordered to pay the costs of the action 'here and in the courts below.'

Winning the case before the Privy Council provided Bennett with a measure of compensation for losing the argument over the Great Waterway Railway in the Alberta legislature. Now his arch enemies, the Sifton Liberals, would be charged with the responsibility of unscrambling the eggs of the Waterways financing! A far sweeter assuagement for the bruised Bennett ego was the short note he received at the conclusion of the hearing from one of the eminent jurists of the Privy Council. It read:

Dear Mr. Bennett: May I take the liberty of congratulating you on your appearance before the P.C. this afternoon. I thought you argued your point extremely well – and may I add we all thought so.

Yours very truly,
Macnaghten[33]

If there was a single high point in Bennett's professional life, this most certainly was it. Bennett cherished that letter for the rest of his life. When, almost a decade later, he was making up his mind to abandon his Calgary law practice and move to London, Macnaghten's letter would have been, to Bennett, assurance that there was a place for him at the London bar – a place, moreover, he would expect to occupy with distinction.

Bennett's participation in the Naval Aid debate on 25 February 1913 provided him with a perfect opportunity to give his views on the future of the British Empire national exposure. Borden's proposal to make a one-time contribution of $35 million to the British navy and to purchase three dreadnaughts was an alternative to the Laurier decision to establish a Canadian navy of three destroyers. Both derived from the Colonial Conference of 1902 at which Joseph Chamberlain had proposed the establishment of an Imperial Defence Council and an Imperial Trade Council. Neither Prime Minister Laurier nor Robert Borden had any interest in these proposals, but Laurier conceded that Canada should assume some responsibility for its own defence and opted for the purchase of the British destroyers while Canada set about building its own ships. The burden of the Conservative argument was that time was the essence of the problem – the pace of the arms race in Europe, and in particular the German super-charged naval construction program, made it imperative for Canada to act quickly. There was no time to go through the costly and time-consuming process of building shipyard facilities to construct capital ships, as the Liberal opposition was advocating. Bennett carried the argument far afield, into the alleged Liberal genesis of the 'nationalist' movement in Quebec to the 'if Uncle Sam wants it I want it' ideology of the American settlers in the west.[34]

Whatever the partisanship of his listeners and beholders, all would have agreed that Bennett's speech rescued the House of Commons from the doldrums into which the Naval Aid Bill had plunged it for many weeks. Every argument that could have been advanced had been made, ad infinitum, ad nauseum. The *Ottawa Journal* described Bennett's speech as 'an oratorical style that has long since gone out of fashion.' The Toronto *Globe* gave it front-page space and described Bennett as 'lashing himself into paroxysms of fortissimo oratory, pounding his desks, shaking his fists and declaiming the great peril, the great menace that threatened to wipe out the whole British Empire.'[35]

In content, the speech ran from appeals to the loftiest levels of idealism to the lowest level of partisan politics, with some cutting resorts to personalities. Bennett impugned the patriotism of Frank Oliver, the former minister of the interior, by telling the House that Oliver, at a public meeting in Calgary, had refused to stand for the playing of the national anthem; that only the intervention of the city police had prevented his meeting from being broken up by outraged patriots and South African war veterans in the audience.

He went back into history to accuse the Liberal cabinet members in Quebec of spearheading the independence movement in that province. He lashed out at Mackenzie King, the Liberal candidate, for his speeches in the town of Berlin, North Waterloo constituency, in the recent election. There was a large body of German-Canadian residents in the riding. King, said Bennett, had quoted from a speech by Robert Borden in which he mentioned the threat of German aggression to Britain and the world, and that he, as leader, was willing to send money to Britain to buy warships to fight Germany. Did they support Borden's position? Members of the crowd roared their disapproval. Fortunately, Bennett noted, the majority of the electors of Waterloo had supported Borden's position in the election and Mackenzie King was defeated. It was the beginning of a personal animosity that would smoulder for forty years.

Word of Bennett's performance spread through the usually unattending majority of the House of Commons over the supper-hour adjournment. When he resumed in the evening the chairs on both sides of the aisle were reasonably full and, for the better part of another hour, the House echoed and re-echoed with alternative waves of cheers and jeers, punctuated with roars of laughter. In a sense, the subject made the speech. The Naval Bill enabled Bennett to give free rein to his emotional attachment to the British Empire, to bare the Bennett soul, as it were:

I cannot conceive of any man who reads the history of this Empire being ashamed to profess his belief that one day he will be able to confederate these great groups of colonies and dominions with the Motherland into a great imperial whole, one grand empire that will be the surest and best and noblest influence we have for peace, truth, justice and freedom. Wherever the British flag has gone, wherever Englishmen have planted the outposts of Empire, there has followed order, justice, liberty, freedom, equality under the law. That is the great thing, the right to worship

God in any way men please under their own vine and fig tree and none may say them nay. Whether they be Mohammedans or Hindus, Buddhists or Catholics, Protestants, or Atheists, it matters not, all have equal rights under that great flag. And I say it is our bounden duty to maintain and sustain that civilization and the Empire that has made it possible.[36]

Bennett had frequently been accused of being an imperialist and, if that was a criticism, he pleaded guilty. His own definition of the word was, 'An Imperialist is a man who accepts gladly and bears proudly the responsibilities of his race and breed.' 'I preach a new parliament,' he said, 'an Imperial Parliament where Canadians, Australians, South Africans and New Zealanders shall sit side by side with the English, Welsh, Scotch and Irish and legislate for this great Empire. I hold out to this house the vision of a wider hope, the hope that one day this Dominion will be the dominant factor in that great federation.'

It was, the *Ottawa Journal* noted editorially, the sort of speech that opponents usually characterized as 'flag-flapping.' But just as there were extremes in flag waving, there are also extremes in depreciating patriotism and imperialism. 'In Canada at the present time when the genius of statesmen is employed in assimilating a large foreign element, there is less danger, perhaps, in "flag-flapping" than in the other extreme.'

Two days later, by a vote of 114 to 84, the House of Commons passed second reading of the Naval Aid Bill, only to have it sequestered in committee for almost two months by a Liberal filibuster. Then, after it was pushed through the House by a closure motion, the Liberal majority in the Senate rejected it until the government submitted it to the electorate as a plebiscite.

There was nothing that transpired in parliament or in the country to indicate that Bennett's imperialist manifesto had cut any political ice. Nor did Bennett pursue the subject further that summer. Indeed, it remained his only noteworthy contribution to parliament that year. His participation in its activities was transitory in the extreme, which gave Bennett ample scope to pursue his other interests. It had been Max Aitken's idea that if a powerful movement towards empire solidarity could be developed in Canada it would force the British Conservatives to become more vigorously supportive of Aitken's own crusade. It was to spearhead just such a campaign that he had urged Bennett to abandon law for a parliamentary career. But if Bennett had hoped to light any such brush fire with his Naval Aid speech he was disappointed. It evoked no enthusiastic response within the ranks of the parliamentary Conservatives, least of all in the prime minister. Borden became much more concerned with how to run a government with a recalcitrant Senate. And out in the countryside the people were much more concerned with the speed at which the great real estate and development boom was turning into a depression.

CHAPTER FIVE

World War I

The gulf that separates politicians of local though prestigious repute from those of national stature was illustrated by Bennett's movement from provincial to the national political stage. In November 1911 he ranked near the top of any list of the half-dozen best-known Calgarians. His reputation as a crowd-moving orator covered the province of Alberta, but he entered parliament as just another small-town lawyer from the boondocks whose speech in reply to the Speech from the Throne could be safely ignored, regardless of how studious or well crafted it might be, or how eloquent the delivery.

That was the normal fate of speeches in reply to the Speech from the Throne. The movers of the reply were usually chosen from the ranks of the freshmen members of parliament. They were expected to pay their respects to the Throne Speech itself and take as long as they liked in extolling the virtues of their riding, region, and province. Their function was to get the debate on the Speech from the Throne under way so parliament could get down to business with the issues of the moment. Additionally, by tradition, neither the newspapers nor the chamber itself paid any attention to the speeches of back-benchers. The best Bennett could have hoped for was a paragraph or two in the papers back home. This was still true a year later when he arose to deliver a stirring oration in support of the prime minister's British Naval Aid Bill. That all ended on 14 May 1914, with his four-hour attack on the Canadian Northern Railway Aid Bill. Thereafter, when R.B. Bennett had something to say, Canadian editors and Canadian politicians sat up and paid attention.

The difference between the railway aid bill speech and the others was two-fold: subject and occasion. The question of whether Canada should contribute $40 million to build a couple of dreadnoughts for the Royal Navy was no family-dividing, violence-triggering issue for ordinary Canadians. For Albertans it was at best a shoulder-shrugging non-issue. It was an even greater bore to Canadians closer to the action, particularly the parliamentarians themselves, for a Liberal filibuster was keeping them in session around the clock. By the time Bennett got into the debate, everything that could be said, pro and con, had been said, ad nauseum. So for fed-up newspaper editors, anything anybody said was by then usable only as a filler on a classified ads page.

In contrast, the Canadian Northern Railway triumvirate, Sir William Mackenzie, Sir Donald Mann, and Zebulon Lash, drew controversial attention wherever they went, whether running a railway into Calgary or operating the streetcars in Toronto. For the last five years, their importuning of provincial and federal governments for construction subsidies and guarantees had caused widespread public debate, particularly as the Canadian Northern had become a lynchpin in Sir Wilfrid Laurier's three-railway transcontinental system. That, of course, was not the way Laurier had planned it; it was only the way it turned out.

Laurier originally had turned his back on Mackenzie and Mann in 1905 when he opted for the Grand Trunk Pacific cross-country project. Later, in 1911, he succumbed to Mackenzie and Mann's blandishments and pushed a bill through parliament to guarantee their bonds up to $30,000 a mile for a 1000-mile line from Montreal to Port Arthur to connect with their western line. But while Laurier had underwritten the beginning of their trans-continental system, his defeat in 1911 had saddled the Borden administration with responsibility for completion of a project his Conservatives had opposed since its inception.

When Mackenzie and Mann appeared on Borden's doorstep in 1912 with a request for a grant of $15 million to enable them to complete a stretch of western trackage, it was a request the

Conservatives could not, politically, refuse. Too many western farmers had vested interests in having the Canadian Northern moving their wheat to market. Bennett was among the Conservatives who approved the grant in 1913. He made a speech roundly criticizing Mackenzie and Mann and all their works, but voted with the Conservative government.

As things turned out, that $15 million did not begin to finish the job and the promoters were back the following year for another $44 million. In the context of the times it was a horrendous sum; the nine provinces combined that year would spend only $46 million. The grand total of all federal expenditures was only $185 million.[1] On this occasion, Bennett did not have to wait until everyone else had spoken; he was slotted into the forefront of the debate, the day after the party leaders. His attitude towards Mackenzie and Mann was, of course, well known long before the Canadian National Railway bill was introduced. He had already expressed his disgruntlement when the matter was being debated in the Conservative caucus. He was more than willing to debate the issue with any wayfaring strangers he could button-hole in the parliamentary corridors, library, restaurant, or barber shop. It was hardly surprising, then, that the members' seats were well filled when he started to speak shortly before four o'clock. So were the Press Gallery and, when he resumed after the supper break, the public galleries. The stage, indeed, had been set for Bennett the previous day when W.F. Nichol, the Conservative member for Kingston, had broken ranks with the party to speak against the bill. Nichol's theme, however, was localized to the injuries Mackenzie had inflicted on the Kingston area. Bennett's indictment was more broadly based. The spectacle of two back-bench Tories foreclosing their futures in the Conservative party by attacking the government was unusual enough to trigger the newspaper editors of the country to prod their Ottawa agencies for extended coverage of Bennett's speech.

In form and substance, it was the best speech Bennett had ever made, perhaps the best speech he would ever make.[2] In the words of the Calgary *Albertan*, the Liberal party newspaper, it was 'the greatest speech of his life, [tearing] to pieces the C.N.R. agreement.' It was Bennett at his best, for he had done his homework with unequalled thoroughness.

He had read and embedded in his fabulous memory the annual reports, auditors' reports, and financial statements issued by Mackenzie and Mann and the Canadian Northern Railway. He had consumed books on railway financing and operations on two continents. He went back into United States history to cite American railway promotion scandals and exact parallels for the promotional antics of Mackenzie and Mann. He had ridden the Canadian Northern and talked to its operating and maintenance workers. And he brought into play his ten years' experience inside the CPR in discussing the Mackenzie and Mann operating inefficiencies.

It was also Bennett at his worst, for once again he could not resist resorting to personal abuse as he had done so often in the Territorial Assembly. His primary target on this occasion was the Honourable Arthur Meighen, another small-town lawyer, from Portage la Prairie, Manitoba. As a newly appointed solicitor-general, it had been Meighen's responsibility to work over the Mackenzie and Mann, Grand Trunk, $44 million request and wrestle it into the kind of proposal that the government could live with politically, that would not unduly outrage the electorate, and that would get through parliament. Not having had the benefit of the immersion course in corporate financing Bennett had been enjoying with Max Aitken, he may well have taken too much on trust and may not have recognized some corporate soft spots. That hardly made him a deserving candidate for the verbal pummelling he received from a brother Conservative. The Liberal opposition benches loved it, of course. It was not often they could enjoy the spectacle of two Conservatives in verbal battle, and they reacted with rounds of applause and mingled laughter.

In a way, Meighen brought it on himself. He had an ego to match Bennett's and could not sit quietly while Bennett worked over his bill. So he interrupted frequently to question Bennett's statements, until Bennett protested to the Speaker: 'I am not going to be interrupted by this impertinent young man!'

(Meighen was four years Bennett's junior.) Later he said: 'When I get through with him the solicitor-general is going to regret that he allowed himself to become Mackenzie and Mann's apologist!'

The burden of Bennett's case was manifold. Mackenzie and Mann were either inexpert construction contractors who could not accurately estimate the costs of their work, or they underestimated in order to return to governments for additional subsidies. Under the tutelage of Zebulon A. Lash, their Toronto partner and the ablest corporation lawyer of his generation, they put together such a maze of subsidiaries and such a plethora of separate stock and bond issues that making financial sense of their operation was extremely difficult. They seemed to possess little talent for operating the projects they built. When such subsidiaries as local freight terminals, express companies, and hotels lost money, they arranged their sale at inflated prices to the Canadian Northern for common stock. The result was a waterlogged railway system that would become an everlasting burden on its freight and passenger patrons.

But it was worse than that, Bennett contended. The country was being saddled with three separate transcontinental railway systems that could bankrupt the country. There was no way a country of five million could generate enough traffic to allow three railways to make a profit, not even if freight charges and passenger fares were set at exorbitant levels. When he got into that section of his speech, the Liberal benches became morosely silent. Bennett was tramping all over one of Sir Wilfrid Laurier's most enchanting dreams.

What Bennett demanded was a royal commission to get out the facts about railway operation in Canada. In the meantime, the government should put the Canadian National into receivership and divorce its operation from the control of Mackenzie and Mann. He recalled that in the CPR's critical periods its directors had pledged their personal fortunes to complete its construction. Mackenzie and Mann were reputed to be multimillionaires but, so far as he could determine, they had never invested any of their own money in their project, yet they owned all the railway's common stock. Only a royal commission which put witnesses under oath could ferret out the truth about CNR financing, he insisted.

Several reactions might reasonably have flowed from Bennett's performance. He might have read himself out of the party and crossed the floor to sit as an independent. The prime minister might have risen to the defence of his solicitor-general and verbally chastised his contumelious back-bencher. Other prominent members of the cabinet, or even the party rank and file, might have turned on him. Nothing of the sort seems to have happened. Instead, he was roundly applauded a week later when he next intervened in parliamentary proceedings. The first occasion was some routine amendments to the naturalization act. His contribution was an impassioned appeal for a complete recasting of naturalization ceremonies. Instead of the perfunctory passing out of printed forms, naturalization should be a ceremony that would glorify Canada's Anglo-Saxon heritage for the foreigners who were being granted entry into the brotherhood of British subjects. His appeal was greeted enthusiastically and he drew even stronger applause when he eulogized the Boy Scouts during discussion of a bill to grant the order a federal charter.

There was nothing Borden did or said at the time that indicated he was at all discomforted by Bennett's speech. In fact he probably welcomed it because it was not a Conservative ox that Bennett had been goring, it was true Grit. It was not the bill before the House that Bennett's barbs were targeted on, but the liaison between Mackenzie and Mann and the Laurier administration. After the Bennett indictment, the Liberals would be forever mud-caked by Mackenzie and Mann. Meighen's pique would eventually turn to gratitude when he realized the job Bennett had done on the Liberal party.

The Bennett speech attracted front-page attention from newspapers across the country. As well it might, for there was hardly a community across Canada that did not have a stake in either the Canadian Northern or the Grand Trunk Pacific, and the latter was also waiting in line for subsidies. Of the Canadian newspapers, the *Globe* in Toronto did the most complete job of reporting it. It gave the speech a column and a half of front-page space and another six columns on two inside pages. Even the financial press sat up and paid attention. The *Financial Post* in Toronto and the *Financial Times* in Montreal devoted long editorials to the debate, both coming down squarely, however, on the side of Mackenzie and Mann.

Ironically, it was in Bennett's home town, Calgary, where the newspapers had the most difficulty with the story. As the three newspapers were being put to bed on the night of 14 May, a story broke over them that would change the economic face of Alberta. The Dingman well had blown in Turner Valley and left 1000 feet of high-quality oil standing in the well casing. The report of Bennett's speech had to share the front pages, the red ink, and the big type with the report of the oil discovery.[3]

The juxtapositioning of the two reports could only have doubly gladdened Bennett's heart when the papers came to his attention. Two years had now passed since he and A.W. Dingman sat on a hummock near the banks of the Highwood River and watched in amazement as W.S. Herron, a rancher friend, ignited a jet of gas that was seeping from a fissure in the surface of the prairie and boiled a pot of coffee on the flame.[4] Where there was gas there had to be oil. The objective of Herron's exercise was to persuade Bennett to invest some money in his Calgary Petroleum Products Company, which would provide the financial backing for Dingman to drill for the oil. Bennett made a modest investment.

For Bennett, it was one of his best investments. Calgary Petroleum Products Company eventually evolved into Royalite Oil and came under the control of Imperial Oil. Bennett became a director and solicitor for each, seriatim. Fifteen years later, he still held 500 of his Royalite shares, which had risen in value from $25 to $200 each. He sold 200 for $200 in the spring of 1929, six months before the Wall Street crash.

When Bennett came home to Calgary a month after his speech, he received a tumultuous reception. His supporters took over the Horse Show Arena for a non-partisan speech-making festival. Everybody who was anybody in Calgary was there, regardless of whether they were Liberals, Conservatives, or dissenters of sundry persuasions. The only absentees were the oil-stock promoters, whose harvesting of dollars was going on, seemingly, around the clock.

The oil boom that engulfed Calgary in the late spring of 1914 had been many weeks in the making. Since late winter there had been periodic reports from the Dingman well site, first of the smell of oil in the cuttings being lifted by the bailer, then of showings of watery concentrate. The volume of concentrate increased to a point where the locals were pouring it in the gas tanks of their cars. Gradually other promoters came into the play and began advertising new companies that were preparing to drill in the valley. Store fronts on Eighth and Ninth avenues in Calgary only recently vacated by bankrupt real estate agents were taken over by oil-stock promoters. For several months Calgarians seemed oil drunk, trading shares back and forth in a frenzy of ever-rising prices. In a single week, ninety new oil companies were incorporated. Beset as he and the other Dingman directors were for tips on which company was most likely to drill the next gusher, Bennett assumed a very statesmanlike posture. Never one to discourage private investment capital, he nevertheless urged his inquirers to look very carefully before they leaped and to make certain the money they were investing was going into the drilling of oil wells, not into the pockets of unscrupulous promoters. Nobody listened to advice like that in Calgary in the summer of 1914 – until, that is, the oncoming Great War cast its awful shadow across the land.

By the end of July, Bennett, who had served in the militia at Chatham, had tried to enlist for overseas service and was told there was no place for forty-four-year-olds in the Canadian militia. On 2 August, two days before the war was officially declared, Bennett wired Sam Hughes, minister of militia and defence in Ottawa: 'Two thousand men here desire to proceed to active service, of whom 1,000 are trained veterans of many campaigns. They anxiously await an opportunity to offer their lives in the defense of the empire.'[5]

Bennett's reaction to the war was one of unrestrainable enthusiasm. He wired Hughes that he was willing to raise and equip a regiment of 1000 men over and above the Canadian contingent being assembled, and he went to Ottawa to confer with him about it. Spontaneous as his reaction had been to the declaration of war, Bennett discovered he was second in line behind A.H. Gault, a wealthy Montreal veteran of the Boer War. Gault was also a captain in the militia and offered to donate $100,000 to pay for equipping *his* proposed regiment. He then set wheels in motion to obtain permission from the Duke of Connaught, the governor general, to name the regiment for his daughter – the Princess Patricia's Canadian Light Infantry. When that permission was quickly granted, Hughes suggested to Bennett that he meld his Calgary recruits into the Gault regiment.[6]

Unlike Gault's outright gift of $100,000, Bennett's offer to 'raise and equip' a regiment had been vaguely couched. Did he mean he would pay for the equipment of a whole battalion out of his own pocket? Or did he mean he would start a campaign to raise money among his friends and other Calgarians for that purpose? At the very least, his announcement raised eyebrows all over Calgary.

Did RB have *that* kind of money, a competence that would enable him to make such a gesture on the spur of the moment? This was Thorstein Veblen's age of conspicuous expenditure, when wealth was something to be flaunted; when, in Calgary, Winnipeg, and Regina, a man's financial standing was judged by the size of the house he lived in – by Lougheed's mansion on Thirteenth Avenue, W.R. Hull's a block to the north, and Pat Burns's another block to the east. A gesture from the denizen of any of these luxurious homes would have evoked no surprise. But R.B. Bennett? What was he doing in the same rooming house, in the same room, in fact, that he had rented at 222 Fourth Avenue West soon after he came to Calgary?[7]

For his first year in Calgary, Bennett had occupied a small room in the Alberta Hotel. He was still there in 1898 when Max Aitken arrived. But when his brother George joined him the next year, they took the large front room on the second floor of the rooming house on Fourth Avenue. It was a nice enough rooming house in a nice enough middle-class district, but in the summer of

1914 it was not the kind of address one would expect of anyone who could equip an infantry regiment.

True, Bennett was frequently seen in the company of the owners of Calgary's show-place homes. Most of them, indeed, were his clients, and he was frequently a guest at their formal dinners, where no one appeared more elegantly attired than he. Indeed, no one appeared on Calgary streets more elegantly attired than Bennett. Nevertheless, his was not a name that would come quickly to mind to anyone compiling a list of the ten most well-to-do Calgarians. Perhaps he did not deserve to be on such a list, perhaps it was just the onrushing war catching him up in an excess of patriotic zeal. Yet it might well have been that Bennett was deadly serious, that his resources *were* sufficient to fund such a project, and that he was more than willing to commit them to it. His income over the previous decade had been substantial and his out-of-pocket living expenses would hardly have exceeded those of his office clerks. By 1911 his annual CPR income alone had reached $10,000. He was the president of Calgary Power, a director of several companies, and a substantial shareholder in others.

Whatever the reality of Bennett's offer, there is no evidence it ever got beyond the talking stage. The first contingent to leave Calgary on 15 August was reported by the *Herald* as being '400 men of the Princess Patricia's (Own) Light Infantry in charge of Major Duncan Stewart.' It noted: 'The honour of being the first men of Western Canada to leave for the front was a striking compliment to both Hamilton Gault of Montreal and R.B. Bennett, K.C., M.P. of Calgary who had financed the regiment and are making this handsome present to the Empire.'

That was the last ever heard of Bennett's gift to the regiment. The Princess Pat's were entrusted to the command of Lieutenant-Colonel F.D. Farquhar, a British officer of the Black Watch and military secretary of the governor general. Gault was promoted to major and named second in command. He served overseas with the regiment, was wounded five times, and lost a leg in battle. The official charter of the regiment, preserved in its Calgary headquarters, acknowledges Gault's $100,000 gift. There is no mention of a Bennett contribution, and his connection is not mentioned in the official history of the regiment.[8] Later, Bennett became the honorary colonel-in-chief of the Calgary Highlanders, at whose mobilization he provided the bagpipes, drums, and a complete set of brass instruments for the regimental band. He was the Highlanders' patron, in everything that term implied.

By the time the first Calgary contingent of the Princess Pats reached Ottawa, parliament was assembling for the four-day session that would provide the Borden administration with all the lawful authority and emergency legislation it would need to fight a war. When it adjourned from 22 August until 2 February 1915, Bennett returned to Calgary and the outer fringes of the war effort. Calgary yielded nothing to any other Canadian community in its enthusiasm for the war. Indeed, by 8 September 1914 this enthusiasm had almost reached the point of mass ecstasy.[9]

The civic authorities had decided that a mass meeting should be held to give the citizenry the opportunity of pledging their collective loyalty to the empire. The format of the meeting was to consist of speeches from leading lights of all the religions in the city, from leaders of all the political parties, and from the mayor, with Bennett delivering the keynote address. The flag-decked Victoria Arena was jammed with perhaps 5000 people an hour before the meeting was scheduled to start. And still they came, in such numbers that the organizers decided to hold an overflow meeting in the Sherman Rink located a couple of blocks away. It too was soon packed to the doors. The schedules were hurriedly reworked so that both crowds would hear all the speakers. Pipe bands were whipped up to entertain with stirring military marches and to lead the crowd in the singing of 'Rule Britannia' and 'Land of Hope and Glory,' with occasional snatches of 'The Maple Leaf Forever.'

In the midst of war-spawned euphoria in Calgary, Bennett received the news that his seventy-year-old mother had died suddenly in the family home at Hopewell Cape, on 1 October. Since the death of her husband Henry J. Bennett a decade earlier,

Henrietta Bennett had lived with her daughters in the New Brunswick village. The elder daughter, Evelyn, was a forty-one-year-old Albert County schoolteacher, and Mildred, who was twenty-five, had returned to Hopewell Cape to be with her mother after graduating from Mount Allison University in Sackville. Brother Ronald, the ship's captain, was now living in Sackville, when he was home from the sea. George, who had enlisted with the first draft of the Princess Pat's Battalion, was in training at Valcartier, Quebec. As the de facto head of the family, Bennett was faced with the problem of what was to be done with, or for, his maiden sisters. Could they be safely left to live alone in the family home in Hopewell Cape? Or might Evelyn return to schoolteaching in Fredericton and Mildred join her there. Or should Mildred move to Calgary and live with him?

The women provided the solution to the problem. Evelyn was unofficially engaged to Dr H.W. Coates, a Methodist clergyman who was living in Fredericton but negotiating for a posting to Vancouver. If Evelyn decided to marry Dr Coates and they moved to Vancouver, Mildred could live with them. The couple would make up their minds over the winter and when, the following spring, they decided to marry, Bennett bought them a modest bungalow. Thereafter, for the next fifteen years, it was to Vancouver that Bennett journeyed for his Christmas visit.

Buying a bungalow as a wedding present for his sister was the sort of gesture that might have been expected of Bennett. Nothing was ever too good for Richard Bennett's family and, fortunately, by 1915, making such a gesture was well within his ability to afford. Following his election to parliament in 1911, he had resigned from the CPR as vice-president of the irrigation subsidiary and exchanged his $10,000 a year retainer for a member of parliament's $2500 indemnity. But he had done so without turning a hair, for his investment income by then probably exceeded the $15,000 a year he received as counsel for Lougheed and Bennett. When the collapse of the real estate market and the onset of the Great War decimated the legal business, there is some indication that Bennett did not collect his full $15,000 a year from the partnership. Whatever the shortfall in his income from the Clarence Block, however, it would have been more than made up by his dividend income, directors fees, and salary for his service as president of Calgary Power. By the time of Evelyn's wedding in June 1915, his income could hardly have been less than $25,000, and it would more than double as the war went on, largely because of the super profit-making of the Alberta Pacific Grain Company.

For the first year in which income particulars became available through income-tax returns – 1917 – Bennett reported a taxable income of $73,329, of which $46,065 came as a dividend from the grain company. Canada Cement, by comparison, provided only $4895. Neither Canada Cement nor Calgary Power ever came close to approaching the money-making ability of Alberta Pacific Grain. The cement industry generally suffered a decline in business during the war, but Canada Cement was able to do a quick detour around that depression by getting into the scandal-tarnished shell-making industry early in the war. Then it obtained a whopping contract from the federal government for cement following the destruction of Halifax by the explosion, tidal wave, and fire in 1917.

Even without his war-related activities, Bennett at the end of 1914 was a very busy man. All Max Aitken's western Canadian promotions were now successfully launched. Bennett's primary concerns were with the Alliance Trust Company, Calgary Power, and Alberta Pacific Grain. While he had, with Aitken's assistance, become a substantial shareholder in Canada Cement, he was not active in its management. The power company and grain company were another matter. As president of Calgary Power, he was constantly involved in its expansion plans – and in Aitken's plans to obtain a number of power sites on the Saskatchewan River from the Borden government. Alberta Pacific Grain Company was embarked on a country elevator construction program that would double the number of elevators it operated in Alberta.[10]

Bennett, clearly, had more than enough to do without his law practice or his membership in parliament, but he had his ear forever cocked for an offer of a war job in the cabinet, or being given charge of any of the myriad new undertakings the war was forcing on the government. When Borden was persuading Bennett to abandon provincial politics and run for parliament in 1911, a cabinet position in the event of a Conservative victory had been discussed. Bennett feared that Senator Lougheed's long service to the party meant that he would have to be in any cabinet Borden would form. Borden admitted it created a problem, but assured Bennett there was always a possibility something might be worked out, given time. There the matter still rested three years later. With the vast expansion engendered by the war, however, time must surely come into play to provide him with the kind of opportunity for service his ability justified. Bennett waited and waited. Despite the crying need for management, no call came, though in the late spring of 1915 he would have been justified in assuming that Borden was thinking about him. The prime minister invited him on a trip to London that would keep them abroad from the beginning of July to the end of August.

Somewhere during the early war years, an aphorism circulated that 'Canada was no more prepared for the Great War than Samoa was prepared for an Arctic blizzard.' If anything, it understated the case. Canada had no army of its own and no officer corps to command it even if it did get one. The ineffable Sam Hughes, the minister of defence until 1916, put 15,000 men 'under arms' by late fall of 1914, but had no place to put them until he cleared 1000 acres of forest and farmland near Valcartier, Quebec. The 'arms' they shouldered as they went through boot camp at Valcartier were Ross rifles, superb Canadian-made hunting guns that would prove disastrously unfit for service in the mud and dirt of the trenches of northern France. It would take two years and a near insurrection to get rid of the rifle, however, along with Sir Sam Hughes. The Canadian-made boots furnished the soldiers disintegrated in the mud of the Salisbury Plains, and the Canadian-made uniforms fell apart in the English rain. There were no facilities to supply and maintain an army in the field, and there was no organization to plan for the production and shipment of foodstuff and clothing for the civilian population. Nor was there any coordination of effort, either military or civilian, between the mother country and its dominions and colonies.

All this came about because the understructure of the British Empire had not kept pace with geographical expansion and political evolution. Canada went into the war, in the eyes of its own government, as a self-governing British dominion. There was, of course, the bothering exception of having to rely on the British foreign secretary to manage all Canadian external affairs. This meant, in the eyes of the British government, that Canada was free to act as it pleased, so long as it did as it was told where British interests were concerned. When the British government advised the king to declare war on Germany, that automatically became a declaration of war on behalf of Canada and all the other dominions. The order was delivered by the colonial secretary of the British government to the governor general in Canada for delivery to the Canadian prime minister.

When Britain went to war and Canada was 'asked' to raise an army, it meant men would be recruited and sent to Britain for incorporation into the British army. That was the first bone of contention to arise between Ottawa and London in the First World War. And it arose within days, perhaps even hours, of the arrival of the first Canadian contingent in England. When Lord Kitchener, the secretary of war, informed Sir Sam Hughes of his intention to break up the Canadian regiments and distribute the men among British units, the outraged Hughes told him he would do nothing of the sort and stormed out of his office. Hughes then cabled Borden his report and went after Prime Minister Asquith and Lloyd George, then secretary of the Treasury. Kitchener was eventually overruled and the right of the Canadians to fight the war as an identifiable Canadian unit was established. The Canadian Corps, however, remained under the command of British generals until after the battle of Vimy Ridge, when Sir Arthur Currie was given command.[11]

It became clear early in the war that if Canada's resources were to be used to best advantage, a better system of communication between governments was necessary. The Canadian cabinet wanted not only to be privy to the overall strategy of the British government, but to decide how Canadian industry could assist in filling British military and civilian needs. It was to this end that Borden visited England in 1915 and took Bennett along as an adviser and assistant. Although they toured the battlefields, visited the Canadian troops in training, and consulted with members of the British cabinet, it was a frustrating six weeks for Borden. He was not able to find any signs of urgency in the conduct of the war. Rather it was characterized by a muddling-through attitude that frustrated and angered the Canadian prime minister.[12]

The closing of the Dardanelles had cut the European allies off from a primary source of bread grains. Britain relied on imported wheat for 78 per cent of its requirements, France for 28 per cent, and Italy for 45 per cent. Yet Britain had no interest in discussing with Canada the possibility of expanding Canadian wheat production to meet its requirements. The British policy had been firmly stated by Reginald McKenna, the home secretary, in a speech in the House of Commons on 8 August 1914. 'On the question of policy our desire has been not to interfere with ordinary trade at all, but to leave the traders to conduct their own business.'[13] The government did, however, have a policy on the price of wheat: the price British farmers received for their wheat would be the ceiling price for foreign wheat. That was typical of other facets of the British war effort. The depression of 1913 had left Canadian factories with a lot of surplus capacity and idle labour that could be utilized for war production. Borden encountered a discouraging lack of interest in getting it put to use.

For Bennett, the journey was a many-sided adventure. Most pleasant was the opportunity for renewing his friendship with Max Aitken, who by then had become immersed in the Canadian war effort in Britain, despite his membership in the British House of Commons. On his visit to Ottawa in the autumn of 1914, Aitken had arranged with Borden and Sir Sam Hughes to become a special representative of the Canadian government in London. He was gazetted an honorary lieutenant-colonel and appointed a special representative of the Department of Defence. That gave him entré to General Headquarters in France and access to the high command, as well as to the Canadian Corps. He was able to report on the activities of the Canadian troops in action, and also wrote dispatches for the government to release to Canadian newspapers. He not only put together a group of photographers to serve the Canadian Corps, but made arrangements for a group of Canadian artists to preserve on canvas an extended record of Canadian participation in the war. Later on he established an office in London to collect and preserve a factual record of Canadian participation, an archive that ranged all the way from official orders to newspaper clippings.[14]

Bennett could only gaze in awe at the scope of Aitken's activities, at his involvement in the internal feuding of the British cabinet while he travelled back and forth to the battlefields as Canada's official witness of the Canadian Corps in action – the first authentic war correspondent. It was, of course, awe mixed with envy, and with the hope that when he got back to Ottawa he would be given a chance to play a useful role in the war effort. That chance would be slow in coming, and it was not much when it did come – the appointment as director of national service in the fall of 1916. In the meantime he enjoyed his English stay as best he could. He was able to renew the acquaintance with Bonar Law and Asquith he had made through Aitken on previous visits. He became friends with F.E. Smith (Lord Birkenhead) and Rudyard Kipling, got to know Lloyd George, toured the battlefields with Borden and Aitken, and visited Paris and met the leaders of the French government.

It was towards the end of his trip with Borden that Bennett learned his brother George had become ill in Flanders and had been hospitalized in northern France. Aitken undertook to keep tabs on George Bennett's enteritis and, when it took a turn for the worse after Bennett returned to Canada, Aitken had him transferred to a London hospital. The illness eventually led to George Bennett's release from the army on a medical discharge, and RB returned to England in late November to accompany his brother back to Toronto and a prolonged convalescence.

The Alberta to which Bennett himself returned in the late summer of 1915 was prospering, particularly for a director of the Alberta Pacific Grain Company. The journey to Calgary was through the finest crop of wheat western Canada had ever grown, and by far. Sixty years would pass before Alberta would again be able to match the thirty-one bushels of wheat per acre it harvested that year. After the British and Canadian governments got themselves sorted out, it would prove a real bonanza to Alberta Pacific Grain. The sorting out, however, would take time.

In the fall of 1914 the British government had passed an order-in-council banning exports of foodstuffs, except under special licence, to all neutral countries from the United Kingdom and from the dominions and colonies. Canada automatically passed a complying order-in-council. This shut off exports of Canadian wheat to Italy, where a profitable market had been developed. France and Britain also stopped importing Canadian wheat in 1914, and Canadian elevators became jammed with wheat. This was sorted out in 1915, when Britain agreed to buy Canadian wheat and the Canadian government commandeered the supplies of all high-grade grain in storage in eastern Canada and rushed it to port to fill British orders.[15]

There was an incidental benefit for Bennett from the trip to Europe – it took him out of the country at the time the Prohibition referenda were reaching their climax in the west. He was thus freed from pressure to declare himself for one side or the other. Southern Alberta had first become privy to Bennett's oratorical skills when he took to the stump as a temperance lecturer soon after his arrival in Calgary, in the run up to the Prohibition plebiscite of 1898. His arguments then, like those of all other missionaries for the cause, were physical, sociological, and financial, and he enthusiastically supported the 'Dry' side. But between the 1898 campaign and the 1911 election his views had undergone a degree of moderation. While he was still totally committed to temperance as a cause and to abstinence as a way of life, he backed away from Prohibition as a way to combat alcoholism.

During the 1911 election campaign he had taken time out to deliver a temperance speech to a Calgary church group. His Liberal opponents circulated reports of that speech to indicate to Calgary drinkers that Bennett was a Prohibitionist who would shut off access to their favourite bar and beverage. In response, on

20 September Bennett issued a statement to the *Calgary Herald*: 'I am a total abstainer and always have been and I am not personally in favor of the liquor traffic. But I realize that ... Any reforms that may be brought about in the matter of temperance must be brought about by education of the people and not through the enactment of regulations restricting the traffic if such regulations be not in accord with the will of the people.'

But what if such regulations did become 'the will of the people?' That was what the 21 July 1915 Prohibition referendum was all about in Alberta. The expressed will of the people was 58,295 for and 37,509 against restricting the liquor traffic.

The moderation of Bennett's attitude towards alcoholic beverages happened more by way of osmosis than otherwise. Most of his Calgary friends used alcohol from time to time, and only Bob Edwards and Paddy Nolan indulged unwisely and too well. It would have been difficult for Bennett to have named a better-living, more 'Christian-living' person than A.E. Cross, a moderate imbiber and the president of the Calgary Brewery. Bennett did not find any conflict between his Methodist temperance lifestyle and his acting for Cross and the Calgary Brewery in a refinancing Max Aitken was arranging. As time passed in Calgary, his own status as a *total* abstainer from alcoholic substances underwent some mild modifications as a result of his social contacts.

Bennett was a frequent guest at dinner at the Cross home and he developed a keen appetite for one of Mrs Cross's favourite desserts. It was built up of alternate layers of cake and whipped cream. As it was constructed, each layer of cake was generously sprinkled with rum before the filling was added, a process repeated for four or five layerings. The best part of a bottle of dark rum went into the cake and, if the cook was not careful, the bottom layers would resemble rum pudding more than cake. Bennett loved that dessert and never passed up a chance for seconds. Mary Cross Dover recalled she suspected the cook gave the recipe extra servings of rum when she knew Bennett was coming to dinner. Later in life he acquired a taste for crême-de-menthe parfaits and brandy-lashed soups, arguing that boiling the latter removed the alcohol. During his residence in the Château

Laurier Hotel during the 1930s he maintained an excellent wine cellar for his guests, as he did when he retired to England. There is, however, no record of Bennett breaking the childhood pledge he made to his mother never to drink, in the normal sense.

The provincial liquor laws that were enacted as a result of the 1915 plebiscites quickly proved to be inoperative. Only a citizen's resources limited the amount of liquor he could acquire by mail order from out-of-province liquor dealers. Drug stores were permitted to sell liquor to holders of medical prescriptions, and export houses established to supply liquor to American customers frequently leaked supplies into the domestic market. By 1916 the Dry forces were demanding the enactment of a national prohibition law to quench supplies at the ultimate source, the distilleries and breweries. In March 1916, H.H. Stevens introduced a bill in the House of Commons to make the manufacture, transportation, or sale of beverage alcohol illegal anywhere in Canada. The proposal at once encountered opposition from members for Quebec, particularly the Montreal area. While Quebec was the only province that had not passed a prohibitory law by this time, it did have a provincial law that enabled local municipalities to prohibit the sale of alcoholic beverages. A large majority of Quebec municipalities had done just that, but they did not include the municipalities in the greater Montreal area – the centre of beverage production and consumption.

The dilemma the House of Commons faced was neatly summarized by Bennett: if the citizens of Quebec municipalities had not persuaded their provincial legislature to pass a prohibitory statute that would abolish sales of liquor in Montreal, what right did the citizens of Alberta or of Saskatchewan have to so?[16] It was Bennett himself who found a solution to the problem. He suggested an amendment based on his own deep conviction that it was the provinces that were best able to determine what served their own social and economic interests.[17] Ergo, it was up to the provinces to pass their own Prohibition laws. As for the House in Ottawa, 'this Parliament should at the present session enact legislation to prohibit the transportation or importation of alcoholic liquor into any province for any use or purpose which is or may

be forbidden by the law of such province.' A resolution embody-
ing Bennett's suggestion was eventually passed by a vote of 104 to
15, but it was so emasculated by the Senate that enforcement was
impossible.

The 1916 debate enabled Bennett to clarify his own ideas. He
was all in favour of an alcohol-free society, by law if necessary, but
it was a condition to be achieved by slow and steady steps that
would carry the overwhelming support of public opinion. Without a convinced public behind it, the law could not be enforced.

If Bennett took no part in the campaign for Prohibition, two
other causes arising from the war attracted his total commitment.
He was the honorary president of the Southern Alberta Patriotic
Fund and president of the Alberta Red Cross. Whenever he was
in the west he was involved with their money-raising campaigns.
He was particularly dedicated to the Patriotic Fund, which was
concerned with raising money to support the wives and children
and, later on, the widows of the army volunteers. Soldiers' wives
with children were eligible to draw $40 a month from the fund,
but as the army expanded it became an onerous task to keep the
Patriotic Fund in a position to meet the demands on it.

From the newspaper reports of the special events that were
being staged everywhere, and almost on a daily basis, it was logical
to assume that the Patriotic Fund was everybody's major charity.
Bennett thought otherwise. When the executive met early in
1916 to confront the latest financial crisis, he was a strong supporter of a proposal that smacked of blackmail. Everybody
seemed to have a story of well-to-do financial 'slackers' who
failed to support the Patriotic Fund to the extent their resources
were deemed to permit. Bennett seconded a motion to publicize
the names of wealthy non-contributors as the only way to 'make
some people realize their fellow citizens are disgusted with
them!'[18]

For a British imperialist like R.B. Bennett, the war was both an
opportunity and an ordeal. It gave him a chance to bear witness to
his Anglo-Saxonism in emotion-tinged speeches across Canada
and into the United States, but it was also an ordeal for him to
contemplate the monumental ineptitude of the Britons who
were conducting the war. Two days after Sir Robert Borden, in

his NewYear's message of 1916, had committed Canada to raising an army of 500,000, Bennett returned to Calgary to report on his second wartime visit to London.[19] It was a litany of disaster over which he sought to spread the best possible gloss. The besetting sin of the British, he said, was their inability to accomplish anything on time. They were late getting to France, late in going to the rescue of Antwerp. Attacks made at Neuve Chappelle and Loos with great heroism and tremendous cost were made useless by failure to send in support at a critical time. The enormous wastage everywhere apparent in the British war effort meant that for every £100 spent, only £60 value was obtained. Such facts, he was quick to emphasize, were to be balanced by the heroism of the soldiers in the field, by the dedication of British workers and British seamen. While compulsory service would soon be necessary, he was confident the British people would accept it to win the war.

He was obsessed by the war – and he had become obsessed by Mackenzie and Mann and the Canadian Northern Railway. As Bennett had predicted, the $44 million the promoters had obtained from the government in 1914 failed to complete the railway. They were back again late in 1915 for another subsidy. So, indeed was the Grand Trunk Pacific. In the midst of all the problems created by the war, Borden's cabinet was once again plagued by what to do about the railway problems, of which Mackenzie and Mann were only a part.

The booming wartime economy had revealed a serious shortage of railway boxcars for moving grain and other foodstuffs to market and for moving military material and supplies to tidewater. These shortages were exacerbated by a shortage of motive power. The situation was further complicated by the need to turn over the railway shops to the manufacture of munitions and vehicles for the army. Finally, there was the need to have all the railway trackage in operating condition. For all these reasons, 'the railway problem' was frequently before the cabinet and the Conservative caucus in the winter of 1916, even before the requests surfaced for subsidies of $8 million for the Grand Trunk Pacific and $15 million for the Canadian Northern.

The CNR proposal evoked a series of objections in both the cabinet and the Conservative caucus. In his diary, Borden noted a meeting with Foster, White, Rogers, Reid, Doherty, Casgrain, and Meighen – the cabinet heavyweights – at which the only point of agreement was that the situation was almost impossible. For himself, Borden wrote, 'I said I would prefer to resign and let the Grits clean up their own mess.' Instead, Borden and the cabinet eventually decided to maintain the railway status quo with the grants and to turn responsibility for finding a permanent solution to the railway problem over to a royal commission.

The internal opposition to the grants became so persistent and unsettling that Borden feared he would be faced with a caucus revolt. On 28 April he brought the matter to a head at a caucus meeting that lasted for more than three hours. In an atmosphere heavy with tension, he wrote, 'I spoke on the railway situation firmly and frankly and won great applause. Placed the facts pretty forcibly before them. It went off much better than I expected. Meighen said my speech settled caucus. Nickle in good mood, Bennett in ugly mood. Many think his mind is becoming affected.'[20]

Borden's speech did not settle anything for Bennett. Borden might have assumed that Bennett, having tackled the issue in 1912 and again with great vigour, even passion, in 1914, would have been content when the matter resurfaced in 1916. After all, everybody in parliament knew where he stood on the Mackenzie and Mann issue. So did most Canadians who had any interest in the subject. And this time the government was adopting his 1914 suggestion of having a royal commission tackle the problem.

In plain truth, Mackenzie and Mann and the CNR were transforming R.B. Bennett into a one-issue politician – worse, into a monumental bore. He took little interest in anything else that was happening in the House of Commons. The index to Hansard needed barely three inches to identify his annual participation in debates, but when baling out the CNR got onto the Commons agenda his reaction was voluminous. It all probably sprang from his seven-year immersion in the inner sanctum of the CPR in Calgary between 1905 and 1912. He was the vice-president of its irrigation subsidiary at the time when a CPR ethos, for want of a better word, was developing in western Canada. The farmers, ranchers, and freight shippers might have hated the CPR, but for its employees it was an awesomely respected institution.

For a CPR engineer, conductor, station agent, or machinist, the height of ambition for his son was to have him follow him onto the CPR payroll. If the son did, 'and kept his nose clean,' he could not only count on a lifetime of well-paid employment, but was assured of freedom to work his way up the ladder to better-paying jobs. Even the presidency of the company was not beyond an office boy's reach. The basic wage scale on the CPR may not have exceeded that of other employers, but the door to promotion was always open. A call-boy got to be a fireman and then freight engineer before he was entrusted with a passenger train. That was the *only* way the CPR made passenger-train engineers. There was a pension at the end of a working life, and CPR doctors who treated employees for free. There were annual passes that took CPR employees from one end of the country to the other, not only for the employees but for their wives and families as well. CPR employees in Laurier's Canada, when they recalled the fringe benefits they enjoyed, stood a little taller than ordinary mortals, and they told a new acquaintance with a touch of boastfulness. 'I work for the C.P.R.'[21]

Bennett had been a CPR employee, and there is evidence that his emotional attachment to the company survived long after his official connection had been terminated. He was well settled into his estate in southern England, in July 1940, when he received a letter from President E.W. Beatty of the CPR asking him to return his pass.[22] The request came as a result of a letter from the Board of Transport commissioner, advising the railway that Bennett was no longer eligible to have the pass the CPR had issued to him for 1940. Bennett returned the pass under protest, pointing out that he was entitled to receive it as a retired officer of the company. When he had retired from the company in 1911 on his election to parliament, he had taken a payment of $5000 in lieu of a company pension at sixty-five, but he was still a retired employee by definition and entitled to receive the pass. He never expected to use his pass again, but it was something he prized for sentimental reasons. Unhappily for Bennett, he had forgotten that it was under his régime as prime minister that the board had amended its regulation to bar retired railway employees from receiving free transportation.

Clearly, the R.B. Bennett who inveighed against Mackenzie and Mann and the Canadian National Railway was not R.B. Bennett the dispassionate thinking machine. He was the CPR pensioner whose thought processes had been CPR-conditioned to react antagonistically towards the CNR. That conditioning blinded him to the realities of life on the western prairies. It made him incapable of conceding that had it not been for Mackenzie and Mann, the CNR, and the Grand Trunk Pacific, the optimum settlement of the west would have been delayed by generations. It was they, between 1900 and 1911, who opened up for settlement the parkland north of the CPR main line. It was the settlement growth along the CNR and the Grand Trunk Pacific that provided the additional population that made it possible for Saskatchewan and Alberta to achieve provincial status. The people were there because the government and the railways enticed them to come. But they were not there in sufficient numbers to provide the traffic that would enable the CNR to earn enough money to pay the interest charges on its debt.

To operate profitably, the CNR would have needed a string of cities of 100,000 population closely placed between Port Arthur and Vancouver. Instead, it had Winnipeg, Saskatoon, and Edmonton and a few hamlets. But that line of hamlets and the surrounding farmers constituted a potent political force in western Canada. Imperative political considerations dictated that the railways had to be kept in operation. There was an additional consideration, equally imperative. As Sir Clifford Sifton, Sir Thomas Shaughnessy, and F. Williams Taylor of the Bank of Montreal kept impressing on Borden, the CNR could not be allowed to default on its bond interest because of the disastrous effect such a default would have on Canada's international credit. Every criticism Bennett made of Mackenzie and Mann, and of their operation of the CNR, might be valid, but nothing he said in 1914, 1915, or 1916 contributed to the solution of Borden's railway problem – for the simple reason that there was no solution. There were only short-gap financial bailouts that would buy time in 1914, pending Mackenzie and Mann's return the following year, and the follow-ing years, for additional short-gap financial bailouts. In face of the awesome responsibilities that devolved on Borden and his col-leagues in prosecution of the war, the frequency with which Mackenzie and Mann surfaced in Borden's wartime diary is as-tounding.[23]

It was these responsibilities that resulted in the railway problem shifting several notches downward on the government's list of priorities in the late spring of 1916. Certainly it was overshad-owed by the need to find recruits for the army of 500,000 Borden had announced at New Year's. It was less important than the need to heal the split that was developing between the Orangemen of Ontario and the French Canadians of Quebec. There was the labour crisis in food production and in the war factories – and later that year Sir Joseph Flavelle would ask the government to consider releasing non-combatants from the army to work in the armament factories. Raising the financial resources required to fund British purchases in Canada as well as Canada's own war effort was reaching the crisis stage that would bring an income tax into operation. Unlike such problems as these, the question of railway financing was one that could be safely, and with compara-tive ease, left until the end of the war.

But not for R.B. Bennett. It was an idée fixe that set him off on another two-hour speech in mid-May 1916, a speech that would win him no friends and exert little influence on the members of the House of Commons who bothered to listen, or had the patience to sit it through. This time Bennett's main talking points were the balance sheets, annual reports, and other financial state-ments of the railways. Once again he had done his homework, including the digestion of voluminous studies of railway financ-ing by Dun and Bradstreet, the United States financial publisher of corporate information. Midway through his speech he became enmeshed in tedious argument over accounting terms and definitions that would have lost him any audience. If Bennett's career in the House of Commons could be said to have had a low point, that was it.

Outweighing all else on Bennett's mind in the spring of 1916, however, was Borden's steadfast refusal to recognize his existence. The prime minister talked to Bennett when an occasion arose, and he was cordial enough at all times. He seemed not to resent or take personally any criticism Bennett voiced of his policies, railway or other. But it was now almost five years since Borden, in their August 1911 meeting in the Windsor Hotel in Montreal, had said that 'the matter to which I had referred must surely be capable of some reasonable solution.' That matter was a position in Borden's cabinet if Bennett would resign from the Alberta legislature and run in the 1911 federal election. Bennett did drop out of provincial politics to run for parliament, convinced he had a cabinet commitment from Borden.

If he had not had a commitment, why would he have run? He had gone on record to a number of people that he was through with politics. He was simply too busy with his law practice and corporate interests to be able to afford the time. He had firmly rejected all overtures from his political friends to change his mind. That had happened only after the meeting with Borden. But in the cabinet that Borden had put together, concededly one of the weakest in Canadian history, no place had been found for Bennett. Then, with the coming of the war and the burgeoning need for talent of all kinds, no opening was made for whatever service Bennett could render. As the Borden administration was approaching the end of its five years in office, the talk increased about a coalition with the Liberals and a second extension of the parliamentary term. Bennett was by then in the process of deciding he was through with federal politics. For five years he had been stealing three or four months a year from his legal practice and corporate responsibilities to waste in Ottawa to no useful purpose that he or anyone else could identify. He had a long discussion with Borden about his future in June 1915 prior to their departure for England, but it was as inconclusive as most conversations with Borden seemed to be.[24] Then, when he discussed his future with Lougheed in 1916, they agreed he should seek an appointment to the Senate.

By the end of the war Bennett would have all the money he would ever need – and a great deal more than he, with his frugal lifestyle and abstemious tastes, would ever be able to spend. A senatorship, he was convinced, would enable him to become a sort of travelling ambassador for the kind of empire he could imagine emerging from the war. He, as a Canadian senator, would achieve the status with politicians in India, Australia, New Zealand, South Africa, and above all London he would not have as a private citizen. Recalling the meetings he had had in London, and the varied opinions he had encountered about the future role of the dominions in the destiny of the empire, he envisioned a most useful role for himself in advancing the common interest of all the components of the empire. He resolved to broach the matter of a senatorship with Borden when the appropriate moment arrived.

That Bennett's thinking was very much attuned to the welfare of the empire is indicated by a strange and cryptic letter he wrote to Max Aitken on 13 July 1916. It began as a congratulatory note on Aitken's baronetcy, an honour Aitken had refused the year before because of the possibility he might return to a political career in Canada. Then Bennett continued: 'I cannot write you what I feel about the Canadian situation. I believe you are sincerely desirous of serving but I do think that if you saw matters from the inside of Canada rather than from the outside you would have some doubts as to whether or not what has been done and is being done are in the interest of the Commonwealth.' After a vague reference to a financial aspect, he continued:

Unless as a result of this war we can consolidate this Empire together it will indeed have been in vain. You will remember that I said to your friend the secretary of state for the colonies that we might win a war and lose an Empire. I only wish I had you in Canada for a fortnight without it being known who you were, so that you might really understand what conditions are from the Atlantic to the Pacific. I am certain you would take immediate steps to see that some things were ended and ended quickly.

However I am not charged with the responsibility for what is taking place but if at times I feel strongly I have endeavored to refrain from giving expression to my views, but the time must come and before very long when I will find it imperative to do so.[25]

What precisely was sticking in Bennett's craw is difficult to identify. His impatience with the progress of the war and the mounting toll of casualties in France was understandable. So was his impatience with Sam Hughes's management of the defence department. The minister's appointees to a shell committee for the British government had become involved in widespread charges of incompetency and graft. The growing bitterness between English and French Canada over the French-language issue in the schools of Ontario and Manitoba was impairing the national war effort. But how any of this could have been seen by Bennett as a threat to the future of the empire is difficult to understand.

Indeed, the obvious threat to the future of the empire was identified by the Canadian government as the intransigent refusal of British politicians to cooperate with the Canadian government in the marshalling of Canadian facilities to assist in the struggle. It was a situation that provoked Borden to write so bitterly to Sir George Perley, the Canadian high commissioner, in November 1915: 'Procrastination, indecision, inertia, doubt, hesitation and many other undesirable qualities have made themselves entirely too conspicuous in this war. During my recent visit . . . a very able Cabinet Minister spoke of the shortage of guns, rifles, munitions, etc. but declared the chief shortage was brains.'[26] It was not until Lloyd George established the Imperial War Cabinet in 1917 that British politicians started treating the dominions as partners and not as messenger boys to be ordered about.

At the time of his letter to Aitken, Bennett was back in Calgary attending to his law practice and his corporate interests. In 1916, as the casualties of the Canadian army increased, triggering the need for increasing recruitment of reinforcements, enlistments in

Canada declined. The government set up a network of home-defence militia units, with the objective of using them to enhance recruitment for the active army. The experiment failed, almost completely, and the failure intensified the bitterness of the conscription controversy that was sweeping the country. Instead of yielding to the demand for conscription, the government decided to continue adherence to the voluntary system of obtaining recruits. To improve the effectiveness of that system, it decided to make an inventory of Canadian manpower to determine the size of the manpower pool that was available not only for the armed forces, but for employment in agriculture and in war production and essential civilian production. In August 1916 it established the National Service Board under a national director and nine provincial directors to take the census.[27]

It was at this point that Borden reached out for Bennett to appoint him to the war job for which he had waited so long. He named Bennett Alberta director of the National Service Board. When Sir Thomas Tait, the national director, resigned in a dispute over staffing, Bennett was appointed to that position.

To put the country in a position to mobilize its human resources to fight a scientifically organized war, Bennett's board divided the population roughly into four groups. The first group were the nineteen to twenty-five year olds – with up to thirty year olds a possibility – who would do the fighting. The second were the farmers, who would provide the food the soldiers and the civilian population would require. The third were the workers in the coal mines and steel mills, who would provide the raw materials to enable the workers in munition plants to make the guns, shells, and bullets the soldiers needed. The fourth category was the government service, including transportation and communications, that would keep the country in operation. His board, Bennett emphasized, was not just another recruiting agency. Its first responsibility would be to inventory the population, then to direct Canadians from less essential occupations into those that were vital to a successful war effort. That would include making a determination of how women might be directed to more highly skilled occupations.

In his keynote speech on his new responsibility on 25 November 1916 in Calgary, Bennett's main emphasis was on production. Not only did Canada have to feed its army overseas, it also had to feed the British army, the French army, and the Italian army, all of whose primary food sources had been cut off by the war. After the needs of the allied armed services were met, there were hungry civilian populations waiting to be fed. So the priority had to be to keep the farmers growing food. It was nonsense, he said, for a thirty-year-old farmer to go off for the front and abandon his farm to weeds. It was nonsense for a twenty-five year old to be working as a store clerk when he belonged in the army.

To compile an inventory of skills required a census of some kind. The board chose a short questionnaire on a printed card which the Post Office would deliver to every adult Canadian male. In addition to name, domicile, and country of birth, there were questions on health, training, and present occupation. The final two questions asked whether the recipient would be willing to change his present work for other necessary work at the same pay during the war, and whether he would be willing the move to another location in Canada.

The questionnaire, when it was completed in early December, triggered a serious confrontation between Bennett and Borden. To Bennett, distributing the questionnaire without imposing some compulsion on the recipients to complete it was a waste of time and effort. He therefore included a compulsory feature in the regulations governing the questionnaire. Borden deleted it, on the grounds, no doubt, that inclusion would be seen as a forerunner to the imposition of conscription for overseas service, then a hot public issue. As Bennett would later write to Borden. 'I should have resigned that day. Men who are now your colleagues openly expressed surprise that I did not. I believed my duty was to obey and not to reason why and, truth to tell, I was also influenced by personal regard for yourself and appreciation of the great burdens you were carrying. I retained my position...with the full realization that I had destroyed my own place and position in this country.'[28] Instead of resigning, Bennett moved to Ottawa to set in motion a propaganda campaign the like of which the country had never seen and would never see again.

A total of 1.5 million questionnaires were distributed to 500,000 Canadian males under sixty-five years of age. The propaganda campaign was to persuade these men to fill in and return the forms to the government. In addition to a nation-wide newspaper advertising campaign, Bennett dispatched 150,000 letters to anybody who was anybody in any position of leadership in the country.

The letter went to university presidents, corporation executives, ministers of all religious denominations, school principals and school teachers, trade-union officers, fraternal organizations, boards of trade, and service clubs. In up to 500 words, though sometimes less, the letters pleaded with the recipients to use whatever persuasive power they possessed to motivate men they knew to fill in and return the printed form. From the response apparent from the news columns of the daily newspapers in the spring of 1917, the recipients took the appeal of the letters to heart. No church service was considered complete that spring unless the sermon was tied in with the appeal for completion and return of the questionnaires. The same was true of the service-club speeches reported in the newspapers.

As a warm up to the distribution of the questionnaire, Bennett joined Borden during the months of December and January on a nation-wide speaking tour. The prime minister concentrated on the battlefield, on the imperative need to win the war to save Canadians from the fate of Belgian women and children. He discouraged thinking about an early end of the war and pleaded for a generous response to the campaigns for reinforcements. Bennett concentrated on the need to make better use of available human resources. 'There are men over there who should never have gone,' he said, 'and there are some here who should have.' Soldiers should be men between nineteen and twenty-five years of age. Those over that age should be put in essential work, and unessential work should be stopped. Young men in munition factories should be replaced with women, at an equal wage.

Bennett divided Canadians into three classes: those who fought, those who worked, and the rich who did neither but were made to pay. He noted that a tax of 25 per cent on corporate profits had been enacted by the government. As for the cries for conscription that were becoming louder, he pleaded for patience even if, as he conceded, the volunteer system did result in uneven sacrifices. It was better that sacrifices be uneven than to use the armed forces to quell riots at home.[29]

It is doubtful whether any other cause got such an outpouring of public support as the national questionnaire. Only in Quebec was there overt opposition, mainly from French-Canadian youths heckling and otherwise intruding on public meetings. In Quebec City, at a meeting attended by leading representatives of both Catholic and Protestant churches and presided over by the mayor of the city, the premier of Quebec, Sir Jean-Lomer Gouin, was interrupted and shouted down by a crowd that stormed out of the meeting when Bennett got up to speak. Elsewhere across the country the meetings were filled with enthusiastic listeners who roundly applauded the patriotic speeches and endorsed the survey idea. In the end more than 1.5 million cards were returned, including 200,000 blanks. The survey turned up 286,976 military prospects in non-essential occupations, an indication that there were enough men potentially available to meet Borden's target of a 500,000 man army.

It was while Bennett was still deeply involved with the National Service Board's affairs in the late spring of 1917 that disaster struck at the Alberta Pacific Grain Company, and missed by only a whisker. That threat, curiously enough, was mounted by the Wheat Export Company, which the British government had established in New York and Winnipeg in 1916 to handle its North American wheat purchases. Until then it had left that business entirely in the hands of the private grain trade.

The private grain trade – the grains futures marketing system – had begun to evolve towards the end of the eighteenth century as a means of reducing the risks involved in making bread in England from wheat grown in North America. The germ of the idea may have derived from the British cotton trade with

America and Egypt, the spice trade with the East Indies, or the sugar or tobacco trade with the West Indies. It eventually came to include them all. By the turn of the century, the futures markets in most commodities were firmly established throughout the world. In Winnipeg, by 1916, the Winnipeg Grain and Produce Exchange occupied the entire seven floors of the biggest office building between Toronto and Vancouver and was planning a ten-storey addition. Its roster of grain brokers included every aspect of the grain business, from the actual growers of the grain to the flour millers.

During 1914 and 1915, the British government obtained all the wheat it required from Canada through the regular facilities of the Winnipeg Grain Exchange. Its brokers placed orders in the futures markets for the wheat it wanted, other agents stored the grain, and still others moved it from the Lakehead elevators to Montreal, Halifax, and New York to await ocean shipping. In 1915 severe problems were encountered in the latter stages. The suddenly emerging war demand revealed a serious deficiency in Canada's supply of boxcars and motive power. Eventually the Canadian government stepped in and passed an order-in-council enabling it to take over the allocation of boxcars to move the wheat to tidewater. The bumper crop of high-quality wheat in 1915 insured that British needs were safe in Canadian hands at least for the immediate future.

If the 1915 crop was the best ever harvested in Canada, the 1916 crop was one of the poorest. The actual yield, though down sharply in Manitoba and Saskatchewan, held up well in Alberta, where it was a shade better than in 1915. But an early killing frost in Alberta, coupled with severe rust infestations, seriously impaired the quality of the crop. In the other provinces, heavy rain storms, followed by long harvesting delays, damaged the grain even more. The 1916 crop went to market seriously lacking in deliverable grades of wheat.

Ordinarily the grain companies were not particularly concerned with the quality of wheat that went through their hands. As part of their 'hedging' operation, they sold futures market contracts to cover the wheat they were buying from the farmers.

In the course of an August day, a grain company might buy 20,000 bushels of six or seven different grades of wheat from thirty different farmers, at ten different elevators. It would issue tickets to the farmers, which they could cash at their banks, and sell futures contracts to deliver 20,000 bushels of wheat in Fort William–Port Arthur in October.

To be deliverable on October futures contracts, the wheat it had purchased in August had to grade no. 1 hard or no. 1, no. 2, or no. 3 northern. Each grade of lesser quality suffered a price discount from the grade above. In practice, the grain trade always accepted the lower grades of no. 4, no. 5, or no. 6 as perfectly acceptable on future contracts at suitably agreed-upon discounts. During the winter of 1916–17 Alberta Pacific Grain continued to buy all the wheat its customers were hauling to market, regardless of grade, and to hedge it through sales of May futures. Despite the drop in quality of the 1916 crop, the price of May wheat futures in December 1916 fluctuated between $1.40 and $1.50 a bushel, well in advance of the price that had prevailed the previous year. The increase in price reflected the rapidly growing demand from Britain and the war-ravaged countries of the Continent. The Wheat Export Company had been a heavy buyer of cash wheat, as well as wheat futures, since the 1916–17 crop came to harvest. The mounting toll of U-boat sinkings on the Atlantic had raised Allied interest in purchases of Canadian wheat and, by January, the Winnipeg price was nearing $2.00 a bushel. Then, in late March, the Wheat Export Company became alarmed at the poor quality of the wheat it was getting, and spread the word it was not going to take delivery of any wheat grading lower than no. 3 Northern on its May and July contracts.[30] Grain cognoscenti began doing their arithmetic and came to the conclusion there was not enough deliverable grade wheat in storage at the Lakehead to fill the Wheat Export Company's purchased May contracts, let alone those of July as well. The inescapable conclusion was that the Wheat Export Company had a 'corner' on the Winnipeg May wheat futures market.

Because of the nature of their hedging operation, all the line-elevator companies in western Canada were 'short' May wheat futures. They, including, presumably, the Alberta Pacific Grain Company, began buying May futures to cover their shortages. That brought an army of speculators into the market and the May futures ran amok. The price rose from $1.90 a bushel to $3.02 a bushel within a single month. If the grain companies had been forced to balance their books with $3.00 or $4.00 wheat, it would have bankrupted them all. On one day, 2 May 1917, the price of wheat jumped thirty-three cents a bushel and the price of flour in Ottawa rose $1.25 a barrel.

That got Ottawa's attention, and negotiations began with the British government.[31] The Winnipeg wheat futures market shut down. Negotiations opened between the Wheat Export Company and the grain dealers to accept substandard grades of wheat at reduced prices. A deal was done and the grain companies were saved. The Canadian government established the Board of Grain Supervisors to buy the entire 1917 crop for $2.25 a bushel and apportion it between Canadian and British needs for the staff of life. To the delight of the western farmers, the Grain Exchange futures market remained closed until the end of the war.

For many leaders of western agriculture, the new system represented the promised land. For years it had been an article of faith of prairie wheat growers that they always got the short end of the wheat prices. In the month of July, before they threshed their crops, the price might soar to $2.00 a bushel. But in October, when everybody was hauling wheat to market, it would be down to $1.25 a bushel. Then, after the farmers had sold all their crop for the low price, the price would go up again. What was needed, the farmers came to believe, was a system that would take the crop off their hands and then feed it into the market as the demand developed during the rest of the year. The Board of Grain Supervisors did just that for the farmers for the next two crop years. Then the board's term expired, everything reverted to the status quo ante, and the futures market reopened. When the price of wheat promptly dropped by a half, to $1.00 a bushel, a clamour set up that eventually led to the establishment of the three Prairie wheat pools in 1923 and the Canadian Wheat Board in 1935.

CHAPTER SIX

Business and Government Affairs

For R.B. Bennett, 1917 was a frustrating year. He had firmly made up his mind to get out of active politics and back to his law practice and corporate interests in Calgary. He had, he was convinced, Borden's firm promise that he would be appointed to the Senate when the Commons prorogued.[1] Alberta would be entitled to two additional Senate seats as a result of its population growth and, as Borden had told Bennett, no one had a better claim to one of them than he. As soon as the national registration was completed he submitted his resignation as director to Borden, but the prime minister refused, not once but twice, to accept his resignation. That kept him in Ottawa when he would much rather have been in Calgary trying to sort out the difficulties that had arisen with his law office.

Ottawa was not fit place for man nor beast in the summer of 1917. The midsummer heat had come early and, by July, the temperature was into the medium to high eighties en route to the nineties in August, with the humidity marching in lock step with the heat. Political tempers fully kept pace with the House of Commons thermometers, as the national mood was exacerbated by deeply emotional reactions to the enlistment-reinforcement crisis. Borden and his Conservative cabinet only a year before, when they opted for a fighting force of 500,000, had been confident such a force could be raised and maintained by voluntary enlistment. Borden had taken a straw vote of his colleagues in July 1916 and only Frank Cochrane, minister of railways and canals, had opted for conscription. When the plans were made for national registration, great emphasis was placed on the government's position that the survey was not a forerunner of conscription. That was still Borden's position when on 14 February 1917, he left for London and the Imperial War Conference. When he returned to Ottawa in May he was convinced that conscription was not only necessary, it was immediately necessary.[2] In the month of April, when the Canadians had lost more than 10,000 in the Battle of Vimy Ridge, volunteer enlistment had produced only 4000 reinforcements.

Nor did the attrition stop with Vimy. The daily national casualty reports in the Canadian newspapers could seldom be fitted into a single column of type. Throughout English Canada, a groundswell of public support for conscription was developing. But how to achieve it? By invoking the Militia Act, or the War Measures Act, or by passing a new Military Service Act? Borden opted for the last, but before bringing such a bill to the floor of the House of Commons he tried to persuade Sir Wilfrid Laurier to join him in a 'national' government. He offered the Liberals half the cabinet positions, even though the Conservatives at the time had a majority of forty seats in the Commons. Laurier and his Quebec supporters spurned Borden's offer, but in the country outside Quebec conscriptionist sentiment was sweeping the Liberal leaders of English Canada. That brought about Bennett's final head-on clash with Borden within the Conservative caucus.[3]

Borden had decided, as a concession that would make it easier for the dissident Liberals to come into a coalition to bring in conscription, that the Conservative party would submerge its identity in a Unionist party. The flaw in that strategy, as Bennett saw it, was that it left the Liberal party completely intact as a party, capable of carrying on to fight the next election, while the Conservatives as a party ceased to exist. Bennett's position was to forget coalition, go to the country as a Conservative party committed to conscription, sweep the country outside Quebec, and win by a thirty-seat majority. It was not simply a disagreement between a back-bencher and a prime minister over a matter of policy. Bennett let himself go in a biting personal attack on

Borden in the Conservative caucus. He challenged Borden's right to commit the party to conscription without recourse to the electors. Borden reacted angrily – 'So much so,' Bennett later wrote, 'that one of my friends stated that he knew one man who would not be appointed to the Senate and I was that man.'[4]

What is to be made of Bennett's emotional eruption, of his involvement in an argument he could not win with the man who held the key to his political future? It might well have been a natural reaction to the fact that he had spent almost six years in Ottawa without being able to influence the course of government in any important, identifiable way. Or it might have been simply that Bennett's health was giving out in the midst of the debate over the Canadian Northern Railway nationalization and the fight over conscription. Until he was approaching his forty-seventh birthday in June 1917, Bennett had enjoyed remarkably good health, considering his unhealthful eating habits. He was a heavy consumer of fatty food and rich desserts, and between meals he munched candy the way other men smoked cigarettes – from force of habit. This addiction gave rise to the legend that he had a firm contract with the Moir Candy Company to keep him supplied with a pound of chocolate creams a day. Despite all this, he enjoyed robust health and immunity to ordinary flu germs and colds. Everything caught up with him during the last week of June, however, when he checked into the Royal Victoria Hospital in Montreal for some unidentified abdominal surgery. The operation was a success and he was out of the hospital and back in Ottawa in time to cast his vote for second reading of the Military Service Bill on 7 July. On 2 August the *Calgary Herald* reported that Bennett had been ordered back to the Royal Victoria to recuperate from a relapse brought on by the Ottawa heat wave.

Bennett took little further interest in the Ninth Parliament and when it prorogued he was back in Calgary, awaiting his appointment to the Senate while he tried to sort out the sadly neglected and disordered state of the Lougheed and Bennett law practice. Since the 1911 election, the day-to-day operation of the law firm had been in the charge of L.M. Roberts and W.H. McLaws. Both had signing authority for the partnership, and Bennett discovered they had hired several other lawyers on improvident terms and had run up a large overdraft at the Bank of Commerce. When Bennett brought all this to Lougheed's attention, the founder was all for firing the pair on the spot. Bennett had a better idea: they should delay the firing until Bennett had an opportunity to complete his probing to see what else might be wrong. Lougheed agreed.[5]

The 1917 federal election intervened, however, and Bennett was off making speeches across the country. Months passed before he got to the bottom of his office problems. It was worse, very much worse, than he had ever suspected. McLaws and Roberts, to accommodate a client of the firm, had endorsed a five-figure promissory note at the Royal Bank on his behalf. The client not only defaulted on the note, but left the country, with Lougheed and Bennett holding the bag.

This, at first glance, was a doubly painful blow for Lougheed. He had taken no active part in the firm for more than a decade, nor had he participated in the firm's earnings. Indeed, he had endeavoured in 1912 to wind up his partnership with Bennett and seek another association. Eventually Lougheed agreed to the reorganization of the Lougheed and Bennett partnership that Bennett devised. It was based on a profit-sharing arrangement with the other lawyers that would generate sufficient funds to pay off the banks.

It was the financial disaster at Lougheed and Bennett that gave birth to one of Calgary's most fetching and longest-surviving pieces of folklore. In the summer of 1917 Bennett acquired a house. Not just *a* house – a showplace house atop Calgary's Mount Royal with a superb three-dimensional view of the city below, a three-storey, twelve-room house with three bathrooms and a grand entrance hall with a circular stairway leading to the second floor. It had a dining room that would comfortably seat a dozen guests, and, to call the servants, a buzzer system keyed to a box in the kitchen, with connections to all the rooms. There were even back stairs for the servants to use to get to their third-floor quarters. It was centred on a lot 200 by 149 feet, of red brick and sandstone construction, set on a full basement with sixteen-inch concrete walls. What all Calgary wanted to know was what so confirmed a bachelor as Richard Bedford Bennett would want with such a house? His Calgary friends concluded he was going to get married and live in it. But to whom? No Calgary women of eligible status came to mind. It had to be someone Bennett had met in the east.

No one knew Bennett better than Max Aitken. Their life-long friendship survived collisions that would have left most normal relationships fatally impaired. Despite Bennett's statements to Aitken that he was never going to marry, Aitken has identified a number of women in whom Bennett had taken more than casual interest during the time he was a member of parliament.[6] One was Evelyn Windsor, daughter of an Anglican rector in Montreal who was serving with the Canadian medical corps overseas. Aitken says he also courted Edith Cochrane, daughter of Frank Cochrane, the powerful Ontario Tory leader. Cochrane discouraged that courtship and his daughter later married another man. Then there was Jennie Eddy, who consulted Bennett frequently in connection with the tangled affairs of the E.B. Eddy trust. Was there more to the Bennett–Jennie Eddy relationship than death duties, taxes, and corporate affairs? Max Aitken was convinced there was not, and it is inconceivable that Bennett would not have discussed such a relationship with Aitken since they were in negotiations over the possible sale of the Eddy company to Aitken's Royal Securities Company.

Whatever the circumstances, Bennett got the house and came home to Calgary without a bride to share it with him. He rented it to a succession of corporate executives, and retained ownership of the Prospect Avenue house until 1939, when he was preparing for his departure for England. Sixty years after his purchase, the Bennett house was still a stopping point on tour-bus junkets around Calgary, for tour conductors to embroider their theories of why Bennett never lived there. The facts are much more prosaic than their imaginative explanations. The house was previously owned by L.M. Roberts,[7] who undoubtedly turned it over to Bennett in liquidation of his debts to the firm.

Not all the Calgary news was bad that summer. Under Bennett's presidency, Calgary Power Company had worked its way into a highly profitable existence. He had been personally responsible for getting franchises in Edmonton and Medicine Hat. The company had at last solved all its water-storage problems, obtained a couple of superb hydroelectric sites, and located contractors who could erect power plants without going broke as well as suppliers of generating equipment that worked to its satisfaction. At the 1917 annual meeting of the company in Montreal, Max Aitken, now Lord Beaverbrook, turned up with a sheaf of correspondence he had had with Bennett five years before. In this exchange he had offered Bennett contingency remuneration of $15,000 (par value) worth of Calgary Power shares a year to become president of the company. As the company was now earning a net profit of $300,000 a year, he suggested it was time to make good on that promise. He moved that $75,000 worth of the company $100 par value common shares be issued to Bennett to cover the five years he had served as president. Bennett protested that the figure was too generous by a third. He suggested it be reduced to $50,000. His suggestion was adopted by the meeting.[8]

The Calgary Power Company was clearly lapsing into a public-utility kind of prosperity that required only minimum calls on Bennett's time and attention. Such was not the case as far as the Eddy company and Jennie Shirreff Eddy were concerned. There was, for example, the maturing on 10 February 1916 of the E.B. Eddy trust. Ordinarily, the trustees would wind up the trust by distributing the assets as required by the Eddy will, but that was not the case with the Eddy trust.

In making a final check of the will and the trust on behalf of Mr Eddy, Bennett discovered a gaping legal discrepancy. Eddy left 125 shares of the Eddy company to each of his key executives of the company: president-to-be W.H. Rowley, general manager G.H. Mullen, treasurer S.S. Cushman, and lawyer J.J. Gormully. The condition attached to the bequest was that they were to serve the company in their present capacities at the present remuneration for the term of the trust – ten years. They were to serve as his executors and trustees for the same period without remuneration. As officers and directors of the Eddy company, they were not to increase dividends on the company shares beyond the current 6 per cent until a $3 million loan from the Bank of Montreal was reduced to $300,000.

At the time of Eddy's death, the four already owned about 900 of the company's outstanding 3000 shares of common stock. The bequests would bring their holdings to 1496, while Mrs Eddy, when she exercised her option to buy young Ezra (Bessey) Eddy's 250 share inheritance, would have 1504 shares. As the earnings of the Eddy company improved steadily after the founder's death, his trustee-executor-director quartet decided to boost the dividend payments well above the 6 per cent limit imposed by Eddy. The increased dividend was maintained for the balance of the term of the trust. When Bennett discovered what had been going on, he cried 'foul.'[9]

The cumulative total of the extra dividends paid out of the treasury of the Eddy company would dilute the value of Mrs Eddy's inheritance when the shares willed to her came into her possession. The Royal Trust Company was called in as trustee for the estates of Rowley and Cormully, who had died in the meantime. A deal was done, and Millen, Cushman, and the estates of Rowley and Gormully agreed to return on grand total of $122,488 to the Eddy company before they obtained their shares and accumulated cash dividends on those shares from the trust. In addition to her shares in the Eddy company, Mrs Eddy inherited $507,456.70 from the trust.

A year later, Bennett became involved in another off-pattern development. It came about in July 1917, with the amendment to the Business Profits War Tax Act of 1916.

Under the original business tax, Canadian corporations were allowed to earn and keep, tax free, 10 per cent of their invested capital and retained earnings. The 1916 tax levied a 7 per cent tax on earnings above that 10 per cent. The 1917 amendment sent the tax rate into orbit. The rate for earnings between 10 and 20 per cent was to be 50 per cent, and above 20 per cent the rate was to be 75 per cent. The earnings of the Eddy company, which had risen sharply to $600,000 in 1916, were running at double that level when the amendment went through. Like all directors, Mrs

Eddy, Bennett, and J.T. 'Harry' Shirreff, Mrs Eddy's brother whom she had appointed as vice-president, sat up and paid attention to the impact the new rates would have on their company. At the same time, a new group of auditors was discovering that the company had never followed the practice of deducting an allowance for depreciation of its plant and equipment before fixing its net profit for the year.[10] That had not mattered in the era before corporate taxation, though it had the effect of exaggerating the profitability of the company. After the 1917 business tax amendment, it mattered a lot.

The first task was to determine how much money was involved. The auditors put the figure at $1,108,357.81. For the tax collectors, that meant the Eddy company in 1916 would have paid substantially less taxes than if it had been making deductions for depreciation. If the depreciation was claimed in 1917, however, it would reduce the company's profits for purposes of taxation by perhaps $150,000. To bring the Eddy company into conformity with the rest of corporate Canada resulted in a long, difficult, and contentious negotiation between the company and the government. In the ultimate settlement, the company was permitted to deduct one-thirteenth of its back depreciation each year for thirteen years before computing its taxes.[11] The extent to which Bennett participated in these negotiations is not known, but the odds are overwhelming against his being able to stand clear of such a fascinating argument for very long.

During the 1917 election Bennett had received a most intriguing letter from Prime Minister Borden. The British government, he explained, had been earnestly considering how it might demonstrate its appreciation for the service rendered to the British Empire by British subjects in the dominions and colonies. It had decided on the 'Order of the British Empire,' and had written to the governor general for the names of worthy Canadians who could be recommended to the king. If Bennett would give his permission, Borden was prepared to recommend him for the honour. Bennett put the letter aside and did not reply to it immediately. Indeed, he did not reply until six months later. And what a reply it would be![12]

What was mainly on Bennett's mind as 1917 was winding down was his promised Senate appointment. Such appointments were by long-established custom the subject of intensive lobbying of the prime minister by supplicants and their supporters. Bennett, convinced he had the prime minister's promise, would have none of that. He refused to remind Borden of his promise or to have his friends do so. He left it strictly up to the prime minister. On 5 February 1918 Borden, now head of the Union Government, filled the new Alberta Senate seats. He appointed Edward Michener, the Conservative leader in the Alberta legislature from 1910 until 1917, and William Harmer, an obscure Liberal party worker who had never run for public office. Commenting on Harmer's appointment the next day, the *Albertan*, itself a Liberal party organ, wrote: 'It has been suggested to the Albertan that A.L. Sifton, always a democrat, is bent on the destruction of the Senate by making it look weak and ridiculous; hence the appointment to that body by Bill Harmer. In no other way can this unexpected appointment, which fell upon an unsuspecting public yesterday, be justified.'[13] The *Calgary Herald*, the Conservative paper, went on at greater length:

If it be true that the new government has got no farther away from cheap political tactics as this appointment shows, we may well begin to worry for the future. Mr. Harmer has performed no public action, nor has he attained any public or personal distinction that would justify his appointment to so honorable a body as the Senate of Canada. His record is that of a civil servant of very ordinary ability whose chief and almost only function has been to act as political manager for Hon. A.L. Sifton. His political reputation has not been such as to command public confidence or respect, nor has he ever placed himself before the public in a light which would cause him to be singled out for public honor or preferment. It needed so callous a politician as A.L. Sifton to make this appointment. It needed so innocent a premier as Sir Robert Borden to consent to it.[14]

If Borden had gone out deliberately to turn R.B. Bennett into a gibbering idiot, he could hardly have made a better, or worse, appointment. Bennett's antipathy for A.L. Sifton went back to his first membership in the Territorial Assembly and had deepened with the years. It was Sifton's impending appointment to the Union Government that provided the final nudge Bennett needed to take himself out of the 1917 general election.[15] If Bennett had been asked to name the Canadian politician he held in deepest contempt, there is little doubt the name of A.L. Sifton would have been at the top of the list. If Borden had chosen a distinguished Albertan in preference to Bennett it would not have been so bad, but a Sifton henchman?

There is no record of Bennett's immediate and explosive reaction to the Senate appointments, but he was hurt and humiliated by what he regarded as Borden's reneging in his promise. He began writing a letter to Borden on 14 April 1918 and did not finish it until three weeks later. It ran to almost twenty pages of handwritten prose, and covered Bennett's relationship with Borden from their pre-1911 conference to the offer of the OBE. It was the approaching deadline for accepting or declining that honour that, Bennett said, evoked the letter.

As for the Order of the British Empire, Bennett regarded it as a splendid idea. 'I am one of those who believes that a distinct value is attached to the wise and judicious distribution of honour by the Crown. I have ever been opposed to the conferring of hereditary titles upon Canadians resident in Canada. But I am convinced that the bestowal of honours has had a very considerable influence in creating and maintaining the almost affectionate relations that now exist between the outlying Dominions and dependencies of the Empire and the Motherland. Britons in all parts of the world are thus reminded that there is a centre of Empire and authority and that they owe allegiance to one Sovereign King and Emperor.'

It was clearly an honour he would be delighted to receive. And it was an honour that would be particularly appropriate for Bennett, since there were few Canadians more deeply committed to the British Empire, or capable of expressing that commitment more eloquently. But was it an honour that was being offered to him in recognition of his commitment to, of his service to, the

British Empire? Or was it being offered as a sop for the reneging by the prime minister on his promise of a senatorship? Aye, that was the rub!

Before Bennett got around to confronting Borden with that question at point-blank range, as it were, he went to considerable lengths to recall to the prime minister the circumstances under which the promise of a Senate appointment was made, as he reminded him of the Montreal meeting at which the cabinet position had been discussed. He described how they had met in the prime minister's temporary office in the Museum Building and what Borden had said about Bennett's entitlement to a senatorship. Bennett had gone into detail about how he proposed to use it to facilitate his rendering of service to the empire. They walked to the temporary House of Commons discussing the matter and continued the conversation as they sat together in the Commons Chamber. As the 1917 session of parliament wound down, Bennett mentioned his impending Senate appointment to several of his friends in the cabinet and other members from the west.

The letter contained considerable posturing by Bennett, along with references to obscure episodes in British parliamentary history, coupled with sly jibes at Borden that were designed more to bruise than to cut. The extent of Bennett's own bruising may be identified by the main concluding paragraphs of the letter:

I can say with a clear conscience that I have at no time sought honours. But I have desired useful and honourable service. I can challenge the criticism alike of friend and foe as to the disinterested character of my efforts to serve my day and generation to the best of my ability. At the end of long years of struggle I am discredited. My experience is wasted. Even my somewhat special knowledge of transportation problems in Canada cannot be utilized by my native land. Yet within the past two months two offers of employment quite directly connected with the war have come to me from men of international reputation. Acceptance involves leaving Canada. That at the moment I prefer not to do. I do not complain. The fault after all 'is with ourselves not with our stars that we are underlings.'

Having regard to the circumstances to which I have alluded I have therefore concluded:

1. That I cannot become the recipient of an honour bestowed upon me by the Crown, on your recommendation, if it is thereby intended to, shall I say, compensate me for my disappointment in not being appointed to the Senate. But –

2. That if your recommendation is made without reference to my not having been appointed to the Senate I will accept the honor.[16]

Borden, so far as can be discovered, never replied to Bennett's letter, so there is no way of assessing how it affected him and how he reacted to it. But there is evidence to contradict Bennett's assumption that the OBE was offered as a sop for not getting the senatorship. The governor general, the Duke of Devonshire, had called Borden in on 11 February 1917 to apprise him of the impending creation of the new order, and suggested Borden himself and Sir Wilfrid Laurier to be a recipient of the first order. Borden was not overly eager on his own account, said he would prefer that the honour go to others, and mentioned several names, including 'Flavelle, Bennett, Marshall and Lady Drummond.'[17] Clearly, Borden had Bennett in mind for an OBE well before he named Harmer to the Senate seat.

Borden's discovery from the letter of how important Bennett regarded his Senate appointment must have come as a shattering surprise. What did Bennett really need with a senatorship? He was well on his way to becoming a millionaire, if he was not one already, and he was a most successful lawyer.

Senatorships, fundamentally, were an integral part of the lubricating device that kept political party machines in good running order. Borden took Senate appointments very seriously, and none was ever made without long discussions with such 'political' cabinet ministers as Robert Rogers of Manitoba, Frank Cochrane of Ontario, and E.L. Patenaude of Quebec. Senate appointments were the sparkling baubles that kept otherwise recalcitrant back-benchers in line, were useful rewards for long-service party worker, and a sometimes solution to the problem of caring for impoverished former members of parliament. But what was there about Bennett that got him so bemused by a senatorship? An equally intriguing question is what Borden might have remembered about his conversation with Bennett on the Senate appointment? Did he remember actually promising Bennett the appointment? Did he take seriously Bennett's idea of using a senatorship to advance the cause of a better-organized empire? Could anybody have done so? Had he, perhaps, simply forgotten all about his conversation with Bennett when he was being lobbied by Arthur Sifton to name Bill Harmer to the Senate? There is not a single mention of Bennett and the Senate appointment in the Borden diaries.

Bennett's name came off Borden's list of recommendations for the Order of the British Empire. That much we know, and it is about all we know. If it were not for the fact that Bennett did not get an OBE, the assumption that Borden had even read the letter might be untenable. It reached Borden's desk at the most critical hour of the First World War, and of Canada's participation in it.

The Haig-Robertson offensive of 1917 had failed ignominiously with 400,000 British casualties, including the 15,000 Canadians killed and wounded at Passchendaele. The need for increased reinforcements that resulted from these casualties intensified the demand for conscription. Then came the total withdrawal of the Russians from the war, which enabled the Germans to move fifty divisions of battle-hardened troops from Russia to the Western front. That gave the Germans substantial superiority in men and material with which to mount the 'final offensive of the war' to destroy the Allied armies before the main American army could reach France. That offensive was launched on 21 March 1918. By the time Bennett's letter reached Borden's office, Field Marshall Haig was preparing to issue his stand-and-die-to-the-last-man order to the British army. Within a month, the British Fifth Army was destroyed and the Germans were within a hair's breadth of winning the war. Long before this the Canadian cabinet was in almost continuous session trying to determine how best to respond to Prime Minister David Lloyd George's cable on 31 March to the Duke of Devonshire:

I would urge the Government of Canada to reinforce its heroic troops in the fullest possible manner with the smallest possible delay. The struggle is only in its opening stages and it is our business to see that our armies get the maximum measure of support that we can give them. Let no one think that what even the remotest of our Dominions can do will be too late. Before this campaign is finished the last man may count.

Until the receipt of the Lloyd George cable, the Military Service Act of 1917 had been working reasonably well towards its military objectives. It had immediately doubled the monthly intake into the army to 6000 men. It was, however, running behind the pace required to reach its goal of 100,000 recruits during the year of 1918. At the same time, the debate over conscription had caused the most severe strain on the civilian front. Vigorous opposition developed among the farm population. At the end of March an armed skirmish in Quebec City caused several deaths, massive property damage, and led to the imposition of martial law.

Canada's problem, simply stated, was that it had undertaken too heavy a burden. It did not have the manpower to fulfil all its war-production goals, food-production goals and military goals. In order to get the Military Service Act through the House of Commons in 1917, substantial concessions had to be made to the civilian side of the war effort. Farmers were explicitly exempted from being conscripted and a series of appeal boards were established to hear applications for exemption. In the run up to the 1917 election, the Unionist party had published a series of advertisements in western papers emphasizing the farmers' exemption.[18] On his speaking tour on behalf of national registration and again in his support for the Unionist cause, Bennett had focused his emphasis on the need to keep the farmers on their farms producing food. But by the spring of 1918, conditions had so changed that something had to give. The government decided it had to choose between food production and reinforcing the army. It opted for the Army and, on 20 April, passed an order-in-council ending the exemption of farmers from military service.

Specifically, it made all males under the age of twenty-three subject to conscription. It also reduced the minimum age from twenty to nineteen years. It did, however, retain provisions for appeals to the tribunals, which were still permitted to grant postponements pending completion of a farming operation and outright exemption in cases of extreme hardship.

By this time the government had done several other things. It had enacted an 'anti-loafing' law, which made it illegal for any adult Canadian male not to be gainfully employed. All civilian males were required to carry on their persons their exemption certificates from the military service tribunals. They were required to produce these certificates on demand by any law officer, civilian or military. It was thus possible for a young-looking male to be accosted several times during a stroll down his street to justify his civilian existence. If he failed to do so, he was subject to instant arrest. That happened in Fort Macleod, Alberta, in early June 1918 to a half-dozen young American homesteaders from the Peace River Country who were on their way back to the United States to enlist in the American army. Four of them, given the choice by a Calgary magistrate before whom they appeared, opted to enlist in the Canadian army instead. Two others, who rejected that choice, were fined $20 for failure to produce the documents and sent on their way south.[19]

The order-in-council of 20 April was quickly approved by the House and Senate and, within a matter of days, the government had a near insurrection on its hands. On 14 May a group of 5000 farmers from Ontario and Quebec stormed Parliament Hill demanding the right to present its case to the House of Commons. The group was accompanied by provincial cabinet ministers from Quebec and the leaders of the United Farmers of Ontario. The farm leaders claimed that the changes would cut Canadian food production by 25 per cent, to which Sir Robert Borden replied that if the government had to choose between food production and reinforcements for the army in France, it was choosing the latter. Despite protest meetings by the organized farmers, it stuck to its position. Orders went out to all farmers on the Military Service Board's rolls who were under twenty-three years of age to report by specified dates to their nearest military establishment for induction into the Canadian army.

In Calgary, Military District 13 consisted of two separate establishments. The headquarters was on a square mile of territory on the western edge of the city where Sarcee Camp was located. In the heart of downtown at the Victoria Park Exhibition Grounds there was a manning pool. On receipt of orders to report for induction into the army, the potential soldiers headed for Victoria Park. On completing their physical examinations, they were fitted with uniforms and introduced to parade-ground drill. Then they were transferred to Sarcee for assignment to battalions and shipment, within a matter of days, to Ontario and Quebec, where they would undergo advanced training to prepare them as reinforcements for the front-line troops in France.

It was to the Victoria Park manning pool that a young Calgary district farmer named Norman Earl Lewis reported on 8 June 1918. A half mile away, young Lewis's father was climbing the stairs to the second floor of the Clarence Block for an appointment with R.B. Bennett. His intention was to retain Bennett to find a way to get his son released from the service so they could complete their pre-harvest preparations on their family farm.

There was no more dedicated conscriptionist in Calgary than R.B. Bennett, but he was a conscriptionist with a difference. He believed in a balanced war effort that gave as high a priority to food production as it did to military service. So, he believed, did the parliament of Canada when it passed the Military Service Act, which exempted active farmers from liability for military service. In face of the bitterness of the debate that had preceded the Military Service Act and the extreme care that had been taken to meet the desires of Canada's million farmers, Bennett was convinced the government's action in amending the law by order-in-council when parliament was sitting was ultra vires. In the venacular, the government was playing dirty pool. It was with some enthusiasm, then, that Bennett agreed to represent the Lewis family.

He applied to the Supreme Court of Alberta for a writ of habeas corpus to compel the army to release young Lewis. He did so, however, in the name of the father rather than the son because, as he explained in court, he did not wish to expose the younger Lewis to the ill treatment the army frequently inflicted on conscriptees who had tried to avoid military service. The court ruled such a petition in error. Bennett then took action in the name of Norman Lewis.

It has long been an accepted practice in British law that when an appeal for habeas corpus finds it way onto a court calendar it is moved to the top of the list, regardless of how cluttered a court schedule may be. The full Alberta Supreme Court composed of Chief Justice Harvey and Justices Hyndman, Stuart, Beck, and Simmons convened to hear the Lewis case on 21 June, with Bennett and A.M. Sinclair for Lewis and James Muir for the minister of justice.[20] After two days of hearings, the court adjourned for a week and brought down its decision on 28 June 1918. The verdict of the court, by a margin of four to one, with only the chief justice dissenting, found that Bennett was right, that only an act of parliament, rather than an order-in-council, could extinguish the rights established by the Military Service Act. The court granted Bennett's petition to have Lewis brought before the court and released, but ordered execution of the order held for two weeks to enable the dominion government to appeal its decision to the Supreme Court of Canada.

All this caused scarcely a ripple on the surface of Calgary, perhaps because the verdict came down on the beginning of the long Dominion Day weekend, which also happened to be the eve of the opening of the Calgary exhibition. Ottawa's reaction was an instant and a trenchantly worded press release: it would ignore the Alberta Supreme Court and proceed with the conscription of young farmers while it awaited the result of the appeal it was launching to the Supreme Court of Canada.

Meanwhile, newspaper-reading lawyers all across the country sat up and paid attention to what Bennett had wrought. They began to troop into court with habeas corpus applications on behalf of other young farmers. In Calgary Leo H. Miller turned up with eleven applications, and other lawyers quickly ran the number of applications on file to twenty and beyond.[21]

When the sheriff attempted to serve the writ of habeas corpus on Lieutenant-Colonel Philip Moore, who was in charge of the Victoria Park barracks, armed sentries refused to admit the sheriff's men to the grounds. The same thing happened when they went to the Sarcee Barracks, where Colonel M.D. Macdonald was in command of Military District 13. The sheriff returned to the Supreme Court empty handed.

The court reconvened after the fourteen day grace period, expecting Moore to appear with Norman Lewis. Instead it was Major J.M. Carson, the assistant judge advocate general, who appeared from Ottawa with a brand new order-in-council that he presented to the court. It not only ordered the Canadian army to ignore the judgment of the Appeal Court of Alberta, but instructed it to pay no attention to any subsequents judgments and to get on with gathering in the conscripts as if nothing had happened. The partial text of PC 1697 read:

Whereas the acting minister of militia and defence represents that military conditions make it imperatively necessary that the principle of this judgement should not be permitted to have effect, and that it is impossible to suspend the operation of the order-in-council pending an appeal if the exigencies of the military situation are to be met.

Therefore his Excellency the Governor General, on recommendation of the acting prime minister, is pleased to order and direct, and doth order and direct, that men whose exemptions were cancelled pursuant to the provision of the order in council of 20th April 1918, above referred to, be dealt with in all respects as provided for in the said order in council, and not withstanding the judgement, or any order that may be made by any court, and that instruction be sent accordingly to the general and other officers commanding military districts in Canada.

In presenting the order-in-council to the court, Carson made it the occasion to impugn the patriotism of those involved with the present proceedings and to lash out at the lawyers who were counselling clients to disobey orders to report for military service. The chief justice replied that the proper procedure was through the courts. And, he added ominously: 'That is the trouble on the other side. The people did not observe the laws. If the military authorities here disrespect the courts I would not be surprised if there was a revolution here.'

By 12 July the confrontation between the military and the Alberta Appeal Court had driven even the German offensive out of the front-page headlines of the *Calgary Herald*. Other lawyers, moving into court on Bennett's coat-tails, as it were, were seizing the initiative. J.E. Varley and Leo Miller asked that writs be issued to the sheriff to arrest Lieutenant-Colonel Moore and to bring him into court along with the draftees. The chief justice, however, held off and gave the military until 2 pm to change its mind and produce Moore. Two o'clock came and went and the military still defied the court. Egged on by the sensational coverage the newspapers were now giving the confrontation, the Calgary public had so jammed access into the court-house itself that Moore would have had great difficulty getting in if he had appeared on the scene. When he did not, the chief justice issued a writ of attachment to the sheriff to bring Moore and the enlistees into court. It waited until six o'clock that evening, in vain. Once again the sheriff was denied entry to Victoria Park by armed sentries.

The issue came to a head the next day, 13 July, when the chief justice was faced with the challenge of upholding the civil law by ordering the sheriff to proceed to the barracks with whatever force he deemed necessary to arrest Moore. If the army defied the sheriff and his force, bloodshed might well have resulted. Into this conflict a prominent local lawyer, H.P.O. Savory, intruded with a suggestion. On behalf of the mayor of Calgary and the city commissioners, he invited the military authorities and the civilian and military lawyers to adjourn to the city hall and try to work out a compromise that would hold until the Supreme Court of Canada had a chance to decide the case.

The crux of the matter was no longer the fine point of legal interpretation. It was the physical bodies of the conscripts. Of the men taken on strength since Bennett launched his action, more than two-thirds had already been shipped east for training outside the jurisdiction of the Alberta Court of Appeal. It would have been a simple matter for the military to ship out all the others along with Moore, and to face the court with a fait accompli. The compromise ultimately reached that night saved everybody's face. Until the Lewis case got to the Supreme Court of Canada, Colonel Macdonald would undertake not to ship out any more conscripts until he had given the sheriff twenty-four hours notice in writing that he intended to do so. Ottawa acquiesced to the compromise, and the Court of Appeal agreed to a stay of proceedings against Moore.

For Bennett, there was a touch of irony in the way the conscription crisis moved to dénouement. He had started the action and drew all the static. But it was the other lawyers who followed him into court who became prominently active in the confrontation between the Alberta Court of Appeal and the Canadian government and Military District 13. Then, when the government filed its action in the Supreme Court of Canada, it bypassed Bennett's Lewis case in favour of an Ontario case involving a young farmer named George Edward Grey, who was under detention for disobeying orders. His lawyer had applied directly to a judge of the Supreme Court of Canada for a writ of habeas corpus, and the application was referred to the full court. By the time the Lewis case reached Ottawa the Supreme Court had already rejected the Grey application and declared, by a vote of four to two, that the order-in-council of 20 April was legal.

And where did all this leave R.B. Bennett? Mud-splattered. The *Calgary Herald*, his staunchest newspaper supporter in western Canada, deserted him. In the midst of the uproar at the court-house on 12 July, it led off its Note and Comment column with this sarcastic jibe: 'R.B. Bennett, K.C. ex-M.P., must be proud of his handiwork.'

In an adjacent column, a leading editorial consisted of an eight-inch animadversion on the role of 'bedevilers' in wartime Canadian society. It defined the species as 'a fellow who takes delight in tossing monkey wrenches into a delicate piece of machinery and grins with pleasure at the resultant confusion.' Its conclusion was that Canada had too many of these bedevilers for its own good, given the abnormal conditions that prevailed. The editorial was obviously focused on the habeas corpus proceedings seeking to block the enforcement of conscription.

When Bennett arrived in Ottawa for the Supreme Court hearing, the *Ottawa Journal* had some scathing comments to make about his oratorical style, his lack of any real influence on the parliament in which he sat, and the gain for the country in his absence from it. The *Herald* reprinted that editorial as a front-page news item. On 20 July, after the Supreme Court verdict, the *Herald* returned to a more extensive examination of the role of lawyers searching for technicalities that could be used to frustrate the legitimate actions of governments in emergency conditions: 'Legal gentlemen who have busied themselves in the effort to put a spoke in the wheel of military action by the government occupy a somewhat unenviable position ... An adverse decision by the Supreme Court ... might have very seriously affected Canada's war activities for months to come. If an ordinary citizen were to attempt anything like that he would be roundly scored, and rightly so. Because a citizen happens to be a lawyer is he specially privileged in such matters?'

Ironically enough, Bennett never did get the Lewis case before the Supreme Court. It was not considered because the judgment handed down in the Grey case, which upheld the legality of the conscription order-in-council, covered all the issues raised by the Lewis case. It was decided that the full Supreme Court would have to consider that appeal. Then the court calendar became too heavy and it was put over until the following session in the early winter of 1919. By then the war was over.

Peace came to Calgary, as it did to all Canada, on the wings of the outbreak of the great influenza epidemic of 1918. In Calgary the schools were closed, along with theatres and churches, and people were required to wear gauze antiseptic masks over their faces. But that did not stop a wild public celebration that went on far into the night of 11 November, and the following day, a solemn thanksgiving service in the new downtown Armories on Eleventh Street at Eight Avenue. Hurriedly organized by Colonel M.D. Macdonald, a half-dozen military units paraded to the service, which featured a speech by Bennett and a religious service conducted by Major G.M. Barrow. Macdonald, despite their recent unhappy confrontation on opposite sides in the Lewis case, welcomed Bennett warmly to the service and thanked him, on behalf of the military, for the splendid armory that he had been able to procure for Calgary when he was member of parliament for the city.

Bennett came through the flu epidemic unscathed, only to be laid low in the spring of 1919 by an attack of erysipelas that left him incapacitated for much of the year. It was an affliction that came and went. His face and upper torso would break out in a rash of dollar-sized blotches, which, as they faded, left him with severe headaches and extremely painful areas. After two or three days, the sore spots would disappear, only to return a week or so later. No treatment for the disease seemed to work and, in the end, his Calgary physician suggested a change of scenery. Perhaps Calgary's dry climate had something to do with it and an extended seaside vacation might have some effect.[22] Bennett spent a good deal of time on the east coast that summer, which enabled him to renew his acquaintanceship with Dr A.S. Mackenzie, president of Dalhousie University. Mackenzie was deeply into planning a rebuilding campaign to celebrate the centenary of the founding of the university. One of the projects they discussed was the construction of a new women's residence on the campus. This appealed to Bennett as something he could take back to Ottawa and present to a wealthy widow he knew, as a project she might like to undertake as a memorial to her parents. As Bennett would later write to Mackenzie, her income that year would probably exceed $250,000, but 'she lives as though she had an income of $100 a month. But she has a good heart.'[23]

The lady, of course, was Jennie Eddy, who early the next year would decide to donate $300,000 to Dalhousie to erect a women's residence to be known as Shirreff Hall in memory of her father and mother, John and Henrietta Shirreff. Her father, she was proud to recall, had been high sheriff of Northumberland County, New Brunswick, for twenty-five years. Mrs Eddy, alas, did not live to see the completion of her project. Shirreff Hall was the first of two magnificent donations she made to Dalhousie, for on her death she set up a $350,000 trust fund to go to the university.[24]

Bennett maintained his interest in the construction of Shirreff Hall after Mrs Eddy's death. He and Harry Shirreff visited the construction site several times. Once, on a visit to Minneapolis, Bennett's eye caught some laminated doors that appealed to him. He sought out the manufacturer, got the details of their construction, and sent them off to Dr Mackenzie. He also mounted a campaign to have each of the eighty rooms in the dormitory provided with running water. That, as Mackenzie discovered when he investigated, was a dumb idea.[25] The drains were forever becoming clogged, and the girls disliked the idea of washbasins protruding visibly into their rooms.

After planting the idea of funding the construction of Shirreff Hall in Mrs Eddy's mind, Bennett returned to Calgary in the late summer of 1919, free of erysipelas at last, to become deeply involved in the affairs of the Red Cross. He was elected chairman of the Alberta chapter and became its delegate to the Winnipeg convention of the western region. The organization was in the process of converting from wartime to peacetime activities, with a long stopover in the reconstruction of war-torn Europe. From Winnipeg it was on to the national convention at Toronto, where Bennett was named to represent the Canadian Red Cross at the international convention at Geneva the following March. At this point Bennett heard from Dr Mackenzie that Dalhousie was going to award him the honorary degree of Doctor of Laws, but he had to beg off attendance at the fall convocation because of his previous Red Cross commitments.

Erysipelas, the affairs of Dalhousie University, and the Alberta Red Cross more or less accounted for R.B. Bennett's year in 1919. Certainly his divorcement from politics was complete. He made no speeches and seems to have conducted no correspondence as the political turmoil mounted in western Canada. The world around him was one with which he was rapidly losing any familiarity.

The trade unions he had supported so enthusiastically twenty years before were now marching to the drums of the militant

British socialists who were setting class against class and tearing the economies of the cities asunder with their strikes. A verbal civil war was raging among consumers, producers, manufacturers, and retailers over who was responsible for the high cost of living. And out in the countryside the farmers were deserting both the Liberals and Conservatives in favour of the class-action Progressive party. The Alberta farmers, who had been given a glimpse of the promised land by three years of high prices, would be brought back to reality by crop failure and a collapse in farm prices. The eternal economic verities were proving ephemeral to the touch. Faith in the future of real estate was a casualty of war. In January 1920 the *Herald* reported there were 690 houses standing empty in Calgary. And Bennett himself would be writing to the Royal Securities Company that there was no point in having the Alliance Trust Company provide it with a note to cover its indebtedness to Lord Beaverbrook since the Alliance Trust might be going into liquidation. Bennett was president of Alliance Trust, a company Beaverbrook himself had promoted in 1911.[26]

Bennett's withdrawal from political activity, however, could not be described as total divorcement. D.L. Redman, who succeeded Bennett as Conservative member of parliament for Calgary West, in 1917 practised law with the Lougheed and Bennett firm. When their paths crossed, in Ottawa as well as in Calgary, they compared notes on the inner turmoil that was shaking Borden's Unionist party. And Bennett's interest in Conservative party politics would certainly have been prodded back to life when Borden resigned and was succeeded by Arthur Meighen. Meighen's efforts to persuade Bennett to join the new cabinet he was putting together in the summer of 1921 proves that Bennett's bitter needling during the Mackenzie and Mann debates had not permanently damaged their relationship.[27]

Bennett was in Ottawa quite frequently in the early months of 1921 after Jennie Eddy was taken ill. She underwent surgery in March and seemed to be making a good recovery when peritonitis set in and she died in her home in Hull on 9 August 1921 at the age of fifty-seven. During her long illness the future of the Eddy company was very much on her mind. With the company's spectacular earning record – before-tax profits in 1920 were $1,427,629 – she would have had no trouble finding a buyer of her controlling interest for several millions of dollars.[28] Instead, she became more convinced than ever that her late husband's establishment of the ten-year trust was the wisest course he could have taken. During her convalescence, her mind turned to devising a way to draw up a will that would utilize the trust idea to further extend the life of the E.B. Eddy Company.[29]

Childless in marriage, Jennie Eddy in 1917 shared her home with her brother Harry, a childless widower. She also had a sister, Edith Richardson, who lived in California. A sprinkling of first and second cousins in New Brunswick and the United States accounted for the rest of her relatives. With the cash she received on the maturing of the Eddy trust in 1916 – $507,406 – plus the subsequent dividends, Jennie Eddy had more than enough cash on hand to meet all the deserving bequests she might want to make. Her solicitor, T.P. Foran, has recalled how she busied herself with drawing up holograph wills for him to translate into proper legalese.[30]

When all the relatives had been taken care of, including an income trust for her sister, down to surviving children of second cousins, Jennie Eddy had enough cash on hand for a handsome bequest to the Presbyterian church and to all the private charities she could think of. And that still left her the controlling interest in the Eddy company to dispose of. What could she possibly do with her Eddy shares that made sense? Leave them to her brother Harry, who was five years her senior and beginning to show signs of developing a drinking problem? The more she thought about it the stronger became her memory of her late husband's injunction – perpetuate the existence of the company that bore his name. She had assisted that process by consenting to the establishment of the ten-year trust to hold her shares. Why not establish her own trust to hold the shares for her brother and R.B. Bennett and then, at the end of the trust, let them worry about what to do? Why not, indeed? According to a biographical sketch of Bennett in the archives of the Conservative party in the National

Archives of Canada, it was her original idea to leave her entire holding of Eddy stock to Bennett. He knew nothing of her intentions and, when he did find out, he insisted they be split between her brother and himself, 1007 shares to Shirreff and 500 to him.[31]

To ensure that the control of the Eddy company remained intact, Shirreff and Bennett had reciprocal wills drawn leaving the shares to each other in case of death. When Shirreff wooed and married a comely secretary in the Eddy office a couple of years later, he had Foran draw up a marriage contract that removed his Eddy shares from his estate. That, as Bennett was quick to point out to Shirreff, would leave his new wife almost penniless if he died. The executors of his estate would be forced to sell a block of his Eddy shares to pay Quebec's succession duties. At Bennett's behest, Foran drew up a new will for Shirreff. It provided that Bennett would establish a trust fund of $250,000 that would pay Mrs Shirreff $1000 a month for life. It also made Bennett liable for the succession duties on Shirreff's estate, estimated at $250,000. (This estimate turned out to be deficient by $100,000.)[32] Then, and only then, would the 1007 shares of Eddy stock pass to Bennett.

Bennett's erysipelas was at last clearing up as 1920 waned. In the winter he had found the energy for a trip to Switzerland for a Red Cross convention, followed by an extended visit with Beaverbrook in London. He was now spending more time away than he was in Calgary. In addition to the increased demands the Eddy company was making on his time, he was a director of the Metropolitan Life Insurance Company of New York, whose Canadian head office was in Ottawa.

On his extended visits to Ottawa, he usually stayed at the Rideau Club, the favourite lunching spot for cabinet ministers, lobbyist, and hinterland lawyers with Supreme Court appearances pending. It was inevitable that Bennett's path would cross that of Arthur Meighen, frequently. Despite their bitter verbal passages at arms over railway subsidies in the Conservative caucus and in the House of Commons seven years before, the two remained firm friends. Indeed, Meighen and Max Aitken seem to have been the only friends who communicated with Bennett on a first-name basis.

Any conversation between Bennett and Meighen was bound to turn to politics and Bennett's political intentions. A combination of fifty-two months of war, the Paris Peace Conference, and the strain of coping with the economic crisis gripping Canada was taking such a toll of Sir Robert Borden's health that his imminent retirement was regarded as a certainty. By Dominion Day, 1920, he had had enough and he retired as leader of the Unionist party and prime minister on 10 July. The government caucus turned almost automatically to Arthur Meighen to succeed him.

Meighen's role as Borden's successor had been taken for granted within and without the party caucus, so that Meighen could have felt no hesitation about discussing Bennett's future with him, discussions that included an offer of a cabinet post in the Meighen administration, if and when it came to fruitition. This, however, was a different Bennett in 1920–1 from the man who, in 1911, had been persuaded by Robert Borden to run for parliament. He was no longer persuadable by vague promises about possible places in the cabinet. He wanted specifics and he wanted them in writing. Meighen's first offer was the Ministry of Railways and Canals, a fitting post for anyone of Bennett's expertise in railway operations in Canada. Bennett turned that offer down. Then Meighen offered the Ministry of the Interior. Bennett rejected that, too. The negotiations went on desultorily during the summer, accompanied by considerable public speculation over Bennett's intentions. Thus, when newspaper reporters questioned him during the Canadian Bar Association convention in Ottawa, they got only vague and noncommital answers. When he returned to Calgary, 'he will he won't' stories appeared in the local newspapers, along with one report that he would seek to win the Calgary West seat as an independent. The speculation ended on 21 September 1921, with the announcement that Bennett had been appointed minister of justice.[33]

The fact was that Bennett had committed himself weeks before to returning to politics as a supporter of Arthur Meighen as leader of the Conservative party. In a letter to Meighen from Calgary on

23 May, Bennett made his return to politics conditional on two minor points: that Meighen should strengthen his cabinet, not only in Quebec but in Ontario as well, and that there should not be an immediate election. His comments upon their mutual relationships are most interesting:

Your political principles are those which I have always supported. I see no reason for believing that either of us has erred in his profession of faith...I have profound faith in the future of Canada. Yet I cannot but believe that if the policies or our opponents are really chrystallized into legislation the very integrity of the Dominion would be menaced...I should not like to think that I have shrunk from discharging my duty merely because the problems that confront us are difficult, the conditions of life onerous and the outlook for the future dark and gloomy.

...I have therefore concluded...to place my services loyalty and unreservedly under your Premiership, at the disposal of the country...Sharing your political beliefs, I feel that to decline an invitation to public service at this time would be a confession of either fear or cowardice...

I need hardly say I am deeply touched and honoured by your consideration. We have had differences, through all of which our friendship has not been destroyed, and we share the same abiding confidence in the future of our country as of the Commonwealths comprising the British Empire.[34]

The election in Alberta was in part a replay of the 1911 contest: the protective tariff versus free trade. This time, however, the Liberals were replaced by the United Farmers of Alberta – the Progressives – who had added a demand for the restoration of the Wheat Board to demands for free trade in farm implements and farm products. Bennett's main opponent in Calgary West was J.T. Shaw, a Liberal-Farmer-Labour candidate. Bennett was delayed in starting his campaign by a gas-rate hearing of the Public Utilities Board, which went on for two weeks at the end of September. He was counsel for the city of Calgary. Then he was off to Ottawa for a week on the business of the attorney-general. During the second half of October Bennett's speech-making included rallies in Calgary West and two or three speeches a day through rural southern Alberta. He also travelled to Saskatchewan to assist the national campaign.

The electors of 1921, however, were no longer willing to listen to reason, so many meetings were poorly attended. They were in open revolt against the established order, against crop failures and low wheat prices, against the high cost of living, against all governments, whether Liberals in Manitoba and Alberta or Unionists in Ottawa. When the votes were counted on 6 December, the Conservatives suffered the greatest defeat in Canadian political history. They were wiped out completely in Prince Edward Island, Nova Scotia, and Quebec and the only successful candidate on the Prairies was Bennett himself, but not for long. On a judicial recount, his twenty-vote majority became a sixteen-vote deficit when the judge ruled all ballots marked with fountain pens and coloured pencils for Bennett were illegal.[35] Bennett was outraged at the decision, even though the election act specifically stipulated that ballots had to be marked by black lead pencils. Subsequently he lost his appeals to the Court of Appeal in Alberta and the Supreme Court of Canada.

The streak of proud stubbornness that Bennett brought to Calgary twenty-five years before was never so sharply etched as it was in those appeals. In the earlier years it was evinced by his carrying, at his own cost, appeals against magisterial decisions in picayune cases involving miniscule penalties. In the intervening years that streak had lengthened and broadened and thickened until 1922 and the Supreme Court hearing of the election appeal. It was, of course, costly from a financial point of view. It was, additionally, an appeal that Bennett could not afford to win from every other consideration. Winning would consign him to another back-bench seat in parliament for the duration of the Tenth Ministry, however long it survived. But this time it would be on the opposition benches, where he would be totally devoid of influence on the affairs of the country and with drastically reduced access to its key administrators.

In a roundabout way, it was the Supreme Court of Canada hearing that touched the spark to the tinder that blew the Lougheed and Bennett partnership apart. This explosion ignited antagonisms of such intensity in Bennett that they bridged

10,000 miles and burned with undiminished vigour twenty years later. At the time of the Supreme Court hearing Bennett's disenchantment was all-embracing – with Calgary, Alberta, Canada, politics, and the practice of law. He bared his feeling in a long letter to Beaverbrook from Calgary on 13 March 1922. It was his first letter to Beaverbrook since before the election and he devoted part of it to an explanation of his reason for running, his assessment of his chances, and his evaluation of the result. Then he went on:

Conditions in Canada have never been as bad as they now are, and in my judgment, the next five months will be the worst that the Dominion has ever known. The western crop, which was very indifferent, has been disposed of. There is therefore no east bound traffic for the railways, and as financial confidence has not returned, there is no purchasing power in this section of Canada. The manufacturers are without orders and until there is some assurance that a crop will be harvested this fall, I look with great alarm upon the future. It is only necessary for me to add that if there is no crop this fall Canada will be an excellent country to leave.[36]

An extreme judgment, surely, but only if the one making that assessment was unaware of the severity of the change in conditions in Alberta. The great crops of the war years and the high prices that prevailed after the closing of the grain futures markets were gone, seemingly forever. With the reopening of the Grain Exchange, wheat prices declined from $2.80 a bushel in 1919 to $1.20 in 1921 – and at a time when drought was coming back to Alberta. Wheat yields that had averaged thirty bushels to the acre in 1915 were down to six bushels in 1918, eight bushels in 1919, and ten bushels in 1921. The bumper crop of 1915 and the high prices of the next three years had launched prairie farmers on land-buying sprees at rising land prices, saddling them with debt burdens they would find impossible to carry with $1.00 wheat. The farm depression was having its impact on the Alberta Pacific Grain Company as well as on its customers. Bennett's dividend income from the grain company in 1921 dropped to $8735 from the $50,000 a year it had been averaging.[37]

Bennett, as he set about composing the letter to Beaverbrook, was obviously deeply concerned with what to do with the rest of his life. He noted that he might be in England soon, that he was seldom in western Canada, and that he did not contemplate living in Calgary much longer. By this time he had announced his decision to retire from the partnership with Lougheed and to leave Calgary, perhaps to move permanently to England. He had written to several of the lawyers with the firm and had spoken to others about his plans in general terms. A.M. Sinclair, who had carried the bulk of the litigation work for the firm for the better part of a decade, expressed his interest in buying Bennett's share of the partnership.[38] Indeed, Sinclair, who clearly felt he had been carrying a disproportionate share of the workload for an inadequate share of the income, was making noises about leaving the firm altogether. And there were reports that W.H. McLaws, who, after his dismissal from the firm in 1918, had abandoned law in favour of a business career in Vancouver, was back in Calgary looking for an opportunity to return to the practice of law. That was where Bennett's law practice in Calgary stood when he left for Ottawa early in June 1922 for his appearance before the Supreme Court on his election appeal. He would also make time to consult with Lougheed on the question of dissolution of the partnership. Sinclair, who was to represent Bennett on the appeal, would join that discussion.

The talks with Lougheed were still in the preliminary stages when Bennett received a cable from England that an appeal he had launched with the Privy Council had been set for immediate hearing. This forced him to rush off to Montreal, before seeing Sinclair, to catch a boat for England. In his opinion, the conclusion of the partnership dissolution was put off until his return to Calgary in the fall of 1922. After the Privy Council hearing, he had plans to spend some time in London before taking a month's holiday on the Continent. There the matter rested until 19 July, when Bennett received a cable from Lougheed in Calgary: 'Acting on Ottawa conversation Sinclair will purchase your interest as mentioned and organize a new firm of myself, Sinclair, Hannah,

Redman, Sanford who will assume present guarantees. Unless immediate steps taken dissolution probable. Cable reply.'[39]

The cable indicates quite clearly that a profound difference of opinion existed between Lougheed and Bennett over what precisely had been talked about during their meeting in Ottawa. Lougheed believed they had discussed Bennett's terms for winding up the firm and selling his interests to Sinclair; Lougheed, in return, had communicated those terms to Sinclair, who had agreed to them. Bennett remembered no such specific details discussed. Rather, his memory was of an agreement to put everything off until his return. Bennett's reply to the cable, when he got over the shock of receiving it, read: 'Cable settlement of important questions involving future activities clearly impossible. Must await my return.'

As the days passed and Bennett did not hear further from Lougheed, he might well have assumed that his cable had settled matters and that the terms of settlement would be worked out when he got back to Calgary. Then, ten days after receipt of the first cable from Lougheed, he received a second cable on 29 July: 'Your cable answering mine so adds to uncertainty of firm affairs that Sinclair and Redman have served notice of dissolution to me. No other alternative now remains than dissolution, of which this is notice.' Bennett's reaction to Lougheed's second cable was remarkably restrained and conciliatory. He replied on 31 July: 'Hoped different termination 25 years association and effort. Greatly hurt action taken during absence. Will hasten return to protect property and professional rights. Sincerely trust avoidance meantime causes possible friction and deplorable bitterness. Still believe friendly settlement whole situation preferable and possible.'

Meanwhile, Alex Hannah, a senior barrister with the firm who had been vacationing in Scotland, came to London to discuss the Calgary situation with Bennett. Hannah, if he could not be described as a friend, was certainly a Bennett loyalist. He reported that the 'partnership' was flying apart and that the 'deplorable bitterness' that concerned Bennett had already settled into the office. It was only to be expected that Bennett's hope for a friendly settlement was doomed. Then, on 3 August Lougheed dispatched a long cable that closed off the possibility of any further negotiation:

You told me Ottawa break-up of office threatened and nothing here further interested you. Also offered to sell Sinclair your interest and requested me to see and make arrangements with Sinclair and the others on my arrival. Redman also had letter from you saying nothing left here for you and you negotiating sale with Sinclair, also to make arrangements with me otherwise a complete breakup. You also wrote Brokovski to see me. You also informed Sanford you were withdrawing. Sinclair requiring confirmation from you sell him your interest, but your reply so unsatisfactory that Sinclair gave notice of immediate withdrawal. Sinclair made arrangements join McLaws followed by Redman. This meant complete break-up of practice founded by me, and to protect my own interest, including old firms obligations, have joined partnership above parties, otherwise I would be main victim of break-up. Old firms interests receiving every protection. Sinclair still willing purchase your interest fair basis and is hopeful you may carry out first arrangement. Present situation result your own suggestion and necessary much regret. If your withdrawal not intended what was the objective of Ottawa instructions and letters to Redman and Brokovski?

Until this point the exchange of cables raised more questions than they answered. Why was Sinclair in such a hurry to obtain Bennett's interest? Why in this legal factory had no one drafted an agreement that could have been examined with 'due diligence' until signings on dotted lines became the next order of business? At the very least, why had Lougheed not worked out a deal with Sinclair on Bennett's behalf and cabled the terms to London for Bennett's approval?

As would become apparent later from the pleadings in Lougheed versus Bennett, there was a disagreement between the two over the fundamental nature of their partnership. Lougheed clearly believed that the original Lougheed and Bennett partnership had been replaced by a partnership that included Sinclair,

Hannah, Redman, et al. Under Lougheed's interpretation, Sinclair, Hannah, and Redman would have shared the liability to the Royal Bank and the Canadian Bank of Commerce that McLaws and Roberts had saddled on the partnership, and Sinclair and Redman thereby had the right to serve notice of dissolution of the partnership. Bennett, however, insisted that only he and Lougheed were partners, and all the others were employees serving under a profit-sharing arrangement. They were entitled to a fixed percentage of the annual profit of the law firm and to monthly drawing accounts against the profits, but, as employees, they could not serve notice of dissolution. They could only quit and go elsewhere.

The combination of Hannah's report on the Calgary situation and Lougheed's third cable destroyed the last vestige of Bennett's restraint. He abandoned his plans for a European vacation and fired his final cable off to Lougheed:

Cable argument futile. Having seen Hannah fully appreciate incompleteness, inaccuracy, insincerity your messages. Only occasion Sinclair mentioned purchasing my half interest partnership, assets and goodwill we recognized impossible without your approval. Accordingly arranged conference Ottawa, failing which you stated matter must stand until my return. As no conference held, offer made or price or terms even mentioned, advised you, replying your message, cable negotiations impossible and must await return. Your subsequent action taken without consideration my wishes during absence firm business and compels govern myself accordingly. Sailing Thursday.

Although it was only five months since he had written disparagingly of Canada and Calgary to Max Aitken and he was now free to establish himself in Ottawa or in England, without further responsibility for the debts of the firm, he chose to rush back to Calgary in a towering rage, to show Lougheed, Sinclair, Redman, and McLaws they were not going to push him around. He cabled George Robinson to lease suitable office space for the new law firm he would be organizing on his return to Calgary, and Robinson chose the best available — the vacant sixth floor of the Lancaster Building, a block west of the Clarence Block. On 14 August he sailed for home from Southampton.

When Bennett arrived in Calgary he learned that Lougheed had begun action in the Supreme Court of Alberta for the liquidation of the partnership and had obtained an order appointing the Trust and Guaranty Company interim receiver for the tangible assets of the firm. The new firm of Lougheed, Sinclair, McLaws, and Redman was now occupying the old firm's offices in the Clarence Block, offices from which all the other 'partners' had been evicted. They had a newly printed letterhead on which they listed the new firm as the successor to Lougheed and Bennett, and had notified all the old firm's clients that this transaction had occurred. Bennett sued for $50,000 in damages, in a suit that never came to trial.

Bennett's first action on his return was to call on Horace Howard, the trust company manager, to demand that he carry out his duties and take everything in the old Lougheed and Bennett office into receivership.[40] Howard rented a vacant floor in the Southam Building at the corner of Seventh Avenue and Second Street West and hired a moving van. Over the next three days they moved everything except the fixtures of Lougheed's office. The seizure included all the office files, furniture, and clients' papers, and they remained under the watchful eye of a woman caretaker-custodian for the next three years. When either firm required access to a client's file, it was necessary to get a court order for a sheriff's deputy to retrieve it from storage. Even when the seizure was complete, it did not satisfy Bennett. Walking past the Clarence Block one day he noticed that the polished brass Lougheed and Bennett nameplate was still attached to the building. He stopped into the Trust and Guaranty Office and ordered Howard to detach the sign and put it in storage. Howard did so, but had less luck with Bennett's demand that the large canvas awnings that shaded the office windows be removed. Lougheed, contending they were permanently part of his building, refused to permit the seizure. Bennett sued.

Bennett quickly got a new partnership in place – Bennett, Hannah, and P.L. Sanford. Other senior lawyers on the old staff

joined Bennett as associates, and later became partners. They were
E.J. Chambers, O.E. Might, and H.G. Nolan. It said something
for the trust and respect Bennett had engendered in his staff that
most of the secretaries and office staff also opted to go with the
Bennett firm. Members of the rival firms passed each other on
the street without speaking, and avoided social contact with each
other wherever possible. At the very least, the Lougheed Bennett
feud provided the Calgary legal fraternity with some of its most
colourful folklore: the story of Bennett, during a court appearance, calling a lawyer who had garnered in one of his trust
companies as 'reprobate barrister' and getting punched in the
nose in response; and the story of an eminent KC, who had co-
opted the Hudson's Bay Company account, being forced to cool
his heels outside Bennett's office for two days before Bennett
would accept the document he had drafted.

The depths of Bennett's lifelong grudge against everyone associated with the other side is illuminated by an experience related
by Major Harry Chritchley of Calgary, who was attached to the
Canadian Army Headquarters in England in 1943.[41] Canadian
headquarters was located on the Tyrrlswood golf course, down
the road a couple of miles from Bennett's country estate at
Mickelham. In the summer of 1943 the officers decided to stage a
garden party at which the band of the Calgary Highlanders
would be invited to perform. Since Lord Bennett was the original
honorary colonel of that regiment, they decided to invite him to
attend. Colonel Carson MacWilliams, a Calgary lawyer, volunteered to convey the invitation to Bennett. When MacWilliams
appeared at the front door of the Bennett mansion, his ring was
answered by Bennett's loyal, long-time secretary Alice Millar. She
recognized him instantly, but when informed of his mission she
replied: 'Oh no, Carson, Lord Bennett would never attend a party
if he knew you were to be there. He would certainly not want to
see you here and I shall not tell him you have been here.' MacWilliams had been one of the students with Lougheed and Bennett
who had gone with Lougheed, Sinclair, and McLaws, twenty
years before.

In 1922, in addition to the need for new professional quarters,

Bennett's return to Calgary faced him with the necessity of finding a new place to live.[42] He had given up his 'digs' with the Smith sisters, but the landladies made a smaller room available in which he could store his 700-book library until he became permanently settled. By the time he left Fourth Avenue for residence in the Ranchmen's Club in 1922, his library contained the collected works of every major British author from Samuel Pepys to Rudyard Kipling. In addition, it contained a fifty-volume edition of the Harvard Classics, the *Encyclopaedia Britannica*, a fifteen-volume edition of Greek and Latin Classics, twenty-five volumes of *Halsbury's Laws of England*, and a ten-volume set of *The World's Greatest Oratory*.

After a year at the Ranchmen's Club, Bennett moved to a suite on the seventh floor of the Palliser Hotel. Identified as room 759, it consisted of a large bedroom with a view and a large adjoining sitting room. A door across the corridor enabled a second bedroom to be added to the suite. That came in very handy when his sister Mildred joined him in Calgary following the death of their sister Evelyn in 1929. Living at the Palliser with his library on Fourth Avenue was an inconvenient arrangement, but Bennett put up with it for several years before he added another connecting room to his suite and turned it into a storeroom for his book. It remained so until he had all his books packaged and shipped to England in 1939.

CHAPTER SEVEN

Largesse

Putting his law practice back together after the departure of Lougheed and Sinclair in the late autumn of 1922 turned out to be easier for Bennett than he might have expected. For one thing, there was not all that much 'business' to put back together. The practice of law, for everybody in it, had fallen on hard times in Calgary, in melancholy contrast with the glory days of the real estate boom before the First World War. For many practitioners, days stretched into months when there was little to do except the pursuit of debtors of local merchants and the foreclosing of mortgages on abandoned real estate holdings.

For Bennett personally, the practice of law was steadily diminishing in interest. For the past five years, the focus of his workaday world was shifting from the law courts to the marts of finance and business. This was true even before Mrs Eddy's death forced him to devote more of his time to the affairs of the E.B. Eddy Company, but was particularly true after 1922, when Bennett and Shirreff decided to spend $3 million on plant improvements – including the installation of a completely new newsprint mill and a modernized sulphite manufacturing facility. The scope of the Eddy operation can be seen from a *Financial Post* progress report on construction in the midsummer of 1924. When completed, the *Post* estimated, the payroll at the plant would increase by 50 per cent from the 1000 to 1400 currently employed. Bennett, of course, took no part in the day-to-day operation of the Eddy company, which was controlled by the president, G.H. Millen, the old E.B. Eddy protégé, and C.V. Caesar, the general manager. But in an operation as large as this one, there were enough policy decisions for the board of directors to keep Bennett's attention focused. In addition, he was already a director of the Metropolitan Life Insurance Company of New York and was about to join the boards of the Royal Bank and Canadian General Electric. He also had substantial shares in a number of smaller companies in Alberta and British Columbia.

By 1922 it could almost be said that Bennett was well on his way to becoming a one-man investment trust, and in the stock promotion boom that would sweep the country later in the 1920s he seemed to be into everything. The developing pattern of his investing is obvious from the list of stock certificates he deposited for safe-keeping with the Royal Bank in Calgary in February 1921.[1] It included certificates of the Spanish River Pulp and Paper Company, Vancouver Milling and Grain Company, Eastern and Pacific Land Company, Western Agency and Development Company, Canadian Cuban Sugar Company, Central Okanagan Land Company, and the Albertan Publishing Company. These, of course, were additional to his other, much larger holdings of Alberta Pacific Grain, Canada Cement, Royal Bank, Bank of Montreal, Merchants Bank, Canadian Bank of Commerce, Canadian Pacific Railway, Dominion Bridge, Metals Limited, and Royal Trust. Stock certificates for these companies were held elsewhere. Indeed, his stock certificates came to be widely scattered – from Montreal, Toronto, and Calgary brokerage offices to various bank vaults in Ottawa and Calgary. This frequently caused considerable trouble for Alice Millar, who handled the details of Bennett's financial affairs. It was not uncommon, when a decision was made to sell some shares, to find the unendorsed certificate in a bank vault in Calgary while Bennett was in Ottawa and the shares had been sold in Vancouver. So it had to be retrieved, sent to Bennett for his signature, and only then deposited with the broker.

Bennett, in good times and bad, was an investor with an unshakable faith in Canadian resource industries. He was not only a buyer of all kinds of mining stock, he was a grub-staker of prospectors and a speculator in mining claims, He and John I. McFarland spend thousands of dollars over more than a decade vainly trying to bring a gold mining property in Asoyoos, British Columbia, into profitable production.

In 1922 Bennett's income from professional fees dropped to $1989, the lowest point reached since his arrival in Calgary twenty-five years before. For the same year his investment income was $30,944 and his income from directors' fees, $5435.[2] Nevertheless, Bennett was viscerally driven to taking every possible action to ensure that every one of his legal clients would take all their legal business to the sixth floor of the Lancaster Building and not to the second floor of the Clarence Block.[3] And for the most part that was what happened. The overwhelming majority of the Lougheed and Bennett clientage stayed with Bennett. He remained the personal solicitor of A.E. Cross, W.R. Hull, Pat Burns, W.R. Pearce, and John I. McFarland, which meant that most of their corporate legal needs also came to rest in Bennett's new office. The way in which his own corporate connections added grist to Bennett's legal mill is perfectly illustrated by the birth and growth of the Royalite Oil Company.[4]

Sir James Lougheed and Bennett had both been bitten by the oil bug when W.S. Herron introduced them to the natural gas seepages in Turner Valley back in 1912. Both became shareholders in the Calgary Petroleum Products Company Herron was promoting to drill the Dingman discovery well of 1914. Bennett was still an active director of that company in December 1920, when a fire destroyed its extraction plant and forced it to shut down operations. The insurance carried on the plant was insufficient to enable the company to rebuild, and for some months it looked as though the end was in sight for Herron's dream. However, two widely separated oil industry developments combined to rescue the project.

A large oil field was discovered in Montana just south of the Alberta border. The Imperial Oil Company decided to build a refinery in Calgary to process the Montana crude oil into gasoline for its Alberta customers. The Montana discovery also encouraged Imperial Oil to intensify its own search for oil in Alberta. There was oil in Alberta, for the Dingman well had produced more than 50,000 barrels before going up in smoke. Bennett was the Alberta solicitor for Imperial Oil and, when the financial bind of the Calgary Petroleum Products Company was brought to the attention of Imperial Oil, a deal was quickly done.

Imperial Oil agreed to acquire the properties of Calgary Petroleum Products Company through an exchange of shares with a new company it would incorporate in the Lougheed and Bennett office – the Royalite Oil Company Limited. Imperial Oil would supply Royalite with enough money to complete a fourth well the old company had started a couple of hundred yards north of the new separator it would build. While all this was being arranged, Mrs Jennie Eddy fell terminally ill and the spring of 1921 found Bennett frequently in Ottawa on Eddy company affairs. As a result, he turned over the details of incorporating the Royalite Oil Company to Alex Hannah and P.L. Sanford. They, with three law students in the Lougheed and Bennett office, became the pro forma incorporating shareholders. Once all the legal formalities were completed, Imperial transferred these pro forma shares to its own nominees and proceeded with the exchange of shares with the Calgary Petroleum Products shareholders. The vehicle chosen to bring that about was the Alliance Trust Company, Lord Beaverbrook's Calgary enterprise of which Bennett was a director. Alliance called in all the Calgary Petroleum Products Company shares and replaced them with Royalite shares. In that exchange Bennett received 1500 and Lougheed 2000 $25 par shares of the Royalite Oil Company.[5] Everything that Imperial Oil had to do to complete its acquisition of Calgary Petroleum Products Company was done through Lougheed and Bennett. When the breakup of Lougheed and Bennett came, Imperial Oil and Royalite automatically took the pathway to Bennett, Hannah, and Sanford. Bennett did not get around to joining the board of directors of Royalite Oil himself until 1925, and became president in 1926. By then the company had brought the spectacular Royalite no. 4 into production – a well that would ultimately yield better than $3 million worth of naphtha and natural gas and set off the second Alberta oil boom.

Long before Royalite no. 4 blew in, however, Bennett's attention was diverted elsewhere – to the climax of the agrarian
revolt in western Canada.[6] The revolt occurred in 1921 when
angry farmers failed to elect any Liberal or Conservative
members to the House of Commons from the prairie provinces.
They followed by electing farmer-controlled provincial governments in Alberta and Manitoba. When political action failed to
achieve their goals, they turned to the economic battlefield – to
crusade for the re-establishment of the Canadian Wheat Board to
market their wheat.

During the war, the Canadian government had closed the
Winnipeg Grain Exchange futures market and established an all-
powerful government board to take delivery of the wheat crop
from the growers and to sell it to domestic and foreign millers.
That action had ushered in the greatest, if the shortest, period of
prosperity in Canadian grain-growing history. The price of wheat
rose from less than $1.00 a bushel in 1914 to $2.63 in 1919. Then
the Wheat Board was abolished, the Winnipeg futures market
reopened, and the price of wheat dropped to $1.99 in 1920 and
to $1.07 by 1923.

The wheat growers, quickly identifying cause with effect –
the Wheat Board with high prices and the Grain Exchange with
low prices – mounted a massive campaign for a return of the
board. Nobody in Ottawa paid any attention. Economists could,
and did, argue that conditions in 1923 were as different from what
had prevailed in 1917 as peace was from war. While European
governments during the war years had bought all the Canadian
wheat they could get their hands on, now they were tightly
controlling the amount of wheat that could be imported. The
difference had produced a collapse of world prices no wheat
board could have prevented. The government, instead of re-
establishing the Wheat Board, set up a couple of royal commissions to listen to the gripes and grievances of the wheat growers
of the west.

Denied the Wheat Board, the farmers turned to the idea of
cooperative marketing of their own wheat through their own
'wheat pool.' Particularly in 1923 there had to be a better way

because, for the first time in five years, they were going to have a bumper crop to harvest – two and a half times as much wheat as the province had ever grown before. Already, in July, the price was down to 80 cents a bushel on Alberta farms. How much more would the price drop when the marketing of the record crop reached its peak in October and November?

The agitation to organize a wheat pool for the 1923 crop began to erupt in the United Farmers of Alberta locals in June and, by early July, it was reaching the clamour level.[7] But the leaders of the UFA, trying to get a grip on the process of governing Alberta, which they had taken over in a landslide in 1921, still paid no attention to the wheat pool agitation. When it could no longer be ignored, they pleaded it was already too late for 1923. The farmers would soon be on their binders and would be far too busy from morning till night to become involved in the huge task of putting a wheat pool in place. For example, the signatures of 30,000 farmers would have to be obtained on contracts binding them to deliver their wheat to the Alberta Wheat Pool. Even the wording of the contract still had to be worked out. Finalizing and then organizing the recruitment drive could take months. It was far too late for 1923.

Then the *Calgary Herald* got into the act. It discovered that Aaron Sapiro, the American lawyer who had organized the Kentucky tobacco growers cooperative and the California raisin grape cooperative, was soon to pay a visit to British Columbia. These cooperatives were widely acclaimed for turning two depressed agricultural areas of the United State into thriving communities. The *Herald* undertook to get Sapiro to come to Alberta to teach the wheat growers how to organize a wheat pool to market the 1923 crop. First the UFA leaders criticized the *Herald* for intruding into the farmers' affairs; then, when Sapiro agreed to come, they leaped for the bandwagon.

Sapiro's prairie crusade began in Calgary with a speech to a joint meeting of the Kiwanis Club and the Board of Trade on 2 August 1923. He emphasized the change the tobacco and raisin grapes cooperatives had made to the social and economic fabric of their localities. Then he spent three hours with the UFA executive and the leaders of the local agitation on the basics of organizing a wheat pool.[8] For cooperative marketing to succeed, he warned, they must first get the signatures of half Alberta's 40,000 wheat growers on five-year contracts. High-calibre grain men had to be located and hired to run the pool. Then they had to make arrangements with the banks to finance their operation, and negotiate contracts with the established grain trade – the people who owned Alberta's 400 country elevators – to move their grain to market. And they had only six weeks at the most to get it done. That evening Sapiro carried his message to 3000 southern Alberta farmers in the Calgary Arena, repeated his performance in Edmonton the next day, and took off for Saskatchewan and Manitoba, for more of the same. Prairie Canada would never be the same again.

When John I. McFarland announced on 4 August that he was an enthusiastic supporter of the wheat pool idea and was prepared to place the Alberta Pacific Grain Company's 283 elevators at its disposal; the *Herald* broke out the biggest, blackest type it owned to headline that front-page news for its readers.[9] McFarland also offered to sell the elevators to the pool if it wanted them on easy terms at a price set by an independent evaluator. A couple of days later Bennett, freshly home from a month in London, checked in with a laudatory interview in support of the wheat pool idea, noting that it would have a desirable secondary effect of attracting more British settlers to Alberta. He joined the pool himself and eventually became a director. When the final draft of the contract with the growers was completed, the pool's provisional executive ordered it submitted to Bennett for his approval.[10] Meanwhile, McFarland joined the original group of seventeen provisional directors of the fledging pool. The membership drive was launched, the farmers by the thousands signed the contracts, and the wheat pool was born.

Bennett's enthusiastic support for the wheat pool idea was a clear indication that while he was a political Conservative, he was no 'economic royalist.' His statement in the *Herald* interview that the wheat pool would encourage the inflow of British settlers to Alberta might have seemed opaque at first encounter. But Bennett, in his many visits to the United Kingdom, must have become aware of the great United Kingdom cooperative movement that the farmers were using to counter the economic power of the milling and baking trusts. There was no one more aware than Bennett of the multiplicity of 'middlemen' exacting toll as the wheat moved from the Alberta farmers' fields and the British consumers' table. He might have fought the UFA 'Progressives' on the hustings, but when he sat down with them at a wheat pool meeting, the gap that separated them narrowed considerably.

As the wheat pool was being organized, another unrelated development in the grain trade involved McFarland and Bennett even more deeply. In the spring of 1923 the large British milling company, Spillers Milling and Associated Industries Limited, began to attract occasional small attention in the Canadian financial press. The company had been experimenting with the shipment of Canadian grain from Vancouver to Liverpool through the newly opened Panama Canal. The tests had been satisfactorily profitable except for one thing: the terminal facilities in Vancouver were unable to handle the volumes of wheat Spillers wanted to ship. It announced it was going to build its own terminal capable of storing two million bushels of grain.[11]

The announcement came to the attention of the Toronto promoters of a failed flour-milling project in Calgary that had run out of money with its construction only half completed. The promoters contacted Spillers and negotiations began for Spillers to take it over. That brought Alberta, the nearest wheat-producing province to Vancouver, to the notice of Spillers directors, who began to wonder about lining up an agency in Alberta to supply them with a steady flow of wheat for their new elevator in Vancouver.

While the Spillers' agents were in Toronto and Calgary negotiating the purchase of the milling company, they opened negotiations with John I. McFarland to have the Alberta Pacific Grain Company become its western Canadian purchasing agent. These negotiations began in the spring of 1923 and continued intermittently until the end of the year. When the agency idea proved impractical, Spillers' attention switched to the outright purchase of the company, with McFarland staying on as president and general manager. That, of course, brought Lord Beaverbrook into the picture, and Bennett and McFarland went to London to work out final arrangements for the sale. Beaverbrook was still a major shareholder.

Eventually a deal was done that called for an exchange of Spillers shares for those of the Alberta Pacific Grain Company Limited. The exact details of the transaction were never publicized, except that it put a value of $197 per share for the Alberta Pacific Grain preferred shares and $200 a share for the $100 par common stock.[12] The split between Beaverbrook, McFarland, and Bennett was not revealed either. Bennett and McFarland were 'in' Alberta Pacific Grain together just as they were 'in' dozens of other investments over the years, but there is no record of the precise division of the interests of the partners in any of these investments. Bennett continued to draw from $2250 to $2750 in director's fees from the grain company up to and including 1926, along with annual dividends of $12,052 in 1923, $25,000 in 1924, $29,378 in 1925, and $7555 in 1926.[13]

An estimate of Bennett's wealth can be made from the dividend-paying securities identified on his income tax returns. In 1923 his liquid assets were worth perhaps $750,000, exclusive of his holding of Alberta Pacific Grain and E.B. Eddy Company. He also held some tax-free bonds, Imperial Oil rights, and other oil stocks and mining stocks that did not pay dividends. By the time he was selected as leader at the Conservative convention in 1927 he was indeed a millionaire, as the newspapers described him.

Despite Bennett's lugubrious assessment of the future of Calgary and western Canada in his letters to Beaverbrook before the wheat pool agitation, he was fated to do much better with his new legal practice with Hannah and Sanford than he had ever done with Lougheed. During 1923, the new firm's first year of existence, he reported an income from professional fees of $14,330, compared with his 1921 professional income of $13,092. That income rose to $19,000 in 1924, to $22,621 in

1925, and to $39,718 in 1926. But when his professional income is compared with his combined dividend income and directorship fees, it was still outnumbered by three or four to one.[14]

Ironically, the less Bennett participated in the work of his new partnership, the more it prospered. Following his defeat in 1921 and his withdrawal from politics, Bennett's own court appearances diminished steadily as court calendars listed the names of his partners when cases from his office were posted for trial. The only case deemed worthy of newspaper coverage that Bennett was involved in over a stretch of five years was the Public Utilities Board hearings in 1921, when Bennett appeared for the city in an inquiry into Calgary's natural gas supply. Bennett's absence from legal confrontations, coupled with his abandonment of political activity, was turning him into a non-person in Calgary. He had joined the Kiwanis Club and attended its meetings. He made speeches on foreign affairs every year or so when any group asked him to. He mastered the ceremonies at infrequent testimonial dinners. Otherwise his comings and goings within the community went unnoticed by either Calgary newspaper. Sending a reporter to interview R.B. Bennett for his opinion on some issue of the day, as happened in the Wheat Pool agitation, was a rarity for newspaper editors. In general, he was away from Calgary much more than he was at home.

It was while Bennett was preparing for his month-long trip to London with McFarland to negotiate with Spillers that a letter arrived in his box at the Palliser Hotel that would launch him into the most improbable charade of his life. The letter was from a case worker of the Children's Aid Society of Toronto inquiring for the address of his brother, George H. Bennett, whose wife, from whom he had been separated for some time, was no longer able to take care of their daughter, Mary Joan, aged four, and had placed her in the custody of the society. The society wished to communicate with Mr Bennett and have him make financial arrangements for the care of his daughter.[15]

George Bennett was the cross that RB had been bearing with steadily mounting impatience for the last five years. After he got George out of the army in 1915 and brought him home to

Canada, the younger Bennett spent a long time in a military hospital in Toronto recovering slowly from the severe case of enteritis with which he was infected soon after he landed in France with the Princess Pat's Canadian Light Infantry. On his discharge, there is some doubt whether he ever returned to employment with the Bank of Montreal. If he did, he did not last, and spent several years drifting from place to place and from job to job. The only knowledge we have of George during this time is contained in a letter Bennett wrote to the governor general, Lord Tweedsmuir, after George's death in 1938. He said in part: 'He came back from the war a wreck and after visiting South America, and other parts of Canada he eventually settled at Fort McMurray. He grew much attached to the country, had a very fine garden – was much beloved by his friends, many of whom write about him with real affection.'[16]

What Bennett did not say was that George had become an alcoholic whose periodic binges prevented him from ever holding a permanent job again, even though his outgoing personality and skill as an accountant enabled him to obtain employment more easily than some of his drinking associates. Nor did Bennett mention George's marriage, his wife, or his daughter, which might give rise to this question: Was RB aware before 1924 that George had ever married, that he even had a wife and a daughter? There is no way of knowing the answer, but Bennett's curious attitude towards his sister-in-law and niece over the next twenty-three years at least makes it not unreasonable to ask the question.

George eventually found his way to Calgary (in 1923?), where his behaviour while drinking became such an embarrassment to his brother that RB ultimately determined he had to get George out of town. It was a need that became instantly more pressing when Alberta, in November 1923, voted to abandon Prohibition in favour of allowing the sale of beer in hotel bars and liquor by the bottle in government stores. George had had little difficulty slaking his thirst during postwar Prohibition. Conditions after repeal would make it more difficult for him to keep that thirst in check. Compared with conditions that had prevailed during Prohibition, Calgary and other Alberta cities would soon become awash in booze. Discretion dictated that George be shielded from temptation by removal to some spot in the deep boondocks beyond the flow of government liquor. But how to find such a spot, and then how to persuade George to move there?

Eventually Bennett recalled that the Alliance Trust Company had title to a house and a number of lots in Fort McMurray, a fur-trading hamlet of one hundred people 275 miles north of Edmonton. Would George consider moving permanently to Fort McMurray? What if the house were turned over to him and provision made for a modest but adequate monthly income, and for as long as he lived? George, who had acquired a genuine liking for small-town life during his prewar sojourn at Outlook, Saskatchewan, was persuaded.

The George problem was solved at last, and amicably. RB must have reacted to George's acquiescence with a deep sigh of relief. He had assumed the role of his brother's keeper even before the death of his father in 1905, even to deciding the career his brother should follow. He early recognized that his young brother was not a scholar and that he would probably do best in a business career. It was everywhere recognized at the close of the nineteenth century that a fine foundation for a business career could be made by entering the employ of a chartered bank. Prior to leaving for Calgary in 1897, Bennett had persuaded his brother to enrol at the Mt Allison Academy and Commercial College, with the idea of preparing for a banking career. Towards the end of George's term, in June 1898, Bennett wrote to the principal of the college asking him for a recommendation George could submit to the Bank of Montreal with an application for employment. J.M. Palmer, the principal, demurred on two grounds: George's deportment was far from exemplary because he had chosen to associate with the rowdier elements of the school, and his marks in English, arithmetic, spelling, and Latin were unsatisfactory. His education 'was indeed insufficient for him entering the work you seem to have in view for him.'[17] Nevertheless, Bennett brought George to Calgary and got him a job as ledger keeper at the Bank of Montreal. He also took him to room with him with the Smith sisters on Fourth Avenue West. They shared the room until, three years later, George won his first promotion with the bank and was transferred to Regina. That was the last Bennett would see of his brother until George returned to Calgary in 1914 to enlist in the first contingent of the Princess Pats. The drinking problem developed later.

With the Fort McMurray solution, Bennett could have been reasonably certain that as far as he was concerned, the George problem was behind him. Then came the letter from Toronto! Having freed himself from George's drunken presence in Calgary, did he now face a lifetime of problems from George's wife and daughter? While he pondered the prospects, he fired off the Children's Aid Society letter to George.

It was no big deal for George Bennett. He wrote to the society with a very simple solution to its problem: place the child in the custody of a convenient convent or children's home and he would pay the shot. Not only did he neglect to send along a payment on account, but he neglected to provide his address. When Bennett returned home from England in May, there was another letter on his desk from the Toronto Children's Aid Society still seeking George's address. It remained there. Unanswered.

Bennett, it can be safely assumed, spent a lot of time thinking about the sister-in-law and niece problem on his trip to England and back. Was he to spend the rest of his life looking over his shoulder for problems being created for him by his drunken brother's estranged wife and abandoned daughter? His answer was 'certainly not.' Sometime during that ocean voyage he must have sworn an oath that, come what may, he personally, was never going to recognize the existence of either one of them. He never did.

On 9 July another letter arrived from Mrs Helen Lawrence, superintendent of the society.[17] She emphasized it was important for them to have George Bennett's address. His daughter was now seriously ill in the Sick Children's Hospital. Her mother had been into the office and had agreed on having her daughter transferred to the care of a convent if her husband would pay for her keep.

R.B. Bennett, the eminent barrister and millionaire corporate director, was not prepared to have his brother's daughter abandoned to the permanent care of public charity in Toronto, but neither was he willing to become involved himself. He eventually persuaded one of his oldest friends in Calgary to help him bridge the gap. J.G. Edgar, who had been a fellow lodger with the Smith sisters during their early days in Calgary, was now a successful businessman. He agreed to act as George Bennett's proxy in supporting Joan Bennett with R.B. Bennett's money. The first step, to ensure that no direct connection would ever be made with R.B. Bennett himself, was a letter to the Children's Aid Society from Alice Millar. It was an amalgam of stretched truth and flat lies:

Some months ago, Mr. George H. Bennett left Calgary, as I understand it, to go to Fort McMurray, Alberta. I have never heard whether or not he got there, and I do not think his brother knows his present where-abouts.

Mr. Bennett is not expected to return until the early part of September, when your letter will be placed before him.[18]

Meanwhile, presumably, little Joan could go on being a charity case in the Sick Children's Hospital. In September Edgar stepped front and centre with a letter to the Children's Aid Society:

Dear Madam:

In the spring Mr. George Bennett was in this city and told me he had certain domestic difficulties, the result of which was he and his wife were not living together. He advised me that he had written his wife that if she would place their only child in a suitable convent where it [sic] would be clothed and fed, given proper medical attention and educated he would provide payment. I now have in my possession $100 to pay on account, cheque for which I enclose herewith, on the understanding that it is to be used for the purposes mentioned.

I do not know Mr. George Bennett's present address, but I learned that the child's mother has seen you and I am therefore sending you the money which I have in my possession. I will be glad to hear from you in due course.[19]

The upshot of all this was that Joan Bennett was placed in the care of the Sisters of St Joseph at St Joseph's College Academy, where she remained for the next fifteen years. Though R.B. Bennett assumed financial responsibility for Joan's care and education, never once did he communicate with her directly or acknowledge a communication from her. The Bennett family fold was locked and bolted against her and, in later years, when Bennett was busy putting trust funds together to take care of a covey of nephews, Joan was never included. Even after he had contributed thousands of dollars to her support, he could not bring himself to recognize her existence by writing to her. When he felt need to get a message to her, he would scribble a note for Alice Millar to send to Edgar or to George Robinson, to be redrafted into a letter of their own wording and sent to the girl over either's signature.[20]

The system of payments Edgar devised in 1924 was the essence of simplicity. The tuition and board at the convent were payable in advance at the rate of $200 per quarter. Incidental expenses in one quarter – for clothes, music lessons, elocution lessons, medical fees, and the like – were added to the invoice for the next quarter. Edgar, and later George Robinson, who managed Bennett's real estate, would pay the invoices and send them to Alice Millar for reimbursement. Occasionally Millar would make financial advances so that Bennett's friends would not be using their money on his behalf. It was all very informal, but Millar always saw that the books balanced.

At the end of 1924 Edgar had a small surplus on hand, so he sent it to the convent with instructions that it be spent on Christmas treats for the girl. That became an annual practice, but it was all there was. There is no record of Bennett, Millar, Edgar, or Robinson ever so much as sending a Christmas card to the child. Indeed, Joan was well into her teens and almost out of high school before Alice Millar wrote to Robinson to find out 'how old she was, and what plans she was making to complete her education.'

Christmas, Easter, and summer vacations became a continuing

problem for Edgar and the convent soon after she moved into St Joseph's. The convent school shut down during all the holiday and school breaks and the pupils were sent home. But Joan Bennett no longer had a home to go to. Her mother was working to keep herself, and had nobody around who could take care of a little child during the day. So the convent, reacting to a plea from Edgar, got together with Mrs Bennett and located a motherly lady with whom Joan could be boarded during Easter, Christmas, and summer holidays for a weekly stipend. It was a responsibility the convent assumed with great reluctance, frequently beseeching Edgar to negotiate directly with Mrs Bennett. Edgar never did so. Some years later after Mrs Bennett moved to New York, this refusal precipitated a head-on crisis when Edgar neglected to pay the cost of Joan's Christmas, Easter, and summer vacations with her mother.[21]

It was while Edgar was putting the finishing touches on his negotiations with the convent that the original George problem resurfaced, to the embarrassment of Bennett and his associates. While George had consented to his banishment to Fort McMurray, that did not mean he was going to stay there without occasional trips to revisit the watering holes of Edmonton and Calgary. On 7 November 1924 the elder Bennett wrote angrily to his brother:

I find that you got from Gordon Edgar at Fort McMurray $50.00, you drew a draft on him for $50, you got $100 from Matheson at Edmonton on the way up. I paid your hotel bill here, $27.50. You got $40 from Matheson on the way down. I paid Miss Millar $1.50 which you got from her. I paid Mr. Edgar $225 for your child, making a total of $639 in the last few weeks.

I only direct your attention to these matters for the purpose of letting you know that you need not expect that to continue, and any drafts you draw will not be paid.[22]

Then he added a long appendix to the letter, stressing that his future assistance was conditional on George's stopping drinking. Anything he did would be 'terminated upon your drinking any liquor or beer.' He closed the letter with an appeal to George to get a job in the bush and 'make a man of yourself, again.'

Long experience had taught George that his brother's bark was indeed worse than his bite. In effect, Bennett turned his back on the George problem by turning it over to Alice Millar, Cluny Macdonnell, the office manager of Bennett, Hannah, and Sanford, and H.R. Milner, Edmonton's leading corporation lawyer and a long-time friend. When George, every three or four months, emerged from the bush on his drinking excursions to Edmonton or Calgary, they would pick up what tabs he left around and see him safely onto the train to Fort McMurray. Then the account would be sent to Alice Millar, who took care of it. Only rarely, at long intervals when things appeared to be getting out of hand, was it ever necessary for Bennett to be apprised of what was going on.

Working out a suitable method for paying George Bennett his monthly allowance proved more troublesome than anticipated. At first Bennett set aside a fund of $20,000 in securities from which George was to get the income, but that required that George exercise some managerial skills to stretch the income over the extended period between dividend dates. It did not work, and Bennett then turned the matter over to Alice Millar for her to get a cheque for $125 into George's hands on the first of each month. Why that system did not work either was never explained, but it was replaced by having the Royal Bank in Calgary transfer funds every month to its branch in Fort McMurray so that George could write cheques on his $125 monthly maximum income. Unhappily, it was not long before George's cheques began to exceed his monthly allowance.[23] In the beginning the bank manager at Fort McMurray paid the NSF cheques, secure in the knowledge that an incoming monthly credit would put George back in good standing. When George's debit balance soared well beyond his monthly income, the bank manager shut down his account. George then wrote a cheque on a Calgary Royal Bank branch where he had no account and Alice Millar solved the resultant crisis with an emergency infusion of Bennett's money. But these, after all, were minor occurrences, like George's periodic drinking excursions to Edmonton and Calgary. He always returned to Fort McMurray and always made peace with the bank. He died in Fort McMurray on 27 January 1938 and was buried there.

Bennett's need to get George out from under his feet in Calgary is both understandable and easy to justify, given the nature of the brother's disability and Bennett's strait-laced persona. The deliberate, rigidly uncompromising attitude he adopted towards Mary Joan Bennett is beyond understanding. True, he assumed responsibility for her maintenance, but it was maintenance at an irreducible minimum compared with the generosity he displayed towards his quartet of nephews. An example of his generosity is to be found in a letter to his brother-in-law, Dr Horace Coates, the father of Richard Bennett Coates. Young Coates had settled on a medical career and Bennett had undertaken to see him through his medical studies, including postgraduate work at Edinburgh University. But first he had to get into Dalhousie University. Bennett wrote to President Carleton Stanley of Dalhousie to get his nephew enrolled in the freshman science class, then he treated him to what must have been the most lavish wardrobe ever closeted by a freshman at Dalhousie – three tailor-made tweed suits, a morning coat, striped trousers, and a dinner jacket.[24] Subject to his father's approval, Bennett said he would like to provide the boy with a regular allowance so he could learn to manage his own affairs. Unhappily, young Coates was unequal to the challenge. He flunked Dalhousie, repeated his failure at two other universities, and ended up temporarily in the nether reaches of commercial Montreal.

Bennett's niggardliness towards his niece, moreover, was in complete contradiction to the behaviour pattern he had been developing during his climb to the top of his profession. From his arrival in Calgary totally committed to the twelve-hour workday, he was the personification of the Methodist Work Ethic. He was also an example of someone who had read and committed to memory John Wesley's sermon on 'The Use of Money,' with its three fundamental rules for humans to live by – 'gain all you can,' 'save all you can,' 'give all you can.'[25] In an interview Bennett gave to the *Toronto Star*, he explained: 'I still think that hard work is the solvent for most of our troubles. But all the hard work in the world won't give that vitally important first chance... Getting your feet off the ground onto the first rung of the ladder.'[26] Making sure that all his nephews got their feet planted on that all-important first rung became one of Bennett's consuming interests, but for Joan Bennett, when her time came, he settled for a secretarial course.

Over the years, Bennett helped a number of people to succeed, including some total strangers. His system for helping others was the endorsed bank loan. The scope of his operation can never be known, for Bennett kept no records of the successful careers he was able to launch. Only the records of some of the failures survive in the form of defaulted loans on which Bennett was forced to make good on his guarantees. One particular case that survives in Calgary folklore is worthy of notice.

The central figure in this legend is Ben Ginsberg, a young South African lawyer who arrived in Calgary at the end of the First World War carrying in his baggage an agency for a South African winery he proposed to establish in the city.[27] Since Alberta was still a 'Dry' province, that agency had only long-term potential. Until Prohibition was repealed, Ginsberg decided to get into the practice of law, but this would entail the renting of an office, the purchase of furniture, and the hiring of a secretary – all requiring money Ginsberg did not have. On the spur of the moment, he went into the Imperial Bank to try to negotiate a loan for $200. To his astonishment, the manager did not reject his application out of hand. Instead, he asked Ginsberg to leave it with him for a couple of days while he checked it over. When Ginsberg returned, the manager greeted him with a warm smile and word that his application had been approved.

Ginsberg went on to a highly successful legal career in Calgary and it was only later that he learned the story behind the bank manager's strange leniency. R.B. Bennett had expressed his concern to the manager that young Albertans graduating from law school in the postwar depression might have financial difficulty getting started in practice. If they came to the banker as prospective borrowers of start-up money and the banker brought the application to Bennett's attention, he would be glad to guarantee a modest loan, sight unseen.

Ginsberg spread the story of Bennett's largesse far and wide, but it is most unlikely that he was the only Calgary lawyer to benefit from Bennett's generosity. None of the others whose loans he guaranteed, however, has testified publicly to the fact. There is no way of knowing the extent of Bennett's loan guaranteeing operation, the ratio of success to failure, or the amount of money that was involved. We do know, from the records that survive of some of the failures, that substantial sums of money were involved.

Peter Welsh and the Alberta Stampede Company are a case in point. In 1912 the Calgary Exhibition Company and Guy Weadick got together and staged the first Calgary Stampede. It was a dismal failure on almost every count. During the next ten years, however, rodeo performers sharpened their skill and audiences became more receptive. When Weadick and the exhibition got together again in 1923, this Calgary Stampede was the first of a long string of outstanding successes. Among the Albertans who enthusiastically greeted the 1923 stampede was Peter Welsh, a Calgary rancher and horse trader, who reasoned that anything that went over so profitably in Calgary was bound to be equally successful in Winnipeg, Minneapolis, and Chicago, not to say even Toronto and Detroit. Welsh rushed out and raised enough money to get the Alberta Stampede Company incorporated and to round up a cast of cowboys, bucking horses, and other livestock. What he needed mostly was enough cash to get his show on the road. His first stop was at Bennett's office in the Lancaster Building. With Welsh's lawyer, fellow Conservative A.R. Smith, Bennett walked Welsh down to the Royal Bank branch on Third Street West and endorsed a note for the Alberta Stampede Company for $3370. Five years later the bank called on him to make good on his guarantee.[28]

Then there was the Rev. William Irvine, Unitarian minister, social gospeller, Non-Partisan League editor, political reformer, Labour member of parliament 1921–5, United Farmers of

Alberta member 1926–35, and Cooperative Commonwealth Federation member 1945–9. Irvine had been elected the Labour member for Calgary East in the 1921 election, the one in which Bennett had been narrowly defeated in Calgary West. When he lost his seat in the election of 1925, Irvine found himself without visible means of support. At forty, with a young family, he began to think of the future and came to the conclusion that his best way to succeed would be as a farmer. He located a half section spread near Bentley, Alberta, twenty-five miles northwest of Red Deer. Unhappily, he ran out of money and approached Bennett for a loan. Bennett arranged to guarantee a loan up to a maximum of $8000 with the Bentley branch of the Bank of Montreal. Irvine was to draw on that loan as needed and he did so from time to time, repaying his borrowing as crops were harvested. By 1932, with the collapse of farm prices for everything he grew, Irvine, like other western farmers, was in trouble, but he still had some of Bennett's money to draw upon. When he applied for the money, the bank held back until it checked with Bennett. On 6 October 1932 Bennett advised the bank that it was perfectly in order to accommodate Mr Irvine up to the maximum of $8000.

Irvine, who belonged to the UFA 'ginger group,' was a member of the opposition during Bennett's term as prime minister. While they confronted each other across the floor of the House of Commons, there is no evidence that there was any personal animosity rankling their relationship. In plain truth, R.B. Bennett was much closer ideologically to the United Farmers of Alberta than he was to some of his Conservative supporters. A former protégé, John Brownlee, was now the UFA premier of Alberta. Bennett appointed Brownlee to the Royal Commission on Banking and Currency, and it was mainly on Brownlee's minority report of that commission that he based his Bank of Canada Act.

Whether Irvine discussed the perilous state of his finances with Bennett before he abandoned farming as a way of life is not known, but it can be safely assumed that he did. On 26 October 1934 the manager of the bank at Bentley wrote to Irvine that his loan with interest now amounted to $8269.90. Inasmuch as

Irvine had quit-claimed his farm to a creditor who had leased it to a tenant, what did Mr Irvine propose to do about his indebtedness to the bank? The reply came from Bennett, in the form of another question. Bennett would now have to liquidate his liability to the bank, so would the manager object if he consulted the head office of his bank with a view of getting the interest on the loan reduced? Jackson Dodds, the general manager of the Bank of Montreal, became involved and ordered the interest rate on the loan from 1 January 1934 to 31 December 1935 reduced to 3¾ per cent simple interest. On 31 December 1935 Bennett sent the bank his cheque for $8579.67.[29] Bennett accepted his loss with equanimity. As he wrote to Jackson Dodds, 'I came into this matter long years before I was in my present place, in an endeavor to assist the sons of Mr. Irvine to make a living on a farm, but Providence decreed otherwise so the Bank got their money and I got experience.' It was an experience that would be repeated again and again.

The Irvine guarantee had run for the better part of a decade. Bennett's backing of the Tweedie loan had almost twice that lifespan. It derived from Bennett's emotional attachment to the Tweedie family of Chatham, New Brunswick. When L.J. Tweedie took Bennett in as a junior partner in 1894, he went far beyond the establishment of an employer–employee relationship. He had Bennett into his home for meals, included him in family outings, and took him under his wing. For his part, Bennett developed an attachment for the Tweedies that neither time nor distance diminished. When a call went out from the Tweedies for help, Bennett answered.

In addition to his success as a lawyer and politician, the elder Tweedie was also a modest success as a businessman and, at the time of his death in 1917, was the owner of the Miramichi Foundry and Machine Works Ltd at Chatham. The company passed to his widow and its management remained in the hands of his son Fred. Caught up as it was in the postwar business slump, the company limped along, providing the Tweedie family with a modest living but not much more. Then, in the middle 1920s, business dropped off and, when it began to lose money – $8000 in fiscal 1927 – Fred Tweedie went to Bennett for financial advice. Bennett was eager to help, not only with advice but with a guarantee to the Bank of Nova Scotia of $10,000 of the company's debt.

The guarantee, seemingly, was negotiated between Bennett and the Bank of Nova Scotia rather than with Tweedie, because the manager of the bank wrote to ask Bennett whether the existence of the guarantee should be disclosed to the company. In enclosing his guarantee, Bennett replied: 'I appreciate your expression of opinion that with this guarantee the company may be able to continue for another year. I see no reason why the company may not know of the guarantee because I told Mr. F.M. Tweedie I would be willing to do something of that nature. At the same time I urged the greatest economy be exercised in the conduct of the company's affairs.'

The company did indeed survive for another year – and for more than a dozen beyond that. But it did so only with additional guarantees from Bennett from time to time. It was hoped, even expected, that when the war came it would be able to cash in on the armaments bonanza. Unhappily, its facilities were too small and too old for that, but too large for the amount of other work that was available. The Miramichi Foundry and Machine Works passed out of existence in 1943. By this time Bennett was long gone from Canada and embroiled in the British government's severe controls of foreign currency. Bennett nevertheless was able to come by $10,000 with which to pay off his guarantee to the Bank of Nova Scotia, which he did on 3 June 1943.[30]

The Irvine guarantee might have been explained as a simple case of one Calgarian, or one member of parliament, doing a favour for another; the Tweedie loan as an illustration of Bennett's filial attachment to that family. There is no way of explaining the $1500 loan he guaranteed for Monsignor Isaie Joury, rector of St Mary's Church in Montreal. Bennett may not have shared the deep antipathy of Ontario Orangemen towards the Roman Catholic church, but he was a dedicated Methodist and he had been a leader of the struggle to keep Roman Catholic separate schools out of Alberta. Roman Catholics and Roman Catholic institutions were notably absent from any list of recipients of Bennett largesse. When Monsignor Joury appeared in Ottawa in the spring of 1936 to plead for Bennett's financial assistance to repair the roof of his church, he must have been viewed by Bennett as an archangel sent to test his good samaritanism.

Bennett was equal to the challenge. He guaranteed Joury's note for $1500 at the Dominion Bank in Montreal. Joury agreed to pay off the loan in monthly instalments and to pay the interest on it. That was the last Bennett or the bank saw of Joury, with but one exception. Some months later, in response to Bennett's calling his attention to the fact that the note to the bank was in default, Joury sent Bennett a pound box of Turkish Delight, a confection Joury said he understood Bennett enjoyed. A year and a half later the bank advised Bennett that it had been unable to locate Joury and passed along a rumour that he had been arrested in New York on a fraud charge. Bennett, on 16 December 1937, sent the bank a cheque for $1520.34 to liquidate his guarantee.[31]

The last item in the Joury file is one of his business cards pinned to a sheet of typewriter paper. Above the card, in large letters, are scrawled the words 'Catholic Church.' Below the card is an angry footnote in heavy pencil over the signature of A.E. Millar, obviously written years later in England. It reads: 'This Priest begged for help and in his conversation lied to Lord Bennett who was extremely annoyed by continuous falsehoods. The amount of the loan was never repaid.'[32] The word 'lied' is heavily underscored.

All the foregoing loans combined could not, however, match Bennett's financial adventures with Jozef Van Wyck who, in the 1930s, was manager of the Canadian National Railways hotels. Bennett had first met him when he was manager of the Château Laurier Hotel in Ottawa. Van Wyck was a survivor of the 1929 stock market crash. During the 1920s he had pyramided his common-stock holdings until, at the peak, they probably exceeded $100,000 in value. At the 1929 crash he had sufficient equity in the portfolio to be able to hold onto his shares, but when the market dropped again in 1930 he was on the point of being wiped out. His liability to the brokerage firm of Osler,

Hammond, and Nanton now amounted to $72,000, and the latest collapse had sliced his equity to $45,000. The brokers demanded that he put up the difference or they would sell him out. Such action would destroy Van Wyck financially, and the discovery of that fact by his employers would certainly cost him his job. He asked Bennett to lend him $72,000 on his $45,000 portfolio so he could hold on until the market recovered.[33] Bennett did — after a fashion.

The first step was to call his friend Victor Drury and persuade his firm, now Drury and Thompson, to pay Osler, Hammond, and Nanton $72,000 for Van Wyck's portfolio of stock on Bennett's guarantee of the account. There was a condition. Van Wyck was to apply all the interest and dividends on his stock to paying interest on the $72,000 loan.[34] That was the deal until Bennett was preparing to leave for England in 1938 and began to sort out his financial affairs. As he would later write to the estates officer of the Toronto General Trusts Corporation after Van Wyck's death:

Mr. Van Wyck and I made a careful review of the whole situation. He was very depressed and so I agreed to take over 1,000 shares of Imperial Oil, 300 shares of Ford and 200 shares of International Nickel for $45,000, that figure being the maximum Mr. Van Wyck at any time hoped to receive for such shares. I realized there was no likelihood of any such value attaching to them in the near future, but as they were to be transferred to a trust it was not a matter of moment to me and I felt I was helping him by taking over such shares at a price far in excess of the then market price, thereby reducing his liability to a reasonable sum. I also waived the accumulation of interest at the end of 1939 which amounted to $6,678.12.

In June 1941 Bennett again reviewed the situation and offered to settle the debt for a payment of $25,000. Unfortunately, Van Wyck died before anything was done to reduce the deficit. His estate was insolvent and, when it eventually wound up, Bennett received a cheque for $8000. His loss on the Van Wyck guarantee could hardly have been less than $40,000. But Bennett bore his loss without a trace of rancour: 'I cannot tell you how sad I felt about the death of Mr. Van Wyck. He was the most lovable man.'[35]

Aside altogether from such large denomination transactions, Bennett had always been a soft touch for any good-doing Calgarians on the prowl. When a group of doctors, in 1919, decided that what Calgary needed was a sick children's hospital and took their desires to Bennett, he arranged for their use of a large house in the near downtown to start the project. Ten years later, when the institution had outgrown those premises, Bennett bought the hospital a much larger house on Eighteenth Avenue West. He was a patron of the Red Cross, the YWCA, YMCA, and of all the organized sports groups for miles around. When the Anglicans got into financial trouble with their St Agnes' Girls School, Bennett came through with a $4000 subscription to help rescue the college.

With Bennett, however, giving was more than dropping money into outstretched hands. He frequently developed a genuine interest in the affairs of beneficiaries of his largesse. One of his earliest projects was to provide medals each year for outstanding students of the Calgary public schools. In early December 1928 he wrote to Alice Millar from Ottawa to remind her not only to send out the medals but to get the names of all the winners so that when he returned to Calgary he could write each one a personal note of congratulations. In the same letter he reminded her to send flowers to George Robinson's mother, to send $100 to the Rev. Mr. Avison, and to 'ask Mrs. Kirby to drop into the office and give her a $50 bill.'

In 1924, at the end of his first year's occupancy of his suite in the Palliser Hotel, his Christmas list was limited to the telephone operators, room maids, and dining-room staff, a matter of a dozen boxes of chocolates. By 1937, his Palliser Hotel list encompassed the entire staff – a matter of 178 boxes. Christmas chocolates also went to sixty-two inmates and staff of the Keith sanitarium, along with twenty-six boxes to the inmates of the old folks home, fourteen boxes to the staff of the children's hospital, and eight boxes to the staff of the Woods Christian Home. In addition to the candy, Christmas bouquets were dispatched to the wives of his former law partners, special lady friends, and wives of Conservative party leaders.[36]

Despite his own strong aversion to smoking and drinking, there were always Christmas gifts of tobacco for hospitalized war veterans and, twice a year, a case of Scotch for the widow of his old friend Bishop William Cyprian Pinkham, Jean Drever Pinkham, whose doctors had told Bennett that a shot of Scotch a day was good for her ailing heart. And all this eight years after Bennett had abandoned permanent residence in Calgary.

Up and down the scale between Christmas chocolates and $10,000 bank guarantees were the vast bulk of Bennett's charitable donations – a stained glass window for a church in Vancouver, a pipe organ for a church in Calgary, gifts to Dalhousie, and scholarships for Calgary high schools. From 1917 onward his charitable donations, but only those that were income-tax deductible, seldom came to less than 10 per cent of his taxable income. But his tithing, as these cases starkly indicate, never accounted for more than a fraction of his giving.

CHAPTER EIGHT

Leader of the Opposition

For the people of the western plains, the wheat crop made the difference – the difference between a habitually glum and a habitually smiling populace; the difference, indeed, between melancholia and ebullience. A bumper crop put everybody to work, stripped cities and towns of idling teenage males for stooking jobs in the harvest fields, put the railways to full speed hauling grain in both directions, and encouraged urban merchants to lay in supplies for fall and winter seasons. A bumper wheat crop ripening in the fields generated the feeling that God was in his heaven and all was right with the world.

The Alberta wheat crop of 1923 was that kind of crop – the best wheat crop but one in the province's history, and one that would not be repeated for another thirty years. A year before, in the wake of four poor crops out of five, Bennett was convinced that Calgary, Alberta, and western Canada should be filed and forgotten. He was in the midst of preparations to sell his interest in Lougheed and Bennett and to relocate somewhere in eastern Canada or the British Isles.[1] With the 1923 crop, however, all such notions went from his head as he watched approvingly the efforts of his farmer friends to organize their Alberta Wheat Pool.

One bumper crop was not enough to lift Alberta from its long postwar depression, but it brought wide smiles to the faces of the beholding populace. The resulting prosperity was not confined to the year in which it was grown. The farmers would still be delivering their crops to market, turning their wheat into cash, well into 1924. That would spell a successful year ahead for Calgary business, including, of course, the law firm of Bennett, Hannah, and Sanford. In particular, it would mean a very good year for the Alberta Pacific Grain Company and its principal shareholders. It may even have been the 1923–4 crop that persuaded the Spillers' directors to buy Alberta Pacific Grain. After the preliminary negotiations in the spring of 1924, Bennett returned to England in July and the negotiations went forward successfully, but by fits and starts, until late August.[2]

Ordinarily, Bennett might have become impatient with such a tedious pace. This summer, however, there was a means of escaping the boredom – the British Empire Festival at Wembley Stadium. After a wearisome day there was always the evening tattoo at Wembley, where representatives from every nook and cranny of the empire were recreating past glories. With British pomp and circumstance, massed choruses, marching bands, and casts of thousands, British history came back to life. There were reenactments of the return of Richard the Lion-Hearted from the Crusades, the signing of the Magna Charta, Waterloo, the burial of Admiral Nelson, the Spanish Armada, Raleigh and Elizabeth, Lucknow, and the opening of Canada.

The euphoria that gripped Bennett at Wembley was still warming his spirits when he returned to Calgary after Labour Day. When the Women's and Men's Canadian clubs invited him to address a joint dinner meeting on the British Empire Festival, he accepted with alacrity and, by all accounts, delivered one of the best speeches of his life.[3] Bennett's emotional performance was such a success that one of his listeners hurried home to write a letter to the *Calgary Herald* urging the Calgary Public School Board to print up several thousand copies of the speech for distribution to the school children of Calgary. It would acquaint them, he wrote, as no textbook ever could 'with the glories of the great British Empire.' It was, unhappily, an impractical suggestion. There was no text because Bennett seldom spoke from one. Preparing such a text in his view was an inexcusable waste of time and energy. He confined himself to scribbled chapter headings, memory jogging phrases, and occasional numbers where specific-ity was required. Other speakers who used that method frequently used typed-out texts of lengthy quotations. Bennett, whose ability to reach into his memory for exact biblical passages or texts of legal precedents was legendary, seldom made use of such stratagems.

A couple of weeks after the Canadian Club speech, Bennett's attention was diverted from the past glories of the empire to the contemporary glories of the Turner Valley. Royalite no. 4 had exploded into production with a roar never before equalled in Canada.[4] When the drilling crew attempted to close the well-head valve to bring the gusher under control, the internal reservoir pressure blew the well-head casing and control valve clear through the top of the seventy-five-foot derrick. The wildly blowing well drenched the countryside with oil. The well site caught fire and burned out of control for several weeks.[5] Once the fire was brought under control, it took the crew several more weeks to bring the well itself under control and direct the flow of natural gasoline and natural gas into Royalite's newly installed separators. It was not until the following January that Royalite no. 4 was placed on steady production of $2000 worth of naphtha and $1000 worth of natural gas a day.

Royalite no. 4 put Royalite Oil Company, Calgary, and R.B. Bennett back into the oil business, in spades. On behalf of Imperial Oil, Bennett organized the Dalhousie Oil Company, which he named for his old alma mater, to consolidate the holdings of a number of small independent leaseholders on a share exchange basis.[6] The Dalhousie shares were originally issued at 50 cents. A year later they were selling for $5 each on the Calgary Stock Exchange, and Bennett's $25 par value Royalite shares were quoted at $300 per share.

The interest in the oil industry in Turner Valley and the expansion of Bennett's participation came at the same time that Arthur Meighen was trying to persuade Bennett to return to politics. It was, for Meighen, a forlorn hope at first. Bennett was simply too busy to give the idea a second thought. He was as deeply interested in politics as he had ever been, but he was discouraged by the Conservative party of Alberta. As he wrote to Meighen in

January 1925: 'In this province the situation is deplorable. The excellent convention which you attended in Edmonton, and at which Mr. Blair was chosen leader, just as well might never have held. He went east shortly after his appointment, fell ill and resigned a few weeks ago. Our friends are without heart... the efforts made in this city are spasmodic and unavailing... the fortunes of our party in this province are at a very low ebb.'[7] There was, however, a single sentence in the letter that demonstrated that while Bennett was refusing to become actively involved in Conservative *party* politics, he was deeply interested in national political *issues*.

If there was any validity to the excuses Bennett gave Meighen for not getting back into politics early in 1925 – that the demands of his business interests and law practice were much too great – how did he happen to succumb to Meighen's pleadings months later when these demands were even greater? There was not only Turner Valley, where he was about to take on the presidency of Royalite and become more deeply involved in Dalhousie and McLeod Oil. There were complex and vexing problems arising almost daily at the E.B. Eddy plant, where the newly installed and costly newsprint machinery was refusing to work the way it should.[8] President G.H. Millen, the driving force in the operation of the company, had been stricken with a serious illness and was confined to his bed. Joseph T. 'Harry' Shirreff, the vice-president, had suffered several sieges of poor health and needed all the help Bennett could give him. How, then, if he could not afford to return to politics in January, could he afford to do so in August 1925?

A possible answer is 'noblesse oblige,' as Gratton O'Leary, *Maclean's* Ottawa editor and a good friend of Bennett's, explained in an article that followed Bennett's succeeding Meighen as leader of the Conservative party:

William Jennings Bryan, when he was talking his 'cross of gold' nonsense, used to say that 'no man can make a million dollars honestly'... It is in the spirit of William Jennings Bryan that some people view with misgivings the selection of Bennett, the millionaire, to lead the Conservative party. To such people, piping on a willow whistle the thin strain that comes from misfits and failures, to whom to be rich is to be wicked, it is inconceivable that a man of broad intelligence, and a civilized philosophy of life, should tire of devoting himself to the piling up of wealth, and enter a wider sphere of activity. Yet, uncommon as this may be in Canada and the United States, it is the usual thing in England. There, a man who has amassed all the money he needs, feels that he owes it to his fellows to become a public servant, and that nothing will bring a greater return in happiness and honor. It is so I believe with Bennett.[9]

Bennett, by the late autumn of 1924 and the sale of Alberta Pacific Grain Company, had all the money he would ever need and twice as much as he could ever spend. At fifty-four, and sound of wind and limb, he was free to travel the world in service to the empire and soon-to-be commonwealth – or he could lean back and let his two most enduring interests, education and politics, chart the course of his life. He had abandoned education for the law thirty years before, but the teacher within was never completely subverted. He never allowed his interest in the public schools and their pupils to diminish. As early as 1902, before his legal career had really taken off, he donated silver medals to outstanding students of the Olds public school.[10] The following year he donated a dozen books to start a school library in the neighbouring town of Didsbury. When the new Alberta provincial government established the University of Alberta at Edmonton in 1906, Bennett led the failed campaign to establish a university at Calgary. Twenty years later he still had Alice Millar drive him around Calgary district rural schools in her Model T to deliver speeches, medals, and awards to the top students. Sixty years later the Calgary Public School Board was still delivering scholarships from the Bennett Trust to its leading graduates.[11] Throughout Bennett's life, he seldom delivered a speech in which there were not references of the schoolteacher at work.

The renewal of his acquaintance with President A.S. Mackenzie of Dalhousie University at the end of the First World War led to an intimate, lifetime involvement with Dalhousie and higher education. After exercising his influence on Jessie Eddy to direct almost $1 million to the university,[12] Bennett joined the board of governors and was active in its affairs until the end of his life. In the winter of 1925, while on a trip to London, his path crossed that of G.S. Campbell, a Dalhousie governor, who was trying to put a fund together to buy a residence for the president. Bennett promptly offered to buy the house – an imposing frame structure that would have done an Upper Canadian lumber baron proud.[13]

His involvement with politics was much more of a love-hate relationship. He was still a youth in short pants when he first became addicted to politics in Hopewell Cape. And it was a form of addiction – if there was a political campaign around he had to have a part in it. His last year in Chatham and first five years in Calgary are proof of his infatuation; then, after his defeat in 1905 he must have convinced himself he was swearing off for good. In 1908 he was pushed back in when he wasn't looking, but became disenchanted and was talked into switching to federal politics. He was thoroughly disenchanted again in 1918, but was persuaded to return in 1921. By 1925, however, there were signs that Bennett's addiction to politics was weakening. Nobody who was not addicted, or who did not love every minute of it, could have made the kind of speeches that normally flowed from Bennett. But he was much warier this time. The first bauble Meighen offered by way of cabinet appointments was spurned by Bennett. It was only after Meighen offered the post of minister of justice that Bennett agreed to return to the hustings.

It may well be, however, that this explanation is too simple, that there were other things working on Bennett. He was always an issue-driven politician. Provincial status for Alberta, public schools, immigration, transportation, political corruption, and American annexation were all visceral issues that drove Bennett to active political participation. In 1925 a new issue was beginning to emerge that captured his attention – the burgeoning stampede of young Canadians, a total of 500,000 since the war, for the economic fleshpots of the United States. That was the sort of issue that Bennett could get his teeth into, and it became the central theme of every speech he made in the 1925 campaign.

In that campaign, Bennett did a lot more than make speeches. He became the de facto leader and organizer of the Conservative campaign in Alberta. By 8 September he had organized two conventions, had three others scheduled, and was on the point of persuading General Griesbach of Edmonton to take charge of eight constituencies in the north.[14] In addition, he had helped to persuade A.A. McGillivray, one of western Canada's outstanding criminal lawyers, to take the leadership of the Alberta Conservative party. When the campaign got underway in early October he was all over the place, with major speeches at Fort Macleod, Medicine Hat, and Lethbridge.

The campaign itself, one of the dullest on record, was to a considerable extent a replay of the 1911 election – free trade versus tariff protection, except that the Liberals had abandoned 'free trade' in favour of 'tariff for revenue.' In a world gone protectionist mad since the end of the war, free trade with the United States was no longer salable. That was particularly so after the American Congress in 1922 passed the Fordney-McCumber Tariff Act that imposed prohibitive duties on almost everything Canada could export, particularly agricultural products.

Bennett was the only nominee at a meeting of the Calgary West constituency called to select a candidate for the 29 October election. In his acceptance speech, he focused his attention on the mass exodus of young Canadians to the United States, a great island of prosperity in a world of depression and debt. The challenge facing Canada was to reorder its affairs in a way that would create job opportunities at sufficient rates of pay to keep Canadians at home. That could be done by following the example set by the United States in raising tariffs to protect Americans. It was, of course, the basic protectionist argument that had carried the Conservatives to power in 1911. This time, however, the annexation threat of 1911 was replaced by the depopulation threat.

The protectionist doctrine might sell in Calgary, where Bennett's personal popularity carried more weight than political doctrine, but what of the large farm vote in the Calgary area? In 1921 he had piled up a comfortable majority of the urban vote, but his loss of the farm vote by 1000 ballots cost him the election. Was he not again antagonizing the very people whose support he needed most? If Bennett gave any thought to such concerns, there is no evidence in anything he said during the campaign.

The Progressive party was at the peak of its power in 1921, when J. T. Shaw, its endorsed candidate in Calgary West, narrowly defeated R.B. Bennett. Since then, as a party, it had fallen on hard times. Its leader, T.A. Crerar, quit in disgust in 1922 when he could not get along with Henry Wise Wood, the leader of the United Farmers of Alberta. The Alberta members of parliament bolted the party, the Saskatchewan members were heeding the siren calls of the Mackenzie King Liberals, and the Manitoba members were wavering back and forth. There was bound to be a diminution in the fervour of the farmers for the low-tariff Progressives, particularly after Fordney-McCumber shut Alberta farmers out of what had been a profitable American market for their products. Bennett set out to make all the trouble he could for the Progressive party by ridiculing individual members of parliament, who squabbled among themselves over which measures of the King government to support and which to reject, while still keeping the Liberals in power.

Indeed, in his attacks on Progressive party candidates, Bennett did not hesitate to tromp all over western farmers' most cherished prejudices – their hatred of 'easterners.' This had probably started with justifiable antipathy towards being overcharged for everything they bought from eastern manufacturers. Then there was the business of being overcharged on railway freight rates. Soon the antipathy towards manufacturers became extended to all residents of Ontario and Quebec. In what was probably the most impassioned defence of eastern Canadians ever heard in western Canada, Bennett said in his final speech of the campaign on 27 October in Banff: 'My opponents ... play the part of agents sewing seeds of hate and envy against our more fortunate neighbors ... [the people of eastern Canada]. They ask you to think of them as people with horns waiting to devour you. How can they hope to build a country on hate and bitterness? They [eastern Canadians] are the same flesh as our flesh. The same blood. They have just as much concern for the future of this country as we, and more because Ontario pays 44%, Quebec 28% and Alberta only 2.8% of the tax revenue of the Government.'[15]

Across Alberta generally, the farmers kept the faith with Henry Wise Wood and the Progressives. But there had been enough withering away of support in the Calgary area to enable Bennett to recapture a fifty-five vote majority of the farmers' votes. He won Calgary West by a majority of more than 4200.

On the national scene the Conservatives wiped out the Liberals in Nova Scotia, decimated the Progressives in Ontario, and emerged from the election with 116 seats, fifteen more than the Liberals but ten short of an overall majority. Once again the Progressives, with twenty-four seats compared with the sixty-four they had held, had the balance of power. The Conservatives gained sixty-six seats, while the Liberals lost sixteen and clearly lost the election.

The only one who refused to concede the election to the Conservatives was Mackenzie King himself. He persuaded the governor general that he was entitled to remain in office until a vote of the House of Commons went against his government. Instead of becoming minister of finance in Arthur Meighen's cabinet, Bennett was forced to occupy a Commons member's seat on the opposition benches from February to July in 1926. Ironically, this would turn out to be the most exciting five months in Bennett's life.

He would become a leading member of the Select House of Commons Committee to Investigate the Department of Customs and Excise. Its blistering report would drive Mackenzie King from office. He would become the majority shareholder of the E.B. Eddy Company. He would become the target for a $250,000 blackmail plot. And he would assume the blame for causing the Meighen administration's defeat on its first challenge in the House of Commons.

The Customs and Excise scandal, which blew up in the House of Commons on 2 February, was a long time in gestation. In a way, it came about as a by-product of the automobile age. The enforcement branch of the Canadian customs service was still geared to the age of the ocean freighter and railway boxcar, when imported goods moved from ship and train into bonded warehouses, where customs duties were assessed and paid. Enforcement then was seeing that goods were properly categorized for duty purposes. It was a system that become wholly inadequate when imported goods moved across the Canadian-United States border by truck over an expanding network of roads, yet it remained almost unchanged. By the early 1920s merchants from Halifax to Vancouver were complaining to the government about the unfair competition they were facing from smuggled goods flowing into the retail trade. When Prohibition was adopted in Canada and the United States, two-way smuggling of alcoholic beverages became the stuff of newspaper headlines and newsreel pictures.

The federal government took little heed of the merchants' protest, so they set up a special organization of their own and hired special agents to investigate the liaison between venal customs enforcement agents and smugglers. Then they placed their evidence in the hands of the prime minister. Nothing happened. Nothing continued to happen until 4 September 1925, when Mackenzie King at long last moved his minister of customs, Jacques Bureau, upstairs to the Senate and appointed G.H. Boivin to succeed him. Nothing changed in the department, however, where the same venal employees were on the job in a hopelessly undermanned enforcement service. The embattled merchants then turned to one of their own, H.H. Stevens – a former Vancouver grocer turned Conservative member of parliament. On the night of 2 February 1926, behind a desk overloaded with documentation, Stevens, in a five-hour speech that went on until 3 am, launched a barrage of charges against the customs bureaucracy and all its works. The immediate result was the setting up of a nine-man parliamentary committee to investigate the Customs Department. Bennett was named as one of the four Conservatives on the committee. Although its hearings were dominated by Stevens, Bennett was nevertheless exceedingly active in questioning the witnesses and in drafting the final, unanimous report of the committee.

During March and April there was a new sensation every other day, but, by the middle of May, the hearings were winding down and the members were ready to begin their unanimous indictment of the government. It was at this stage that Bennett's participation in the committee's affairs was interrupted by the death of J.T. 'Harry' Shirreff. He had been ill for some weeks at home, but his death on 20 May was quite unexpected. It confronted Bennett, as soon as the funeral was over, with the responsibility of coming up with half a million dollars, cash.

Bennett and Shirreff had identical clauses in their wills leaving to each other the shares they held in the Eddy Company. Bennett held 501 shares and Shirreff, 1007 shares. Bennett's inheritance was conditional on his setting up a $250,000 trust that would pay Mrs Shirreff $1000 a month for life and provide $250,000 to pay the death duties Quebec would levy on Shirreff's estate.[16] Bennett had well over $500,000 in securities stashed away in safety deposit boxes, exclusive of what he would receive from the sale of Alberta Pacific Grain. His own holdings of Eddy stock were worth at least $1.5 million. Although any half-million dollar loan request should be easy for any bank to grant, the negotiations took time, particularly when Bennett was deeply involved in parliamentary affairs following the tabling, on 18 June, of the Customs Committee's indictment of the Mackenzie King administration. It set off two weeks of the wildest turmoil ever witnessed in a Canadian parliament. Successions of motions, counter motions, points of order, and points of privilege were argued, interspersed with battering-ram attacks on the government. On one occasion the Speaker was kept in his chair for nine consecutive hours. Bruce Hutchison has written that the Progressives, who had kept the Liberals in power for six months, 'were nauseated by the reeking stench of corruption and even Woodsworth had wavered, feeling, as he said, like a man in a mud bath.'[17]

The parliamentary sessions started early and ended late, often well after midnight. In the last week of June Bennett remembered a promise he had made to his friend A.A. McGillivray, the Alberta Conservative leader, to return to Alberta to assist him in the provincial election by making a couple of speeches. As Mackenzie

King was at last going to the governor general to ask for a dissolution, to avoid sure defeat on the condemnatory motion on the Customs inquiry, Bennett was travelling back to Calgary. Lord Byng, however, refused King's request to have parliament dissolved, and called on Meighen to form a government. Meighen did so, and immediately ran afoul the Dominion Elections Act.

The act required that when a new cabinet was appointed, each cabinet appointee had to resign his seat in the House of Commons and, at a special by-election, seek the approval of his constituency to the cabinet appointment. Since compliance would have deprived the Conservatives of a dozen votes on any division, Meighen seized upon a dubious technicality. He made up a cabinet composed exclusively of *acting* ministers, who served without pay pending the holding of the by-elections. The Liberals challenged the legality of Meighen's stratagem with motions and amendments that kept the House of Commons in a turmoil.

On his first confidence vote in the House of Commons, Meighen was defeated by a single vote when T.W. Bird, the Progressive member for Nelson, who was paired with the absent Bennett and honour bound not to vote, nevertheless cast the vote that proved the margin of difference. Meighen was granted a dissolution, and went down to defeat in the election he called for 14 September. Bennett always blamed himself for causing the defeat. Grant Dexter of the *Winnipeg Free Press* recalled:

I asked him why he thought he could have prevented the constitutional issue from arising. He replied that any competent House of Commons man, given the Customs and other scandals, could have prevented Mr. King from ever being heard on the subject. He would have roared out his denunciations, refused to answer silly questions about the shadow cabinet, and so on. I watched R.B. in Parliament from 1926, when he entered the house, until 1936, when I went to Europe for three years. I am a good Liberal but I am very much inclined to think he was right. He was exactly the kind of debater who could have done this.[18]

Bennett, however, had no time for casual ruminations over what might have been when he got back to Ottawa from Calgary that July. There was a letter on his desk that demanded his attention, even as he was being sworn in as minister of finance in Meighen's pre-election cabinet. It was from Mrs Edith Jessie Richardson, the sixty-five-old sister of Jennie Shirreff Eddy and J.H. Shirreff. It demanded $250,000, or she would launch a suit to break Shirreff's will, with disclosures that would proved exceedingly embarrassing to Bennett.[19]

Edith Richardson, as the last surviving Shirreff, clearly regarded Bennett as an interloper who had taken an unfair advantage of her sister and now her brother to enrich himself at her expense. She had, indeed, been making something of a nuisance of herself to Bennett since Jennie Eddy's death. Mrs Eddy had made her sister the beneficiary of a life interest in the income from a $375,000 trust fund. The trust was to pay Mrs Richardson $19,000 a year for life, and when she died it was to go to Dalhousie University.[20]

Mrs Eddy had some firmly fixed ideas about gravestones, one of which was the smaller the better, within the limits of good taste. She stipulated in her will that a gravestone costing no more than $2000 was to be erected on the Shirreff family plot in the cemetery at Chatham, New Brunswick. Mrs Richardson felt herself under no compulsion to be bound by any such limit. Some time after Jennie's death she went shopping for a memorial at the shop of the McIntosh Granite Company of Toronto, found a gravestone to her liking, and ordered one made and erected for $4800.[21]

When Bennett discovered what Mrs Richardson was about, he notified the company of the limit Mrs Eddy had placed on the cost of the memorial stone. Mrs Richardson persuaded the company to proceed with the $4800 stone, which it did. The company billed the estate for $4800. Bennett sent a cheque for $2000 and told the company to collect the balance from Mrs Richardson. Mrs Richardson refused to pay and, eventually, Bennett made the payment through the Montreal Trust Company, trustee for the estate. Then, because of Mrs Eddy's limitation, Bennett, as executor of her will, felt compelled to reimburse the estate for the $2800 it had paid out.

Mrs Richardson was convinced that only some legalistic hanky panky on the part of R.B. Bennett could have resulted in his becoming principal heir to both her sister's and her brother's estates. Immediately after the funeral of her brother she went to Toronto and retained the services of R.T. Harding to investigate the home life of the late J.T. Shirreff and anything else he could find that would enable her to challenge the validity of Shirreff's will.[22]

Harding talked briefly to Bennett, but his main questionees were the servants in the Shirreff home, who provided him with some colourful accounts of the violent relationship they alleged to exist between Shirreff and his wife.[23] They told him that Mrs Shirreff suffered from pre-menstrual trauma, during which she violently attacked her husband, physically as well as verbally. Shirreff, on his part, had a drinking problem which his doctor was trying to treat, but which was intensified by his wife, who served him whiskey against the doctor's orders. It was, presumably, the gossip obtained by Harding that persuaded Mrs Richardson that the Shirreff will might be vulnerable to a challenge in the courts. Instead of taking that action, however, she wrote to Bennett on 28 and 29 July demanding that he pay her $250,000, failing which she 'made a veiled threat of publicity or legal action.' Bennett gathered up the Richardson letters and sent them off to T.P. Foran, the lawyer for both Mrs Eddy and her brother, with the request that Foran act for him in the Richardson blackmail attempt. Foran took the blackmail threat in charge and effectively disposed of it.[24]

As far as his speech-making safari to Alberta was concerned, Bennett might just as well have stayed in Ottawa. The result for the Conservatives was a gain of three seats, to a total of four, in a legislature of sixty dominated by forty-three United Farmers of Alberta. Nor did Bennett do as well for the Conservatives that September in the federal election. He won his own seat in Calgary West, but he was the only Conservative elected in the three prairie provinces. Across the plains, the Conservatives polled

200,000 votes and lost every seat but one. The Liberals cum Liberal-Progressives polled 250,000 votes and won twenty-nine of the fifty-five prairie seats. Across the country, the Conservatives outpolled the Liberals by 83,051 votes, but lost the election by 125 seats to 91.[25]

The loss of the 1926 election was a shattering surprise to Meighen, who lost his own seat, and to Bennett, who had never worked harder in any election. He was clearly convinced that both the custom's scandal and the population drain to the United States would be cutting issues with the electors, and he made the most of both. But nowhere in Canada did the custom's scandal send angry electors rushing to the polls to throw the rascals out – perhaps because, in any confrontation between customs duties dodgers and minions of the law, public sympathy is usually with the smugglers. Nor was there much evidence that Mackenzie King's 'constitutional issue,' his attack on Lord Byng for refusing to grant him a dissolution, aroused any more interest. The truth probably is that the election was lost by inadvertence – by Meighen's effort to extricate himself from his reputation as the father of wartime conscription. That reputation, and the Conservative party's identification as the conscriptionist party, gave the Liberals a clean sweep of the sixty-five Quebec seats in 1921 and sixty-one seats in 1925. After the 1925 election, Meighen decided to try to make peace with Quebec, and on 16 November he delivered his famous speech in Hamilton, Ontario, in which he seemed to abandon Canada's 'Ready, Aye Ready' stance whenever Britain called for military support.

Henceforth, Meighen announced, when that call came, the Canadian government would determine what its policy would be, along with what measures it would take to prosecute the war effort most effectively. It would then submit its package for approval of the Canadian electorate. But the Hamilton speech failed to win friends in Quebec or to gain Conservative votes at the Bagot by-election then being waged. It so outraged Conservative voters in Ontario that the party lost fifteen seats in 1926 and the election.

Once the shock waves of defeat subsided, Meighen's personal

defeat in Portage la Prairie made it a comparatively easy matter for him to make up his mind to retire both from the leadership of the Conservative party and from politics. But it was no easy matter for the Conservative party to accept Meighen's decision. In the hiatus between the ballot-marking on 14 September and King's formal accession to power on 25 September, Meighen, in the words of the *Ottawa Journal*, 'has been showered with letters and telegrams from all over Canada urging him to retain the leadership of the party, and no fewer than four seats were offered to him. Sir Henry Drayton, it is understood, being among those who were willing to give up his constituency for his chief.'

But Meighen had made up his mind, and, after two hours of fruitless effort to change it, the post mortem convention of party leaders, members of parliament, and senators that assembled at Ottawa on 11 October voted to accept his resignation. It also named an executive committee to begin the process of selecting the time and place for holding a national convention to elect a new leader.

What Bennett made of his own future in the Conservative party emerged much later. There was the immediate question of electing a temporary leader of the opposition in the House of Commons, with the idea always floating free in the back of the party mind that the temporary leader would ultimately succeed to the permanent leadership. When the members of parliament turned to the business of selecting one of their number, Bennett's name was among those advanced. He refused to stand and, after a couple of ballots, Hugh Guthrie was selected.[26] With a quarter of a century of active participation in Ontario politics behind him, Guthrie certainly had a valid claim to the leadership on the ground of seniority. But Guthrie's was, in the eyes of many veteran Conservatives, a blemished experience. For sixteen years he had been one of Sir Wilfrid Laurier's important Ontario lieutenants. Then he had switched allegiance to Sir Robert Borden's Union Government in 1917 and, after the war, served as Arthur Meighen's minister of militia. He was, of course, persona non grata in Quebec.

The October caucus decided that, for the first time in history, the new leader should be chosen at a national convention of the Conservative party. Bennett was one of the five members of a special committee – Sir George Perley, Major-General A.D. McRae, J.R. Shaw, and J.D. Chaplin – named to plan the convention.

The most important members of that committee, as far as the Conservative party and R.B. Bennett were concerned, was A.D. McRae. McRae's acquaintanceship with Bennett went back over twenty years, to the time when Bennett handled CPR legal affairs and McRae was a partner of McRae and Davidson, who marketed many thousands of acres of CPR farm land in the Regina-Saskatoon corridor. By the time of the First World War, McRae could afford to abandon the land-developing business to enlist in the Canadian army, where he became its quartermaster-general, and went on to serve as director of organization for the British wartime information department. After the war he moved from the prairies to British Columbia, made another fortune in fisheries and forestry products, and dabbled with little success in provincial politics as a maverick Conservative. He switched to the federal field and, in the 1926 election, was elected for Vancouver North. If Bennett needed somebody to persuade him that the leadership of the Conservative party was his for the seeking and that he owed it to his country to take on the responsibility of leadership, McRae was Bennett's kind of persuader. But he was a lot more than that. A superb organizer, he quickly gravitated to the chairmanship of the organizing committee. In the process of organizing his provincial delegations and special committees, he never lost a chance to extol Bennett's virtues as leader of the party. Eventually, at a meeting in Ottawa on 22 February, the expanded committee, composed of eight representatives each from Ontario and Quebec, one from Prince Edward Island, and three each from all the other provinces, selected Winnipeg as the locale and 11 October as the assembling date for the leadership convention. It also named McRae as chairman of the ten-member organizing committee. That translated into McRae not only organizing the Winnipeg convention, but becoming the organizing genius of the national Conservative party itself.[27]

When Bennett eventually made up his mind to run for the leadership is not known, but it was probably at some time during the ten-week session of parliament that began on 7 February and ended on 14 April 1927. His contribution to the budget debate completely overshadowed Hugh Guthrie's performance. It harkened back, in many ways, to his performance on the railway debates of the previous decade. The publisher of the *Calgary Herald* thought so highly of it that he cleared out two full pages to publish it almost verbatim.[28] It was, indeed, a speech full of ideas. He advocated the establishment of a sinking fund that would ultimately take Canada out of debt. To bring that off, he urged the issuing of 4 per cent government bonds to which the chartered banks and insurance companies would be required to subscribe percentages of their reserves, capital, and premium income. Most of all, he urged the enactment of a universal retail sales tax, an imposed levy on every transaction of whatever kind where money changed hands.

Bennett threw himself into the House of Commons proceedings in that spring of 1927 as he had never done before. The index to the House of Commons Hansard requires thirty column inches to list his intervention in the debates, a scant six inches less than it took to list those of the Conservative party house leader himself. There was one particular issue that he clearly enjoyed more than anything else in his political life – the debate over the extension of the charter of the Montreal, Ottawa, and Georgian Bay Canal Company, the promotion of Sir Clifford Sifton and his family from which the Siftons hoped to extract profits running into the millions of dollars.[29]

The Georgian Bay Canal project first surfaced in 1894. When it came before the House of Commons again on 7 February 1927 it was to renew its charter for the fourteenth time in thirty-three years, and nothing had yet happened to advance it an inch towards actuality. The original concept was that of providing an all-Canadian shipping route for Canadian wheat from western Canada to Montreal that would cut 800 miles off the Great Lakes–Welland Canal route. The canal contemplated construction of no fewer than twenty-seven locks to connect the Ottawa River, via

Lake Nipissing and the French River, with Georgian Bay. When successive Canadian governments refused to provide the subsidies the project required, one promoter after another was forced to abandon it. Hope kept springing eternal, however, and new promoters kept emerging from the financial-engineering underbrush. The Montreal, Ottawa, and Georgian Bay Canal Company charter was about to expire into nullity in May 1927 when the Sifton family, which had acquired ownership of the charter several years earlier, decided to make it the vehicle for a gigantic hydroelectric power company promotion.

The Montreal to Georgian Bay waterways contained a number of power sites which, theoretically, would fall to the canal company that controlled the waterway. The difficulty was that during the twenty-five-year hydroelectric boom, serious constitutional issues had been raised over the ownership of power sites. The governments of Ontario and Quebec contended, and so convinced the courts, that federal control of waterways was limited to navigation; hydroelectric power was a natural resource owned by the provinces. What was more, Ontario had established Ontario Hydro, which developed a number of sites under provincial ownership. Nevertheless, the Siftons, convinced they had the assurance of the Liberal government's support for the project, applied for a charter extension for the Montreal, Ottawa, and Georgian Bay Canal Company Limited. They did so by way of a private member's bill introduced into the House of Commons by E.R.E. Chevrier, MP for Ottawa. Chevrier inadvertently got Bennett's attention, and thundering opposition, very early in the debate. The *Ottawa Citizen*, which had previously supported the project, had reversed its position and now actively opposed it. Chevrier attributed this reversal to the fact that Southam, publisher of the *Citizen*, was now a director of the International Pulp and Paper Company, which owned a hydro power plant on the Ottawa River and might be unfavourably affected by the Georgian Bay project. In developing his argument, Chevrier listed the names of all the International directors. The list contained the name of R.B. Bennett, and Bennett let fly with a barrage of demands that Chevrier withdraw his innuendo that his position in the House of Commons was influenced by that membership. Chevrier's motion, for the House of Commons to approve of his bill in principle and send it to the Railway and Canals Committee for detailed consideration, produced the most prolonged and bitter debate of the 1927 parliament. Ordinary private members' bills passed through the House of Commons in chunks. They were allotted an hour for debate two nights a week and, on a regular night, fifteen or twenty bills, mainly divorces in the 1920s, were heard. But not when the Georgian Bay Canal Bill got onto the order paper. From the day of its introduction, 25 February, until it was eventually given second reading on 28 March, it practically monopolized the time allotted to private members' bills. In all, a total of twelve separate one-hour sessions were taken up by Bill 78. There were few of those sessions in which Bennett did not actively participate. Highlighting that participation was the extraction from the prime minister himself that he had discussed the project with one of the Sifton sons.

When the project got before the railway committee, it attracted such opposition from the public power advocates of Ontario that it received the unanimous rejection by the committee as a measure 'not in the public interest of Canada' and its charter was allowed to expire. That was the joyous conclusion for Bennett of his almost thirty years of active dislike of the Siftons and all their works.

With the business of the House of Commons concluded on 14 April, it was adjourned until the following January. This cleared the way for Bennett to spend the rest of 1927 in a campaign for the leadership of the Conservative party and in familiarizing himself with the operation of the E.B. Eddy Company, of which he was now the owner of 1508 of its 3000 shares of capital stock. The plant stretched for two miles along the north shore of the Ottawa River from the Chaudière Falls to the Gatineau River and was composed of twenty-seven buildings in which, at its peak, 2500 people were employed. The company's lumbering and pulpwood operation harvested upwards of 40,000 cords of wood a year: cut it, trimmed it, hauled it, and then floated it down the Gatineau River to Hull and piled it in huge pyramids to await consumption. It consumed 45,000 tons of coal a year, along with thousands of watts of hydro power. In a single month it turned out 4000 tons of newsprint, 947 tons of speciality papers (including 333 tons of wrapping paper), 7831 cases of toilet paper, 10,782,000 grocery bags, and 20,386 cases of matches.[30]

Within the general categories of manufacturing there were many varieties and specialities. Under the heading of Specialty Paper Products was the cardboard department that turned out almost 10 tons of product a day, a bristol board plant, a bond paper plant, and a book paper plant. Behind all this production was an immensely complicated back-up organization that included several winter bush camps, a steam railway, machine shops, and stockpiles of raw materials and industrial products to be kept sorted and flowing. Embroidered into the fabric of the operation was an ever-increasing army of white-collared workers.

It may have been much too complex, too far flung, too specialized, and too generalized for any outside lawyer to master, but with the death of Harry Shirreff it suddenly became incumbent on R.B. Bennett to make an effort to be on top of it all. After all, it was now mainly his money that was involved, and how could he be sure his interests were being well served if he did not understand what was going on? No one realized this better than Bennett, but from the day he acquired majority ownership of the company until he sold it to Garfield Weston in 1943 it remained inscrutable for him.

The audited balance sheet of the company assessed its plant and equipment at $6 million. Such an asset ought to return a profit of at least 6 per cent annually. Why did it not do so? Why were huge sums invested every year in capital improvements and replacements if earnings were not increased? Why did the annual forecasts of production, sales, and profits seldom turn out to be correct? Bennett asked, but the explanations never made sense to him. Now that he was the majority stockholder in the company, he was prepared to make his presence felt.

Once the details of the Conservative party's defeat in 1926

were taken care of, Bennett was able to find time from his parliamentary duties to confer at length with C.V. Caesar, the new general manager of the Eddy company, to ventilate the questions about the Company's operation that had been troubling him. A couple of months later, on 5 May, Caesar dictated a five-page letter in which he outlined the steps being taken to enhance the profitability of the operation. The reforms included everything from improvements to the toilet facilities in the tissue paper mill to prevention of flash fires in the 2000 tons of coal regularly kept in storage.[31] Two days later he supplemented the summary with another four-page memorandum. Taken together, the letters read like a book of instructions on how not to run a paper mill. They could also be interpreted as a catalogue of the problems that were inevitable in trying to keep in operation an old-and-not-well-maintained paper mill.

Bennett's response to Caesar's earnest effort to explain and to justify was typical of his life-long reaction to the E.B. Eddy Company and all its works – unsatisfied, impatient, and brusque to the point of unfriendliness. For example, this passage from his reply to Caesar on 23 July: 'I am not unmindful of your devotion to the Company and its interests. On the other hand I cannot but think that I am probably to blame for having left you with responsibilities in connection with a manufacturing enterprise with which you are not familiar. I will discuss the whole matter with you when I am east . . . Effective and efficient control of the industry is lacking and the result is unnecessary cost, waste and lack of a coordinated effort.'[32]

Part of the explanation for Bennett's unfavourable reaction to Caesar may lie in an utter coincidence. It was while he was in the midst of wrestling with the Eddy company puzzles that F.B. Feeley floated into his orbit, stayed for a year, and disappeared without a trace. Whether Feeley was self-cast in the role of informer or special agent, or whether he had been recruited by Bennett, can never be known. He supplied Bennett with long, closely typed letters, sometimes every month, sometimes every couple of weeks, in which he identified errors of omission and commission in the daily operations of the Eddy establishment.

Feeley appeared to be an occupant of a lower-middle-management slot in the Eddy company head office. In one letter he mentioned that in the past he had informed Mr Shirreff of various management and operational faults and, from the phraseology of the earliest letter on file, there is indication that he was a volunteer rather than a conscripted informer. On 26 May 1927 he wrote Bennett at the Château Laurier:

Dear Sir:

Circumstances prevent me from using a typewriter just now and trust you will pardon me for taking the liberty I am again taking in placing further information before you.

Permit me to refer to your last wire and remark that you certainly put the fear of the Lord into a lot of them here. At present they are passing the buck and have now placed the responsibility on the Woods Department. But when you have a mill superintendent who knows very little about the practical end, what can you expect?

Your sulphite plant was running at one third capacity while you are using sulphite bought from Howard Smith . . . You were informed 'b' mill was making better paper now because of the overhauling of the machine. Partly true, but they are also using better sulphite than a year ago.

Terrible complaint in this morning from Wright and Co [about] the poor finish, loose cores and [softness of newsprint rolls]. The Detroit newspaper is threatening to cancel contract and refuse payment for unsatisfactory paper.[33]

The true state of affairs was never placed before you . . .

For Bennett, that reference to poor-quality newsprint was a real shocker because the first crisis to arise after his assumption of control of the company concerned newsprint. It developed while he was entangled in the aftermath of the Conservative party defeat. In November 1926 a newspaper in Rochester, New York, refused to accept seven carloads of newsprint delivered to it. Caesar rushed to Rochester to join the company's American sales agency in a conference with the publishers. Ultimately they agreed to take five of the cars, but could not be persuaded to accept the other two on any terms. Six months later the manager of Wright and Company, the New York newsprint sales agency, wrote directly to Bennett to complain about the quality of the newsprint being produced by the Eddy company. Six months later still he would be complaining to Caesar that the publishers of the Buffalo, New York, paper were threatening to take their business elsewhere if the quality of Eddy newsprint was not improved.

The burden of Feeley's litany of complaints – unnecessary costs, waste, lack of coordinated effort – conformed perfectly with Bennett's own assessment of the situation. Specifically they ranged all the way from the trivial to the important – from boozing it up in the accounting department and wasting time reading the paper in the men's toilet, to misplacing, for two whole weeks, a half ton of specially fabricated steel rods for a paper mill, and over-ordering, by twenty barrels, the amount of tar needed to repair a roof. The surplus was placed in storage and, during an Ottawa heatwave, the containers burst at the seams and coated a huge expanse of warehouse floor with tar to the depth of three inches.[34]

Feeley kept up his letter-writing campaign until early in 1928, when he wrote to Bennett that he had been fired and disappeared from Bennett's orbit as quickly as he had entered it. In that one year he had poisoned Bennett's confidence in his company. For as long as Bennett controlled the Eddy company, he was never satisfied with its performance and could never bring himself to congratulate any of his key personnel for a job well done.

With the adjournment in April 1927 of the House of Commons, Bennett returned to Calgary and the exciting challenges of the new Turner Valley oil boom. By this time Royalite had its wild no. 4 well under control and it was flowing 500 barrels a day through its new pipeline into the Imperial Oil refinery in Calgary. The company was preparing to drill another half-dozen wells to tap the rich reservoir no. 4 had discovered.

Unhappily, over the next five months, the Eddy company would continually intrude on the oil business and the Conservative party convention. That process began in mid-June, when

Bennett received a telegram from Ottawa reporting that V.M. Drury had made an offer to buy all the shares of the minority stockholders of the Eddy company. Since Lord Beaverbrook had sold his Royal Securities Corporation to Izaac Walton Killam in 1919, Drury had been operating his own brokerage business in Montreal, Drury and Company. He also represented Beaverbrook's interests on a number of Canadian corporation boards of directors and was, along with Bennett himself, a director of the International Paper Company of New York. On 23 June Bennett wired Drury: 'Confidential. Have just been asked my attitude regarding your purchase shares at seventeen hundred. Wired I had no right to object and if I had I would not. stop. Believe your offer will be accepted.'[35]

By this time all the other minority shareholders except G.H. Millen were dead and their estates were being administered by the Royal Trust Company, which also held Millen's shares. While Bennett's telegram was on its way eastward, a much longer wire from H.S. Smith was on its way to Bennett from New York. Smith was president of the Wright company, sale agents for the United States for Eddy's newsprint production.

Smith had got wind of Drury's attempt to buy up the minority shareholdings of the Eddy company, had moved in with a higher offer, and persuaded the trust company to hold off acceptance of the Drury offer until he, Smith, could buy Bennett's shares. He offered Bennett $2050 a share for his 1508 shares, subject to his being able to buy the minority shares at the same price.[36] Bennett turned Smith's offer down and the trust company then accepted Drury's offer. Drury became a director of the Eddy company and, a year later, when Millen died, Bennett persuaded Drury to take over the presidency of the company, a position he held until the outbreak of the Second World War.

Bennett's out-of-hand rejection of Smith's offer to buy him out of his Eddy shares casts some doubt on whether, by the summer of 1927, he was firmly committed to running for the Conservative leadership. In view of the continuing problem the Eddy company was having with its newsprint quality, to say nothing of the depth of Bennett's disenchantment with its operation generally, one might have expected a more favourable reaction to Smith's purchase offer. Bennett could hardly have visualized the leadership of the Conservative party as less than a full-time job. There was no way he could retain his majority ownership of the Eddy company and remain aloof from its operational problems. The Smith offer would have appeared to any objective outsider as a most fortuitous opportunity for Bennett to begin the process that was inevitable for the national leader of a Canadian political party – the divestment of his business interests and the breaking off of his corporate connections. Yet in passing up that opportunity Bennett never even asked for a better price. It may well have been that, 1500 miles west of Parliament Hill, the corporate world had too much going for it. The Canadian stock market was also positioning itself for the long roller-coaster ride up to Black Thursday, 1929. Canada's special pulp and paper boom was sooner or later going to catch the Eddy company up in its profitable clutches. The chartered banks were all earning great profits and paying great dividends on Bennett's shares.

In the summer of 1927, there was no real Conservative party leadership campaign under way. Canadian newspapers could find nothing at home to write about, not when they had sensation after sensation emanating from the United States. Nobody mesmerized the editors of Canadian newspapers like Charles A. Lindbergh after he completed his solo flight to Paris from New York on 21 May. For the next couple of months few Canadian newspapers went to press without a Lindbergh story someplace, usually on the front page. And if there was not Lindbergh, there was Aimee Semple Macpherson, Big Bill Tilden's epic tennis court confrontations with Henri LaCoste, Bobby Jones's pursuit of his second British Open Golf championship, the Judd Gray–Rush Semple murder trial, or Lita Grey's interminable divorce suit against Charlie Chaplin. On quiet days there were the Chicago gangster shoot-'em-ups and the continuing saga of the Babe Ruth–Lou Gehrig struggle for the home-run championship of the American Baseball League.

When the Conservative convention subcommittee went out to Winnipeg in early June, they discovered that the province was deeply into a provincial election from which its politicians could not be diverted. When the ballots were counted on 29 June, the Conservatives managed to elect fifteen members in an assembly of fifty-one, which was twice as well as the Liberals did. The Bracken Progressives managed to return to power with twenty-nine seats.

In the wake of Meighen's defeat, the consensus of the newspapers seemed to be that if Premier G. Howard Ferguson of Ontario would run, he would win the Conservative leadership easily. Ferguson had evicted the United Farmers of Ontario from Queen's Park in 1923 and had won a smashing re-election in December 1926. But Ferguson quickly took himself out of the race by vigorously denying any interest in moving from Toronto to Ottawa – and he kept on denying any interest for the rest of the summer. The only really active candidate was Hugh Guthrie, the acting leader of the opposition. Guthrie made a number of speeches in Ontario embroidering the theme that the Conservative platform builders ought to be paying more attention to the needs and aspirations of the Prairie provinces, where the party had a solid base of 200,000 voters on which to build. When the newspapers tried to get Bennett to commit himself and he refused, the *Toronto Star* commented that he would be well advised to stay out of the race, and recalled the biblical comment on the difficulty camels experienced with needles' eyes. The *Ottawa Journal* responded by inviting its readers to 'look whose talking!' Joseph Atkinson, publisher of the *Star*, and 'Holy Joe' to its readers, was a multimillionaire.

In the summer of 1927 the *Ottawa Journal*, in an attempt to inject some interest into the leadership campaign, set off some trial balloons. On 7 July it gave front-page space to a story that Charles A. Magrath, chairman of Ontario Hydro and former Conservative member of parliament for Lethbridge, was going to be a candidate. It thought Magrath's wide and favourable reputation in both Alberta and Ontario made him an ideal candidate for the leadership. When no one paid the slightest attention, it followed with a story that Sir Henry Drayton's campaign was picking up steam all across the country. No one paid any attention to that story either.

The *Manitoba Free Press*, on 1 September, devoted a full column on its editorial page to a summary of the Conservative party leadership, concentrating in particular on Guthrie and Bennett. It noted that Bennett had been questioned in Toronto and Calgary about whether he would accept the leadership if it were offered to him by the convention but that he not only refused to answer, but refused to discuss the leadership situation in any way.

According to the *Free Press*, however, Guthrie's flirtation with the west had aroused antagonism in Quebec and eastern Canada. Sir George Perley, the treasurer of the convention organizing committee and old friend of Bennett, was organizing a dinner for him in Montreal to launch a 'draft Bennett' campaign that would subvert Guthrie's drive for the leadership. Any undue favouritism that Guthrie would show the west was bound to inflame Quebec, already a Conservative wilderness. The *Free Press* approvingly quoted a paragraph from an *Ottawa Journal* editorial: 'While Mr. Bennett has declined to discuss the leadership there is no reason to believe that he would refuse the post if it were offered him. It may be doubted if the cause of either Mr. Bennett or the party would be served by an organized push from Montreal or any other part of Canada . . . Political writers believe the choice will lie among Mr. Bennett, Hon. Hugh Guthrie and Sir Henry Drayton but the possibilities by no means are limited to those three.'

As for Bennett himself, he had other things on his mind after September 1927 besides the Conservative leadership. One was the sale of the Eddy match subsidiary to Ivar Kreuger, the Swedish match king. Kreuger, a reputed multimillionaire, was perhaps the most famous of the international financiers of the 1920s. He had emerged from the First World War as the head of the Swedish Match Company and, by 1927, was reputed to control half the world's match production. He had brought this about, according to legend, by putting together a whole series of national match monopolies – by lending large sums of scarce American currency to the countries of central Europe, the Middle East, and

South America in return for being granted a match manufacturing monopoly in the countries involved.

A Kreuger subsidiary at Berthierville, Quebec, owned a competitor of the Eddy match company, and a third plant, the Canadian Match Company at Pembroke, Ontario, was owned by Bryant and May of London, England. All three competed so vigorously in the Canadian market that all were losing money. Early in the summer Kreuger was in contact with Bryant and May and with Bennett with a view of buying both plants. On 2 July Kreuger cabled Bennett from London: 'Have last night signed agreement to sell World Match Corp. to Bryant and May at same time securing for ourselves substantial interest in their whole business. Trust this operation will help to achieve a permanent general agreement all different interests in Canada.'[37]

What Kreuger was telling Bennett was that the way was now open to create a Canadian match monopoly that would put an end forever to the price war in matches in Canada. The problem was to get Bennett and Kreuger to the conference table at a time when the impending leadership convention was at the top of Bennett's priorities and Kreuger was travelling the world on other monopoly errands. Eventually Bennett found a gap in his schedule and wired Kreuger that he could arrange to meet him in New York during the last week of September.[38]

The importance of the deal Bennett negotiated with Kreuger was that he concluded it and escaped with a whole skin. It would turn out, with Kreuger's suicide in Paris in 1932, that he had swindled the sharpest bankers and brokers on Wall Street for fifteen years and had flim-flammed the chartered accountants of two continents with sophisticated new bookkeeping scams. The national match monopolies he claimed to have established across the world frequently never existed. When they did, they seldom made anything like the profits his books set forth. Kreuger had taken the world's biggest and smartest bankers, brokers, trust companies, and accountants for an estimated $477 million, but not R.B. Bennett. The Canadian Match Company, which eventually emerged from the negotiations, never missed a dividend as long as Bennett was a shareholder.

By the time Bennett got back from New York, the Winnipeg convention was all set to welcome the 1500 delegates who would soon be arriving from across the country. With both General McRae, the main organizer of the convention, and Sir George Perley actively promoting Bennett's leadership, it was not surprising that the newspaper reporters had elected him the favourite candidate.[39] At this same convention, Bennett's sister Mildred, at the age of thirty-nine, discovered active party politics as an enduring purpose in life. Thereafter, until her marriage in 1931, the Bennett brother and sister were inseparable.

The depth of affection that existed between Richard and Mildred Bennett was wonderful to behold, and bafflingly so in face of the age difference that existed between them. Mildred was born into the Bennett family nineteen years after Richard, and eight years after her youngest brother. Her brother Dick was by then preparing to wind up his schoolteaching career at Douglastown and depart for Dalhousie law school, so there was no chance of normal familial bonding during their formative years, certainly not during the couple of weeks he spent with the family at Christmas time. The best guess is that the bonding occurred when Mildred was into her late teens and Bennett began taking her along on his frequent junkets to London. After graduating from Mount Allison College at Sackville, New Brunswick, Mildred lived at home at Hopewell Cape with her mother and her elder sister Evelyn, so she was free to go touring whenever the invitation came. Business took Bennett to London, but Mildred's presence took them to the Continent and through rural England, Italy, and Egypt. Later, when she was living with Evelyn in Vancouver, she accompanied Bennett to Australia and the Orient as well.

If Mildred Bennett was ever gainfully employed in Vancouver, it cannot be proved by any extant records in the city directories. She was listed only once – as secretary of the Vancouver Little Theatre. After Bennett moved to the Palliser Hotel, Mildred became a regular visitor to Calgary and Bennett added an adjoining room to his suite for her. When she met General McRae is not clear, but he put her to work in Ottawa in the new national office of the Conservative party. She quickly involved herself in Bennett's leadership drive and became his emissary to the women delegates at the Winnipeg convention.

Mildred Bennett switched from the leadership campaign to the federal election campaign with hardly a pause for breath. She moved permanently to Ottawa to take up residence with RB in the Château Laurier and in the national office of the Conservative party. In Vancouver she had matured from a pretty girl into an extraordinarily charming woman; and in Winnipeg she discovered she possessed an untapped reservoir of basic political savvy and an urge to put it to use.

Bennett himself may have been hard to pin down before the convention, but that did not mean he was not totally committed to the party itself. The party had emerged from the 1926 election so financially strapped that it had to give up the lease of its Ottawa office and disband its headquarter staff. McRae and Bennett dug into their own pockets to re-establish a new national office on Wellington Street, complete with a battery of mimeograph machines that would turn out a blizzard of political propaganda. Bennett was one of McRae's group of twenty-five wealthy Conservatives who were prepared to contribute $2500 a month for the next two years to put the party back on its feet.[40]

For Bennett, that was only the beginning. As he would write to J.T. Boyd, president of the Manitoba Conservative Association, soon after becoming leader, he had already subsidized the party to the tune of $300,000. And that was long before his investment in the *Regina Star*, which would cost him another $350,000.

In deciding to hold their convention in Winnipeg in an attempt to regain the following it had lost to the Progressive movement, the Conservatives were faced with the necessity of holding their convention in the barn-like Amphitheatre Rink. It was the only building in town capable of accommodating the 2500 delegates and alternates expected to attend. Built during the Gay Nineties as a horse-show arena, it had been converted into a skating rink during the First World War. It retained a musty skating-rink odour throughout the year. A large speakers' platform was erected for the convention along the north end of the ice area, with a curtain separating the platform from the end-zone seats. Delegates sat at tables extending from the platform to the south end of the rink, while alternates and visiting spectators used the regular hockey seats.

As things turned out, the reason for the assembly, the election of the new leader, became almost anti-climatic. The event that stood the convention, and the Conservative party itself, on its collective ear was the head-on collision between Arthur Meighen and G. Howard Ferguson.

The convention opened on Monday morning, 10 October, with all the trimmings of a love feast. The leaders of the party were introduced to prolonged applause, and Sir Robert Borden was greeted enthusiastically when he delivered his keynote speech. The same was true for Arthur Meighen when he took the podium after the noon adjournment. Meighen was not scheduled to speak, but when he asked for the opportunity it was granted as a courtesy to a former prime minister. No one among the 1574 delegates and 800 alternates had the foggiest notion of what he was going to say. What he said was a spirited, even biting, hour-long defence of the speech he had delivered in Hamilton earlier the previous year, the speech that had outraged the imperialist right wing of the Conservative party and cost the party fifteen seats in Ontario, and the election, in 1926.

The speech evoked rounds of applause as it was being delivered, particularly from the Quebec and Prairie tables, and Meighen was cheered when he finished – except by Premier Howard Ferguson of Ontario. Ferguson stormed from his seat among the convention personages and grabbed the public address microphone. He was, he said, as angry with Meighen's convention performance as he had been when Meighen came to his home before the Hamilton speech to give him a preview of it. He reminded Meighen that the speech had been made in Hamilton during the Bagot, Quebec, by-election and described it as a farfetched attempt to curry favour with the anti-British electors of Quebec. That being the case, he should have gone to Quebec to deliver it instead of inflicting it on the Conservatives of Ontario.

In contrast with the enthusiasm Meighen's speech had generated, Ferguson's performance roused many of the audience to anger.[41] Choruses of boos erupted from the western Canadian delegations as well as from Quebec. Soon hecklers in the public section behind the platform were making their presence felt. As Ferguson persisted with his criticism of Meighen and his thesis, so did the volume of abuse. Only the forceful intercession of the chairman produced a semblance of order. After perhaps half an hour, Ferguson closed with a threat to bolt the party if the convention endorsed Meighen's speech. As he made his way back to his seat, the Ontario premier was greeted with a chorus of booing that almost drowned out the applause.

Nothing came of the confrontation. Nobody moved a resolution approving or condemning either point of view. But the explosion became the big story of the convention for the one hundred reporters covering it for Canadian newspapers. For the most part, the delegates were content to let the issue lie dormant while they busied themselves with drafting resolutions on immigration, taxation, tariff policy, and wheat marketing. The contestants for the leadership were nominated on Tuesday evening and the election was run off Wednesday afternoon.

To the people of Winnipeg, the Conservative leadership convention was the biggest sporting event their town had seen in years and they treated it as such. Newspaper crowd estimators guessed the attendance to exceed 6000 people. Certainly, there was not a vacant seat to be found during the nominating process for the six candidates who agreed to run. Each candidate was entitled a nominator and a seconder, who could speak for twenty minutes, while the candidate could speak for twenty-five. Although few of the nominators used up their allotted time, the proceedings dragged badly and it was late in the evening before Bennett got his turn. The order of speaking was determined by drawing the names from a hat. Hugh Guthrie came first, followed by C.H. Cahan, Robert Rogers, Sir Henry Drayton, R.B. Bennett, and, after midnight, Dr Robert Manion.

If the Winnipeg audience came expecting an evening of rousing speech-making from some of the ablest political orators in the country, they were disappointed. The pedestrian quality of the speeches, however, did not prevent the supporters of the various candidates from bursting into applause at the slightest provocation. And if the applause that greeted the speakers when they were introduced was a criterion, there was little doubt how the vote would go when the ballots were cast the following day. Bennett was the clear favourite, though the applause for Manion did rival Bennett's. Much of the enthusiasm for Manion derived from the fact that he was a wounded war veteran, the only soldier candidate.

Bennett's speech, like all the others, was big on history and the building of Canada, but short on constructive proposals. Anyone who had listened to Bennett's speech during the budget debate of the previous March would have been disappointed that he had not returned to the 'forward look' of that speech. But Bennett was preaching to the converted, and he knew it. The *Manitoba Free Press* said he 'scored an easy victory,' gaining 246 more votes on the first ballot than his nearest rival, and two more than the required 50 per cent of the votes cast on the second ballot. The first round of the election went Bennett 594, Guthrie 345, Cahan 310, Manion 170, Rogers 114, and Drayton 31. The second vote went Bennett 789, Guthrie 320, Cahan 266, Manion 148, Rogers 37, and Drayton 3.

The spontaneity of the crowd's reaction to the announcement of Bennett's victory caught the convention managers completely by surprise. One moment Senator Gideon Robertson, the returning officer, was standing alone by the microphone reading off numbers and names. The next moment the entire stage was jammed with cheering delegates and the assemblage on the floor of the amphitheatre was stampeding after them. The French-Canadian delegates were particularly enthusiastic, greeting Bennett's victory with a boisterous rendition of 'Il est gagné ses epaulettes.'

Somewhere within the cheering madhouse on the stage were the five defeated candidates who were trying to get to the microphone to move the traditional motion that the election be made unanimous. They had to wait and wait, until a semblance of order could be restored. Only then could Bennett come to the microphone for his acceptance speech.

It was a far better speech than his nomination speech, full of quotable quotes and passages that came straight from the heart:

One night long ago I had a dream – I don't believe in dreams because they usually indicate only a bad digestion – but I thought I was here in my dreams: that I had been called upon to say something to this vast audience, and I am going to say it to you now, what that something was, because it was very real. They were not the words of a human person; they were the words of the Man of Galilee: I looked it up the next day because it stayed with me. 'And whomsoever of you will be the chiefest, shall be servant of all.'

. . .

Men and women, you have honored me beyond my deserts, beyond any deserts I ever may have, you have made me, for the moment, the chiefest among you, and please God I shall be the servant to all.

. . .

It has been said that I am a man of great wealth. It is true. I got it by my own untiring efforts in this great western land. I look upon it as a solemn trust to enable me to serve my country without fear or regard for the future. No longer can the claims of my business or my profession be upon me.

. . .

You have determined for me that henceforth I must dedicate my talents and my time and such qualities as I may have, the fortune that God has been good enough to give me, to the interests of my country through the great party to which I am privileged to belong.[42]

Once the euphoria of the convention had evaporated, the business of settling into the leadership of the Conservative party took considerable adjustment. Bennett moved from the Rideau Club to a suite on the second floor of the Château Laurier Hotel. He took over the opposition leader's offices from Hugh Guthrie, including the staff and the superbly qualified principal secretary, W.A. Merriam, who would prove an admirable transition smoother for Bennett. The City of Calgary staged a civic reception at the Palliser Hotel to which everybody who was anybody in southern Alberta was invited. And Bennett was deluged with mail from people who had read about his dedicating his fortune to the welfare of the party and had advice for him. Mostly it was advice from Manitoba, Saskatchewan, and the province of Quebec to finance the purchase of daily newspapers devoted to advancing the interests of the Conservative party.

Bennett quickly discovered that divorcing himself from his business interests was more difficult than he previously would have thought. He had barely embarked on his trans-Canada familiarization tour when the Eddy Match Company deal with Ivar Kreuger came unstuck. He had to rush over to London to spend a month putting it back together again with Bryant and May. Becoming detached from his Imperial Oil–Royalite Oil Company association took him well into 1928. But at last he was free to begin the process of leading the Conservative party of Canada and, as he was doing so, the Wall Street crash signalled the collapse of the world economy and the onset of the greatest economic depression the world had ever known. It was Bennett's execrable luck to assume the mantle of prime minister of Canada when everything was going from bad to worse, although the Depression, in a way, eased his way to power.

Collapsing prices for natural products and reduction in factory orders in 1930 created serious pockets of unemployment in the Maritimes and western Canada. Appeals were sent to the federal government to make loans or grants to the provinces to enable them to relieve unemployment. The demands triggered Prime Minister Mackenzie King's famous declaration on 3 April 1930, 'I would not give a single cent to any Tory Government.'[43] Then a day or so later he raised the ante from a penny to 'one five-cent piece' and opened the way for Bennett to sweep him from power in the 1930 election.

Illustration Credits

Notes

CHAPTER 1: HOPEWELL CAPE, NEW BRUNSWICK

1 Saint John Museum, Saint John, New Brunswick, Alma Russell Papers

2 National Archives of Canada, R.B. Bennett Papers, microfilm 543,883

3 After Bennett's death, Lord Beaverbrook arranged that the University of New Brunswick should become the repository for Bennett's papers, and he contributed copies of his own extensive correspondence with Bennett to the collection. In addition, he hired Robert Rogers of the University of Toronto to organize, catalogue, and compile a summary of the collection. Rogers also spent some time in New Brunswick interviewing Captain Ronald Bennett and a dozen of Bennett's surviving contemporaries from his school days in Hopewell Cape and his teaching days in Douglastown. Later on, Bennett's long-time secretary Alice Millar corresponded with other contemporaries, notably Carrie Reid and Alma Russell. She also harvested a large collection of correspondence from the Calgary area, along with some letterbooks from the early years of the Lougheed and Bennett partnership. There is a strong suspicion, however, that she edited out a great deal of material that might have reflected unfavourably on Bennett, along with an immense amount of material from the E.B. Eddy Company files. None of the extensive correspondence with Jennie Shirreff Eddy survives. The entire Bennett archives have been microfilmed by the National Archives of Canada.

4 Ibid., microfilm 544,520ff

5 Bennett Papers, microfilm 543,322–6

6 *Census of Canada*, 1871

7 Bennett Papers, Rogers's interviews, microfilm 543,904–10

8 Ibid., Bennett diaries, 1888–9, microfilm 544,470
9 Ibid., interview with Alma Russell, microfilm 543,804
10 Ibid., interview with Mrs Robinson, microfilm 543,766
11 Ibid., interview with Alma Russell, microfilm 543,804
12 Ibid., microfilm 543,769
13 Ibid., interview with R.V. Bennett, microfilm 543,882
14 Ibid., interview with Mrs Robinson, microfilm 543,766
15 Ibid., microfilm 543,803
16 Ibid., interview with Annie Morrison, microfilm 543,893–4
17 *Ottawa Journal*, 21 May 1932; Bennett Papers, microfilm 544,789–90
18 Bennett Papers, microfilm 543,925
19 Ibid., Rogers's interviews, microfilm 543,893
20 Ibid., Bennett diaries, 1888–9, microfilm 544,470ff
21 Lord Beaverbrook, *Friends: Sixty Years of Intimate Personal Relations with Richard Bedford Bennett* (London and Toronto: Heinemann 1959), 3–10; A.J.P. Taylor, *Beaverbrook* (New York: Simon and Schuster 1972), 11
22 Beaverbrook, *Friends*, 6
23 Bennett Papers, Bennett diaries, 1888–9, microfilm 544,470ff
24 *Ottawa Journal*, 19 Feb. 1906
25 Dalhousie University Law School calendars, 1890–3
26 Bennett Papers, microfilm 543,927; 544,647; 545,454
27 House of Lords Records Office, London, Beaverbrook Papers, vol. 66, file 55
28 Taylor, *Beaverbrook*, 11
29 Beaverbrook Papers, Aitken to Bennett, April 1897

CHAPTER 2: CALGARY, NORTH-WEST TERRITORIES

1 Grant MacEwan, *Calgary Cavalcade: From Fort to Fortune* (Saskatoon: Western Producer Book Service 1975), 93
2 Leishman McNeill, *Tales of the Old Town* (Calgary: Calgary Herald 1966), 13ff
3 Edward McCourt, *Saskatchewan* (Toronto: Macmillan 1968), 84
4 MacEwan, *Calgary Cavalcade*, 79
5 Calgary Bar Association Archives, Calgary Bar Association, Minutes, 1890
6 Ernest Watkins, *R.B. Bennett: A Biography* (Toronto: Kingswood House 1963), 30
7 These and all other details of financial arrangements between Lougheed and Bennett are from the pleadings, Lougheed vs. Bennett, 1922, Institute of Law Research and Reform, University of Alberta, Edmonton.

8   *Calgary Herald* interview, 2 Jan. 1939
9   J.F. Perry, ed., *They Gathered at the River* (Calgary: Central United Church 1975), 32
10 Calgary city directories, 1902–25
11 J.W. Grant MacEwan, *Eye Opener Bob: The Story of Bob Edwards* (Edmonton: Institute of Applied Art 1957), 92
12 *Alberta Tribune,* 28 Oct. 1898
13 M.C. Urquhart, ed., *Historical Statistics of Canada* (Ottawa: Statistics Canada 1983), 320
14 National Archives of Canada, Bennett Papers, microfilm 543,748
15 D.J. Hall, *Clifford Sifton,* I: *The Young Napoleon, 1861–1900* (Vancouver: University of British Columbia Press 1981), 154
16 *Calgary Herald,* 25 Sept. 1897
17 Ibid., 17 Sept. 1897
18 Douglas Owram, ed., *The Formation of Alberta: A Documentary History* (Calgary: Historical Society of Alberta 1979), 33ff
19 Lord Beaverbrook, *Friends: Sixty Years of Intimate Personal Relations with Richard Bedford Bennett* (London and Toronto: Heinemann 1959), 16–20
20 Bennett Papers, interview with George Cloakey, microfilm 544,006–15
21 Ibid.
22 *Alberta Tribune,* 28 Oct. 1898
23 *Calgary Herald,* 28 Sept. 1898
24 Ibid.
25 *Calgary Weekly Herald,* 18 Nov. 1899
26 Ibid., 25 Jan. 1900
27 Ibid.
28 Ibid.
29 *Encyclopedia of Crime and Justice* (New York: Free Press 1983), vol. 1, 1023–5
30 *Alberta Tribune,* 20 Jan. 1900
31 *Calgary Herald,* 21 July 1900
32 Ibid., 18 Sept. 1900
33 *Albertan,* 20 Sept. 1900
34 Bennett Papers, interview with George Cloakey, microfilm 544,012
35 Ibid.
36 Glenbow Archives, Calgary, Calgary Brewery Company Papers, A.E. Cross file b22c1
37 Paul F. Sharp, *The Agrarian Revolt in Western Canada: A Survey Showing American Parallels* (New York: Octagon Books 1971), 94

38 Bennett Papers, microfilm 545,454
39 *Calgary Herald*, 7 July 1902
40 Ibid., 21 July 1902
41 Bennett Papers, microfilm 545,669
42 Henry Borden, ed., *Robert Laird Borden: His Memoirs* (Toronto: Macmillan 1938), 9
43 Bennett Papers, Borden correspondence, microfilm 545,760–78
44 Ibid., 545,778
45 Sharp, *Agrarian Revolt*
46 Bennett Papers, microfilm 544,038–43
47 Ibid., microfilm 545,158
48 *Calgary Herald*, 10 Sept. 1904; Regina *Morning Leader*, 12 Sept. 1904
49 *Urban History Review* (Feb. 1984): 45–8
50 *Calgary Herald*, 11 Sept. 1904
51 Ibid., 22–30 March 1904
52 Pleadings, Lougheed vs. Bennett, 1922
53 Watkins, *Bennett*, 75

CHAPTER 3: FRONTIER POLITICS

1 Regina *Morning Leader*, 15 March 1901
2 Douglas Owram, ed., *The Formation of Alberta: A Documentary History* (Calgary: Historical Society of Alberta 1979), 118
3 Ibid., 234
4 Lord Beaverbrook, *Friends: Sixty Years of Intimate Personal Relations with Richard Bedford Bennett* (London and Toronto: Heinemann 1959), 25
5 National Archives of Canada, R.B. Bennett Papers, microfilm 546,480ff
6 Ibid., microfilm 550,575; 545,620
7 R.C. Brown and Ramsay Cook, *Canada 1896–1921: A Nation Transformed* (Toronto: McClelland and Stewart 1974), 12–16
8 Ibid., 76
9 *Eye Opener*, 17 June 1905
10 Hugh Dempsey., ed., *The Best of Bob Edwards* (Edmonton: Hurtig 1975), 7
11 *Eye Opener*, 24 Feb. 1906
12 Dempsey, ed., *Best of Bob Edwards*, 18
13 Owram, ed., *Formation of Alberta*, 299–346
14 *Ottawa Journal*, 19 Feb. 1906

15 Bennett Papers, microfilm 545,595
16 A.J.P. Taylor, *Beaverbrook* (New York, Simon and Schuster 1972), 17
17 G.W. Edwards, *The Evolution of Finance Capitalism* (London and Toronto: Longmans Green 1938), 178
18 Beaverbrook, *Friends*, 29
19 *Calgary Herald*, 15 Feb. 1901
20 Bennett Papers, interview with John Brownlee, microfilm 543,846
21 *Edmonton Journal*, Jan. and Feb. 1910, various dates, and 3 March 1910
22 Ibid., 10 March 1910
23 Trans Alberta Utilities, *75th Anniversary* brochure, 1986, 4
24 *Calgary Herald*, 7 Oct. 1907
25 Bennett Papers, microfilm 596,690
26 House of Lords Records Office, London, Lord Beaverbrook Papers, vol. 66, file 44
27 Bennett Papers, microfilm 596,690
28 Taylor, *Beaverbrook*, 36, 37, 40
29 Beaverbrook Papers, vol. 66, file 57

CHAPTER 4: MEMBER OF PARLIAMENT

1 Lord Beaverbrook, *Friends: Sixty Years of Intimate Personal Relations with Richard Bedford Bennett* (London and Toronto: Heinemann 1959), 31–2
2 Ibid.
3 M.C. Urquhart, ed., *Historical Statistics of Canada* (Ottawa: Statistics Canada 1983), 240, 515, 545
4 R.C. Brown and Ramsay Cook, *Canada 1896–1921: A Nation Transformed* (Toronto: McClelland and Stewart 1974), 370
5 John W. Dafoe, *Clifford Sifton in Relation to His Times* (Toronto: Macmillan 1931), 396–70
6 *Calgary Herald* and *Albertan* campaign reports, 1911
7 *Henderson Calgary City* directories, 1908–10
8 Barney Toole to James Gray, June 1948
9 *Calgary Herald*, 21 Sept. 1911
10 Canada, House of Commons, Hansard, 1911–12, vol. 1, 14–28
11 Beaverbrook, *Friends*, 35
12 Between 1908 and 1929 Bennett and Foran were in prolonged disputes with Quebec over succession duties on the estates of E.B. Eddy, Mrs Eddy, and

J.T. 'Harry' Shirreff. The wills, financial statements, and correspondence are spread across the Bennett Papers, National Archives of Canada, microfilm 580,000–82,000.

13 *Ottawa Journal*, 12–19 Feb. 1906
14 Ibid., 20 Feb. 1906
15 Revised Statutes of Quebec, 1906, c. 11
16 *Ottawa Journal*, 20 Feb. 1906
17 Bennett Papers, microfilm 544,124 and 544,475
18 Ibid., microfilm 580,790
19 Ibid., microfilm 576,125
20 House of Lords Records Office, London, Lord Beaverbrook Papers, vol. 65, file 47
21 Ibid.
22 Ibid.
23 Bennett Papers, microfilm 582,074
24 Ibid., microfilm 596,788 and 596,799. The bonds provided sufficient funds to pay for the optioned companies, and the common stock was distributed as bonuses to the bond purchasers. Bennett took down $200,000 in bonds and received $350,000 in common shares.
25 Pleadings, Lougheed vs. Bennett, 1922, Institute of Law Research and Reform, University of Alberta, Edmonton
26 Ibid.
27 Beaverbrook Papers, vol. 65, file 47, 12 Jan. 1912
28 Ibid.
29 Ibid., vol. 66, file 42, 19 Nov. 1909
30 Ibid., 10 Dec. 1909
31 Ibid., vol. 65, file 13, 1 Sept. 1913
32 Ibid.
33 Bennett Papers, microfilm 600,367
34 Hansard (revised), 25 Feb. 1913
35 *Ottawa Journal*, 26 Feb. 1913; Toronto *Globe*, 26 Feb. 1913
36 Hansard, 26 March 1913

CHAPTER 5: WORLD WAR I

1 M.C. Urquart, ed., *Historical Statistics of Canada* (Ottawa: Statistics Canada 1983), 202, 215
2 Canada, House of Commons, Hansard, 14 May 1914

3 *Calgary Herald*, 15 May 1914

4 Philip Smith, *The Treasure Seekers: The Men Who Built Home Oil* (Toronto: Macmillan 1978), 18

5 Glenbow Archives, Calgary, M 26, Hilda Brandt Papers, scrapbooks of undated newspaper clippings, files 2–24

6 Ibid.

7 The Henderson Calgary directory identified this as Bennett's residence when he moved to the Ranchmen's Club.

8 Princess Patricia's Canadian Light Infantry (PPCLI) Regimental Archives, Currie Barracks, Calgary

9 Brandt Papers, clipping file

10 Charles F. Wilson, *A Century of Canadian Grain: Government Policy to 1951* (Saskatoon: Western Producer Prairie Books 1978), 72ff

11 Ralph Allen, *Ordeal by Fire: Canada 1910–1945* (Toronto: Doubleday 1961), 70

12 National Archives of Canada, Robert Borden Papers, war file–Perley, 1–15 May 1915, microfilm 169,989 to 171,404

13 Mitchell W. Sharpe, 'Wheat Buying, 1914–1918,' *Canadian Journal of Economics and Political Science* (Aug. 1940): 372

14 A.J.P. Taylor, *Beaverbrook* (New York: Simon and Schuster 1972), 87ff

15 *Canadian Annual Review, 1915* (Toronto 1916), 694

16 Hansard, 1916, 222ff

17 Ibid.

18 Brandt Papers, clipping file

19 *Calgary Herald*, 3 Jan. 1916

20 Borden Papers, Borden diaries, April 1916

21 The author had several uncles and cousins infected with this CPR 'disease.'

22 National Archives of Canada, R.B. Bennett Papers, microfilm 376,013

23 Borden diaries, 15 June 1917

24 Ibid., 9 June 1915

25 Bennett Papers, microfilm 556,576

26 National Archives of Canada, Borden–Perley Papers, MG 26, microfilm 169,989 to 171,484

27 *Canadian Annual Review, 1916* (Toronto 1917), 325–35

28 Bennett Papers, microfilm 597,211

29 Brandt Papers, clipping file

30 Sharp, 'Wheat Buying,' 378

31 *Ottawa Journal*, 5 May 1917

294 Notes to pages 186–211

CHAPTER 6: BUSINESS AND GOVERNMENT AFFAIRS

1 National Archives of Canada, R.B. Bennett Papers, microfilm 597,201
2 Ibid., Sir Robert Borden Papers, Borden diary, 16 May 1917
3 Bennett Papers, microfilm 597,206
4 Ibid.
5 Pleadings, Lougheed vs. Bennett, 1922, Institute of Law Research and Reform, University of Alberta, Edmonton
6 Lord Beaverbrook, *Friends: Sixty Years of Intimate Personal Relations with Richard Bedford Bennett* (London and Toronto: Heinemann 1959), 84–5
7 Calgary Land Titles Office, certificate of title
8 Glenbow Archives, Calgary, Calgary Power Company, file M 1546, Directors' Minutes, 1 Aug. 1917
9 Bennett Papers, microfilm 576,125–31
10 Ibid., microfilm 580,790
11 Ibid., microfilm 577,595
12 Ibid., 597,201
13 *Albertan*, 6 Feb. 1918
14 *Calgary Herald*, 6 Feb. 1918
15 Ibid., 17 Nov. 1917
16 Bennett Papers, microfilm 597,201
17 Borden diary, 11 Feb. 1917
18 *Calgary Herald* and *Albertan*, various dates, autumn 1917
19 *Calgary Herald*, 11 June 1918
20 Ibid., 24 June 1918
21 Ibid., 5 July 1918
22 Bennett Papers, microfilm 555,012
23 Dalhousie University Archives, President's Office Correspondence, file M, Bennett to Mackenzie, 16 Feb. 1920
24 Ibid., Bennett to Mackenzie, May 1920
25 Ibid., Mackenzie to Bennett, 24 April 1922
26 Bennett Papers, microfilm 556,576
27 Ibid., microfilm 608,882
28 Ibid., microfilm 580,790
29 Ibid., microfilm 580,210
30 Ibid., microfilm 579,491
31 Ibid., microfilm 581,938
32 Ibid., microfilm 579,477

33 Ibid., microfilm 608,888
34 Ibid., microfilm 608,882
35 *Calgary Herald*, 15 Dec. 1921
36 Bennett Papers, microfilm 596,838
37 Ibid., income tax returns, microfilm 556,587–98
38 Pleadings, Lougheed vs. Bennett, 1922
39 Ibid.
40 Ernest Watkins, *R.B. Bennett: A Biography* (Toronto: Kingswood House 1963), 98
41 Gray interview with Harry Chritchley, Calgary, Sept. 1987
42 *Henderson Calgary City Directory, 1923*

CHAPTER 7: LARGESSE

1 National Archives of Canada, R.B. Bennett Papers, microfilm 555,496–500
2 Ibid., income tax returns, microfilm 556,688
3 J.J. Saucier, *The Bennett Firm Revisited* (Calgary: the author 1982), 1
4 Glenbow Archives, Calgary, Royalite Oil Company Limited, Minute Books
5 Ibid.
6 Leonard D. Nesbitt, *Tides in the West* (Saskatoon: Modern Press 1962), 45–6, 56; Paul Sharp, *The Agrarian Revolt in Western Canada: A Survey Showing American Parallels* (New York: Octagon Books 1971); Charles F. Wilson, *A Century of Canadian Grain: Government Policy to 1951* (Saskatoon: Western Producer Prairie Books 1978)
7 *Calgary Herald*, daily during last half of July 1923
8 Ibid., 3 Aug. 1923
9 Ibid., 5 Aug. 1923
10 Nesbitt, *Tides in the West*
11 *Financial Post*, 16 May 1924
12 Ibid., 12 Sept. 1924
14 Ibid., microfilm 556,688ff, 556,739–832
15 Ibid., microfilm 561,156
16 Ibid., microfilm 561,154
17 Ibid., microfilm 543,485
18 Ibid., microfilm 561,157
19 Ibid., microfilm 561,158
20 Ibid., microfilm 561,160
22 Ibid., microfilm 561,292

23 Ibid., microfilm 561,181–2 and 561,188
24 Ibid., microfilm 561,045, 566,856
25 A.C. Coutler, ed., *John Wesley* (New York: Oxford University Press 1964), 268–91
26 Bennett Papers, microfilm 543,740
27 Letter from Ed. Bredin to Gray, 16 June 1986
28 Bennett Papers, microfilm 555,545
29 Ibid., microfilm 599,570–1
30 Ibid., microfilm 603,982
31 Ibid., microfilm 599,583
32 Ibid., microfilm 599,581
33 Ibid., microfilm 607,369ff
34 Ibid., microfilm 607,303–4
35 Ibid., microfilm 607,372
36 Ibid., microfilm 603,091-2

CHAPTER 8: LEADER OF THE OPPOSITION

1 National Archives of Canada, R.B. Bennett Papers, microfilm 596,938
2 *Financial Post*, 22 Aug. 1924
3 *Calgary Herald*, 19 Sept. 1924
4 Ibid., 15 Oct. 1924
5 Ibid., 23 Oct. 1924
6 *Western Oil Examiner*, 20 Feb. 1926
7 Bennett Papers, microfilm 033,159
8 Ibid., microfilm 578,739
9 *Maclean's*, 15 Nov. 1927
10 Bennett Papers, microfilm 545,842
11 Calgary Board of Education Archives, trust deed
12 Dalhousie University Archives, Board of Governors Minutes, May 1920, 274
13 Ibid., 10 July 1925, 304
14 Bennett Papers, microfilm 039,820
15 *Calgary Herald*, 28 Oct. 1926
16 Bennett Papers, microfilm 579,498
17 Bruce Hutchison, *Mr Prime Minister* (Toronto: Longmans 1964), 223
18 Ernest Watkins, *R.B. Bennett: A Biography* (Toronto: Kingswood House 1963), 123

19 Bennett Papers, microfilm 579,681
20 Ibid., microfilm 569,688
21 Ibid., microfilm 580,668–9; 581,289
22 Ibid., microfilm 579,681
23 Ibid., microfilm 580,164
24 Ibid., microfilm 579,681–4
25 M.C. Urquhart, ed., *Historical Statistics of Canada* (Ottawa: Statistics Canada 1983), 618–20
26 *Ottawa Journal*, 11 Oct. 1926
27 J.W. Aldred, 'The Public Career of Maj.-Gen. A.D. McRae' (Master of Arts thesis, University of Western Ontario, 1970); Margaret A. Ormsby, *British Columbia: A History* (Toronto: Macmillan 1964), 420–5
28 Canada, House of Commons, *Debates*, 20 Feb. 1927
29 Ibid., 28 Feb. 1927 and following days; D.J. Hall, *Clifford Sifton*, II: *A Lonely Eminence 1901–1929* (Vancouver: University of British Columbia Press 1985), 326–34
30 Bennett Papers, microfilm 576,127–32; 575,912–13
31 Ibid., microfilm 575,846
32 Ibid., microfilm 575,824
33 Ibid., microfilm 576,247
34 Ibid., microfilm 575,847
35 Ibid., microfilm 575,687
36 Ibid., microfilm 575,689
37 Ibid., microfilm 575,706
38 Ibid., microfilm 575,948
39 Charles Bishop column in Southam newspapers, 8 and 10 Oct. 1927
40 Bennett Papers, microfilm 17,515
41 *Winnipeg Tribune*, 11 Oct. 1927; *Manitoba Free Press*, 11 Oct. 1927
42 Bennett Papers, microfilm 3698; 4550
43 Hansard, 3 April 1930, 1227–8

Index

American immigrants, 32, 64, 71,
118–20, 124
'anti-loafing' law, 200
Archibald, F.S., 54
Asquith, Herbert H., 164, 166
Atkinson, Joseph E., 276
Autonomy Bill, 84–5, 89

Bank of Canada Act, 243
Bank of Montreal, 35, 110–11, 174,
234, 243–4
Bank of Nova Scotia, 72–3, 76, 245
Banking and Currency, Royal Com-
mission on, 243
Barker, C.H., 72
Barrow, G.M., 207
Bawlf, Nicholas, 136; see also N.
Bawlf Grain Co.
Beatty, Edward Wentworth, 173
Beaverbrook, Lord. See Aitken, Wil-
liam Maxwell
Bennett, Evelyn. See Coates
Bennett, Mrs George, 232–3, 235–
6, 238
Bennett, George H., 4, 35, 161, 166,
232–6, 238–40
Bennett, Hannah and Sanford, 220,
226, 231, 239, 251
Bennett, Henrietta Stiles, 3–8, 84,
160
Bennett, Henry, Jr, 3
Bennett, Henry John, 3–8, 84
Bennett, Mary Joan, 232–3, 235–8,
240–1
Bennett, Mildred, 4, 84, 161, 222,
279–80
Bennett, Nathan, 5

Bennett, Richard Bedford, 15, 24,
40–2, 59, 72, 83–4, 199, 204,
206, 222, 234, 239, 250–1; 1898
territorial election campaign, 45–
51; 1900 federal election campaign, 60–3; 1905 provincial election campaign, 86, 89–92; 1909
provincial election campaign, 99–
100; 1911 federal election campaign, 113–15, 118–23, 167–8;
1921 federal election campaign,
213–14; 1925 federal election
campaign, 255–8; 1926 federal
election, 263–4; Aitken friendship
begins, 16–18, 21–3; Aitken's
business ventures with, 94, 105–
10, 112, 135–6, 139–43, 162,
191, 209, 231; Aitken's letters
from, 81, 93, 114, 127–8, 133–4,
140–1, 177–8, 215; birth and
childhood, 3–11; Borden, relations with, 68–70, 129, 155, 163,
165–6, 176, 179–81, 186–8, 193–
8; Calgary, first sight of, 28–31,
33; Canadian Northern Railway,
hostility towards, 150–5, 171–2,
174–6; Chatham, NB, council
candidate, 21; Conservative party
leadership bid, 265–7, 269, 276–
7, 279–80, 282–5; court cases argued, 36, 54, 56–8, 73–5, 144–5,
201–2, 205; Eddy company involvement, 129, 132–5, 191–3,
207–11, 223–4, 226, 253, 258,
260, 262–3, 269–75, 277–8, 285;
Edwards, relations with, 85–6, 89;
Great Waterways challenge, 100–5;